FRANCIS FRITH'S

WINDERMERE

PHOTOGRAPHIC MEMORIES

NORMAN BUCKLEY became a researcher and writer of walking guidebooks thirteen years ago, after a long career in environmental health. For the past twelve years he has lived in the English Lake District, which has been the inspiration for several of his books, including the ever-popular 'Level Walks' series. However, his walking and writing are by no means confined to the United Kingdom, and he is the author of several books on Europe. In recent years Norman and his wife June have acted as walking consultants to a major holiday organisation, with properties both at home and abroad. He holds post-graduate diplomas in both Environmental Management and in Lake District Studies.

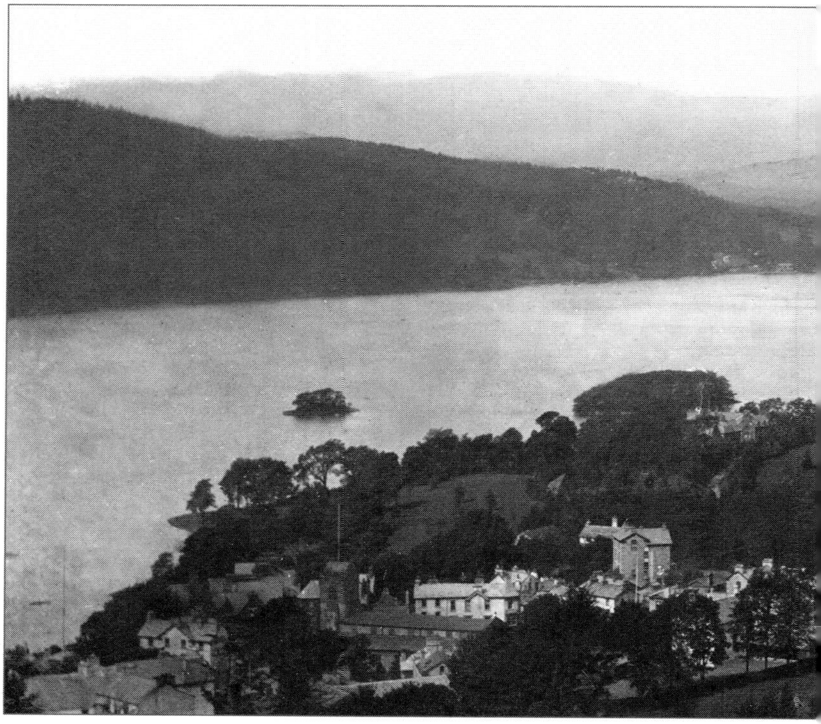

FRANCIS FRITH'S
PHOTOGRAPHIC MEMORIES

WINDERMERE

PHOTOGRAPHIC MEMORIES

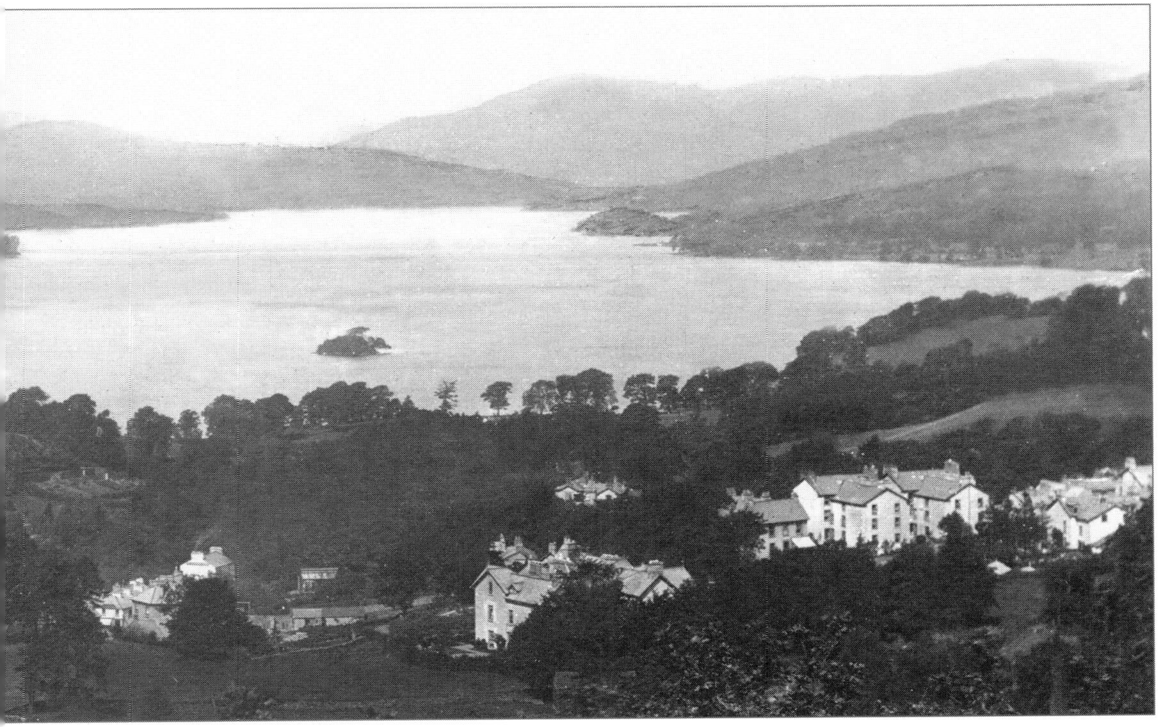

NORMAN A BUCKLEY

FRITH
BOOK Co

First published in the United Kingdom in 2003 by
Frith Book Company Ltd

Paperback Edition 2003
ISBN 1-85937-661-4

British Library Cataloguing in Publication Data

Francis Frith's Windermere Photographic Memories
Norman A Buckley

Frith Book Company Ltd
Frith's Barn, Teffont,
Salisbury, Wiltshire SP3 5QP
Tel: +44 (0) 1722 716 376
Email: info@francisfrith.co.uk
www.francisfrith.co.uk

Printed and bound in Great Britain

Front Cover: Windermere, Newby Bridge 1914 *67414*
Frontispiece: Windermere 1887 *20434*

AS WITH ANY HISTORICAL DATABASE THE FRITH ARCHIVE IS CONSTANTLY BEING CORRECTED AND IMPROVED AND THE PUBLISHERS WOULD WELCOME INFORMATION ON OMISSIONS OR INACCURACIES

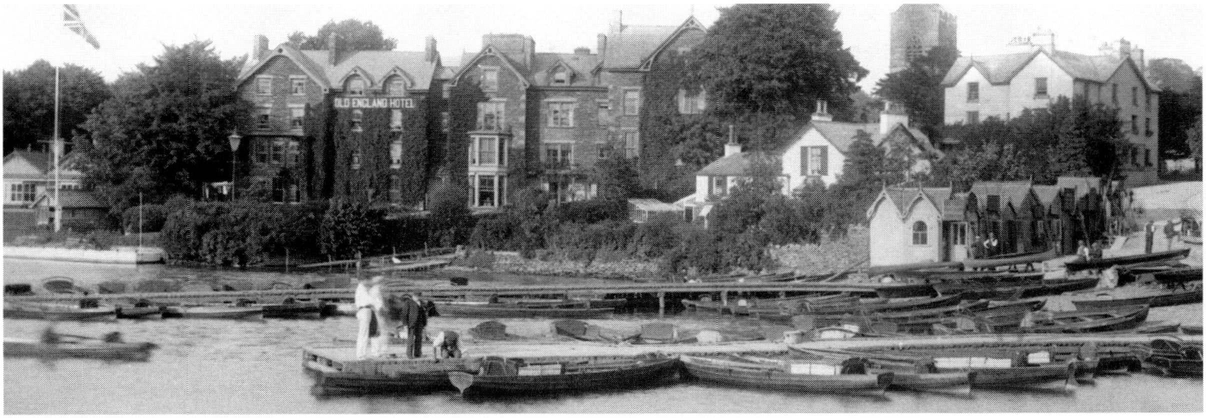

CONTENTS

FRANCIS FRITH
VICTORIAN PIONEER

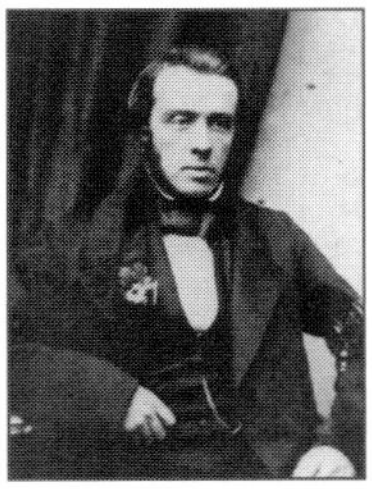

FRANCIS FRITH, founder of the world-famous photographic archive, was a complex and multi-talented man. A devout Quaker and a highly successful Victorian businessman, he was philosophic by nature and pioneering in outlook.

By 1855 he had already established a wholesale grocery business in Liverpool, and sold it for the astonishing sum of £200,000, which is the equivalent today of over £15,000,000. Now a multi-millionaire, he was able to indulge his passion for travel. As a child he had pored over travel books written by early explorers, and his fancy and imagination had been stirred by family holidays to the sublime mountain regions of Wales and Scotland. 'What a land of spirit-stirring and enriching scenes and places!' he had written. He was to return to these scenes of grandeur in later years to 'recapture the thousands of vivid and tender memories', but with a different purpose. Now in his thirties, and captivated by the new science of photography, Frith set out on a series of pioneering journeys up the Nile and to the Near East that occupied him from 1856 until 1860.

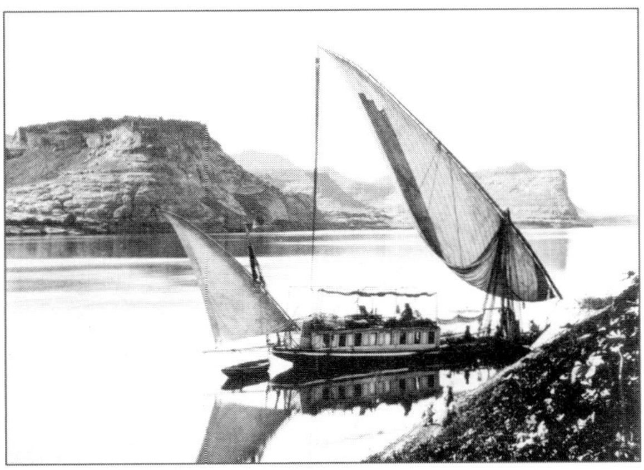

INTRIGUE AND EXPLORATION

These far-flung journeys were packed with intrigue and adventure. In his life story, written when he was sixty-three, Frith tells of being held captive by bandits, and of fighting 'an awful midnight battle to the very point of surrender with a deadly pack of hungry, wild dogs'. Wearing flowing Arab costume, Frith arrived at Akaba by camel seventy years before Lawrence of Arabia, where he encountered 'desert princes and rival sheikhs, blazing with jewel-hilted swords'.

He was the first photographer to venture beyond the sixth cataract of the Nile. Africa was still the mysterious 'Dark Continent', and Stanley and Livingstone's historic meeting was a decade into the future. The conditions for picture taking confound belief. He laboured for hours in his wicker dark-room in the sweltering heat of the desert, while the volatile chemicals fizzed dangerously in their trays. Back in London he exhibited his photographs and was 'rapturously cheered' by members of the Royal Society. His reputation as a photographer was made overnight.

VENTURE OF A LIFE-TIME

Characteristically, Frith quickly spotted the opportunity to create a new business as a specialist publisher of photographs. He lived in an era of immense and sometimes violent change.

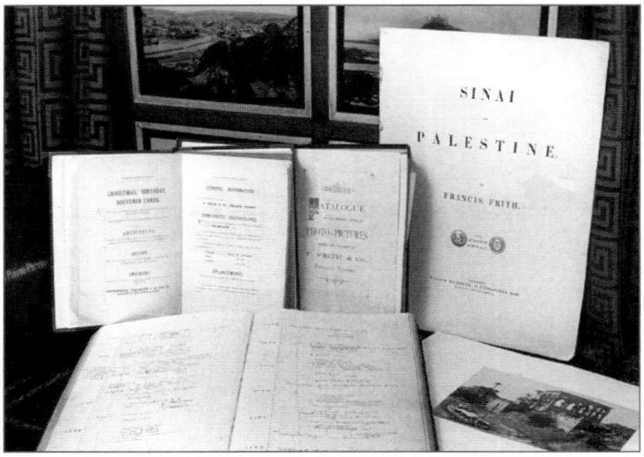

For the poor in the early part of Victoria's reign work was exhausting and the hours long, and people had precious little free time to enjoy themselves. Most had no transport other than a cart or gig at their disposal, and rarely travelled far beyond the boundaries of their own town or village. However, by the 1870s the railways had threaded their way across the country, and Bank Holidays and half-day Saturdays had been made obligatory by Act of Parliament. All of a sudden the working man and his family were able to enjoy days out and see a little more of the world.

With typical business acumen, Francis Frith foresaw that these new tourists would enjoy having souvenirs to commemorate their days out. In 1860 he married Mary Ann Rosling and set out on a new career: his aim was to photograph every city, town and village in Britain. For the next thirty years he travelled the country by train and by pony and trap, producing fine photographs of seaside resorts and beauty spots that were keenly bought by millions of Victorians. These prints were painstakingly pasted into family albums and pored over during the dark nights of winter, rekindling precious memories of summer excursions.

THE RISE OF FRITH & CO

Frith's studio was soon supplying retail shops all over the country. To meet the demand he gathered about him a small team of photographers, and published the work of independent artist-photographers of the calibre of Roger Fenton and Francis Bedford. In order to gain some understanding of the scale of Frith's business one only has to look at the catalogue issued by Frith & Co in 1886: it runs to some 670 pages, listing not only many thousands of views of the British Isles but also many photographs of most European countries, and China, Japan, the USA and Canada - note the sample page shown here from the hand-written Frith & Co ledgers recording the pictures. By 1890 Frith had created the greatest specialist photographic publishing company in the world, with over 2,000 sales outlets - more than the combined number that Boots and WH Smith have today! The picture on the nest page shows the Frith & Co display board at Ingleton in the Yorkshire Dales. Beautifully constructed with mahogany frame and gilt inserts, it could display up to a dozen local scenes.

POSTCARD BONANZA

The ever-popular holiday postcard we know today took many years to develop. In 1870 the Post Office issued the first plain cards, with a pre-printed stamp on one face. In 1894 they allowed other publishers' cards to be sent through the mail with an attached adhesive half-penny stamp. Demand grew rapidly, and in 1895 a new size of postcard was permitted called the court card, but there was little room for illustration. In 1899, a year after Frith's death, a new card measuring 5.5 x 3.5 inches became the standard format, but it was not until 1902 that the divided back came into being, so that the address and message could be on one face and a full-size illustration on the other. Frith & Co were in the vanguard of postcard development: Frith's sons Eustace and Cyril continued their father's monumental task, expanding the number of views offered to the public and recording more

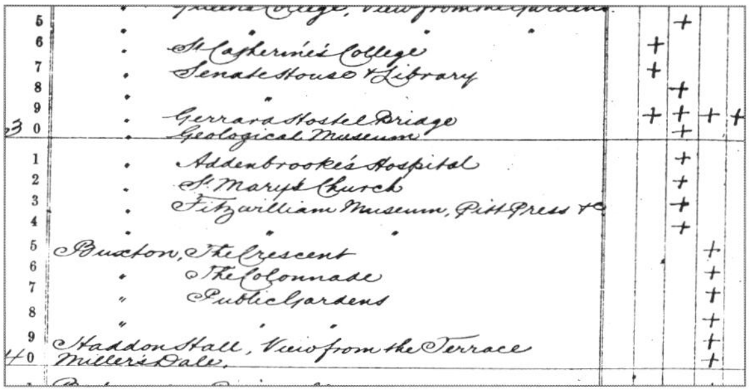

5
6 " St Catherine's College
7 " Senate House & Library
8
9
30 " Gerrard Hostel Bridge
Geological Museum
1 " Addenbrooke's Hospital
2 " St Mary's Church
3 " Fitzwilliam Museum, Pitt Press &c
4
5 Buxton, The Crescent
6 " The Colonnade
7 " Public Gardens
8
9 Haddon Hall, View from the Terrace
40 Miller's Dale

and more places in Britain, as the coasts and countryside were opened up to mass travel.

Francis Frith had died in 1898 at his villa in Cannes, his great project still growing. The archive he created continued in business for another seventy years. By 1970 it contained over a third of a million pictures showing 7,000 British towns and villages.

FRANCIS FRITH'S LEGACY

Frith's legacy to us today is of immense significance and value, for the magnificent archive of evocative photographs he created provides a unique record of change in the cities, towns and villages throughout Britain over a century and more. Frith and his fellow studio photographers revisited locations many times down the years to update their views, compiling for us an enthralling and colourful pageant of British life and character.

We are fortunate that Frith was dedicated to recording the minutiae of everyday life. For it is this sheer wealth of visual data, the painstaking chronicle of changes in dress, transport, street layouts, buildings, housing, engineering and landscape that captivates us so much today. His remarkable images offer us a powerful link with the past and with the lives of our ancestors.

THE VALUE OF THE ARCHIVE TODAY

Computers have now made it possible for Frith's many thousands of images to be accessed almost instantly. Frith's images are increasingly used as visual resources, by social historians, by researchers into genealogy and ancestry, by architects and town planners, and by teachers involved in local history projects.

In addition, the archive offers every one of us an opportunity to examine the places where we and our families have lived and worked down the years. Highly successful in Frith's own era, the archive is now, a century and more on, entering a new phase of popularity. Historians consider the Francis Frith Collection to be of prime national importance. It is the only archive of its kind remaining in private ownership. Francis Frith's archive is now housed in an historic timber barn in the beautiful village of Teffont in Wiltshire. Its founder would not recognize the archive office as it is today. In place of the many thousands of dusty boxes containing glass plate negatives and an all-pervading odour of photographic chemicals, there are now ranks of computer screens. He would be amazed to watch his images travelling round the world at unimaginable speeds through internet lines.

The archive's future is both bright and exciting. Francis Frith, with his unshakeable belief in making photographs available to the greatest number of people, would undoubtedly approve of what is being done today with his lifetime's work. His photographs depicting our shared past are now bringing pleasure and enlightenment to millions around the world a century and more after his death.

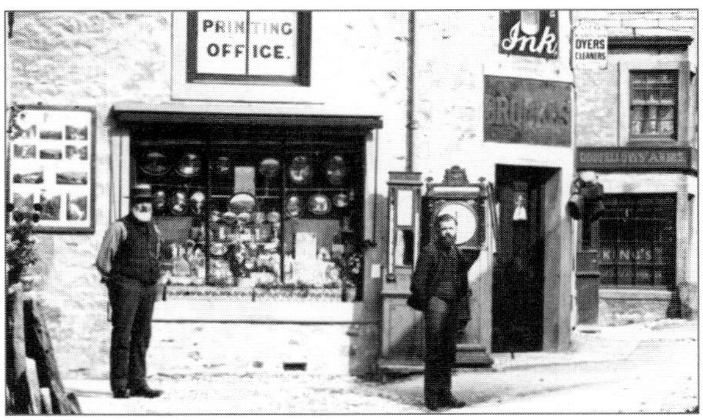

WINDERMERE
AN INTRODUCTION

ENGLAND'S largest and, arguably, prettiest lake, more than ten miles long, is situated in beautiful countryside at the southern end of the Lake District. Many of the best-loved mountains are visible from the lake and its shores. The name Windermere is derived from the name of a Norse tribal leader, 'Vinder' or possibly 'Vinander', whose 'mere' (lake) this became as the incoming 10th-century settlers pushed ever further inland from their landing places on the Cumberland and Lancashire coasts.

These photographs of settlements around the lake range from Waterhead in the north to Lakeside and Newby Bridge in the south, with Bowness-on-Windermere roughly half way between. Also included in this book are several small towns and villages situated some distance from the lake, but quite properly regarded as within the Windermere area. The more important of these will be briefly introduced at the appropriate place. To avoid confusion, it should be mentioned that the village known as 'Windermere' is one and a half miles from the lake shore at Bowness; to distinguish it from the lake of the same name, it is referred to as 'Windermere village'. The term 'Windermere Lake' sometimes used in other publications is incorrect.

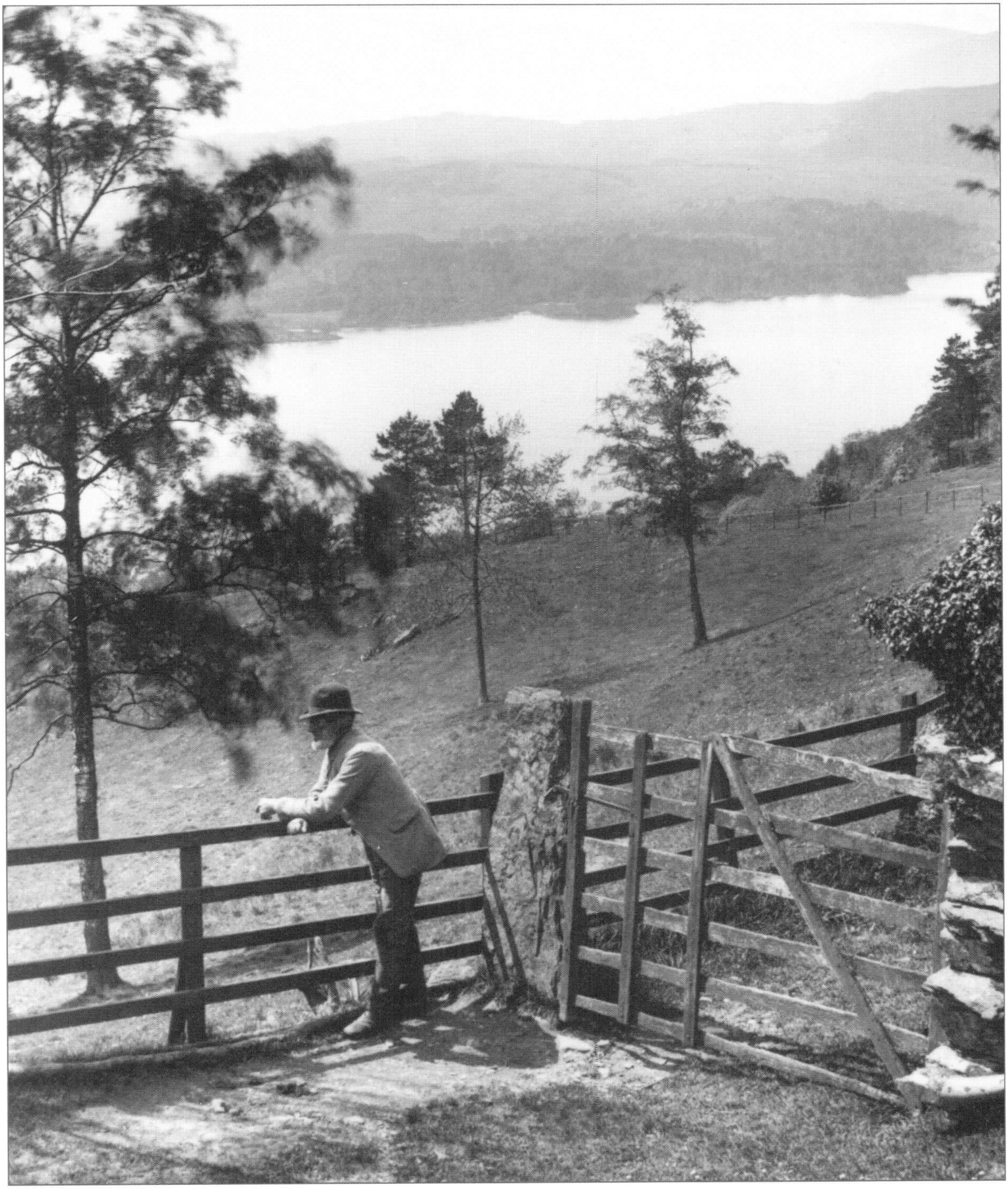

WINDERMERE *1886* 8663

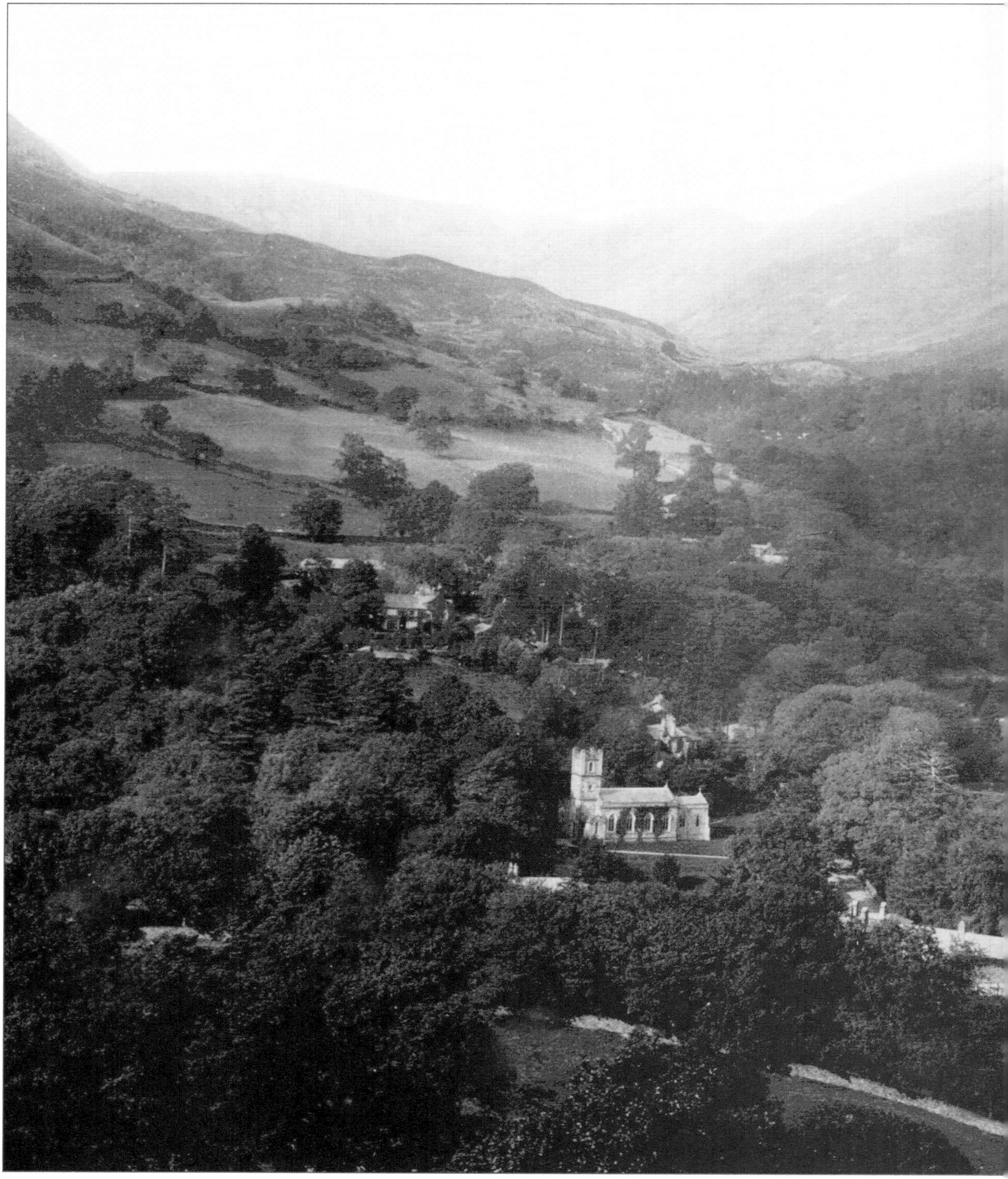

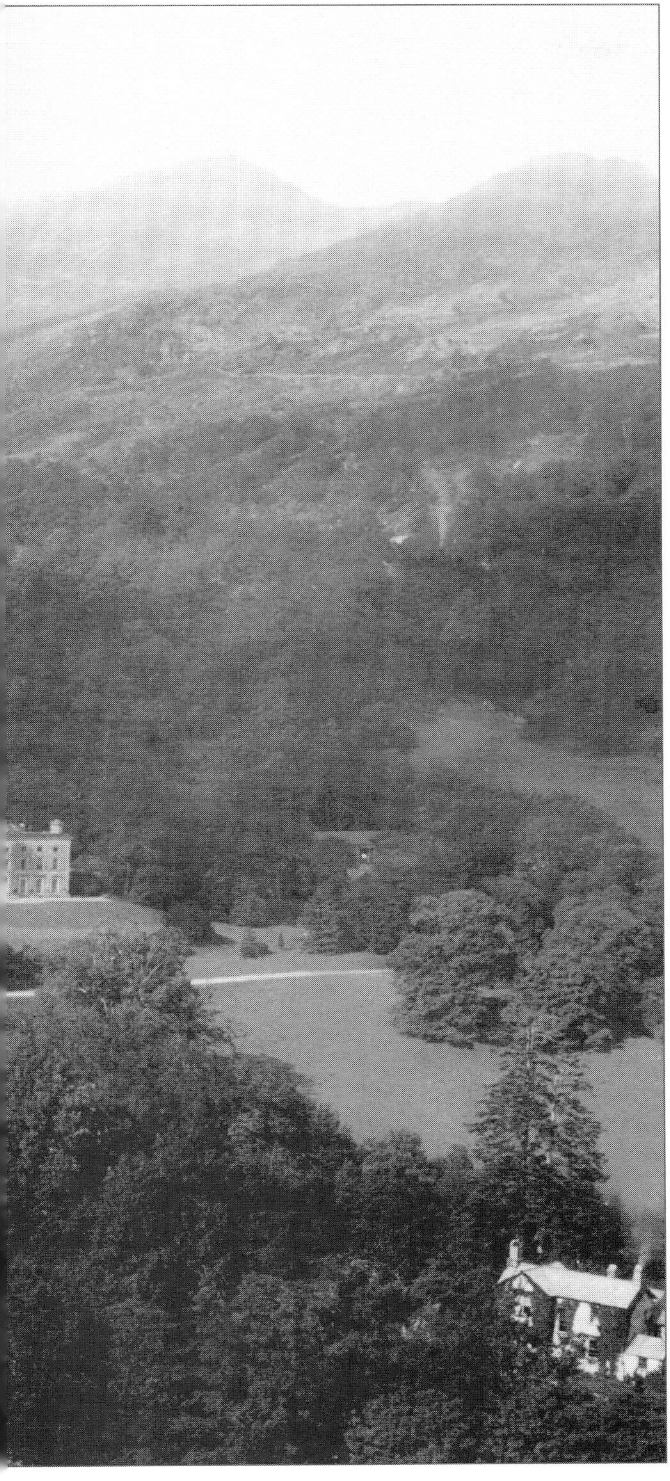

AMBLESIDE
AND ITS SURROUNDINGS

THE little town of Ambleside, nestling beneath steep mountainsides, is a very popular focal point on the road to the north from Windermere. The really old part of the town, with Stock Ghyll ('ghyll' means 'stream') and several former mill sites, rises steeply to the north-east from the largely Victorian town centre, where numerous shops selling outdoor activity clothing jostle with old inns and cafes. A short distance to the north, the lovely Vale of Rydal carries the main road to Grasmere, Keswick and the north of the district.

One mile to the south, the almost separate community of Waterhead sits by the head of the lake, the northern terminus for the lake steamer services and a focus for other boating activity. At Waterhead, the site of the Roman fort of Galava is owned by the National Trust and is open to visitors.

RYDAL WATER
Rydal Vale 1888 20533

The high viewpoint emphasises the rich woodland of the vale, with the prominent solid block of the present Rydal Hall, built in the 17th century, and the church of 1824. The church was paid for by Lady le Fleming of Rydal Hall. Her close neighbour at nearby Rydal Mount was William Wordsworth, who had his own pew in the church; so did the family of Dr Arnold of Rugby School fame. Dr Arnold had a house at Under Loughrigg, a little further down the vale.

WINDERMERE
from Loughrigg 1892
30480

From the rocky lower slopes of Loughrigg we can see the little town of Ambleside nestling below the bulk of Wansfell Pike, with the northern end of Windermere visible in the distance. The spacious parish church of St Mary, with its rather incongruous high spire, was built by Gilbert Scott between 1850 and 1854.

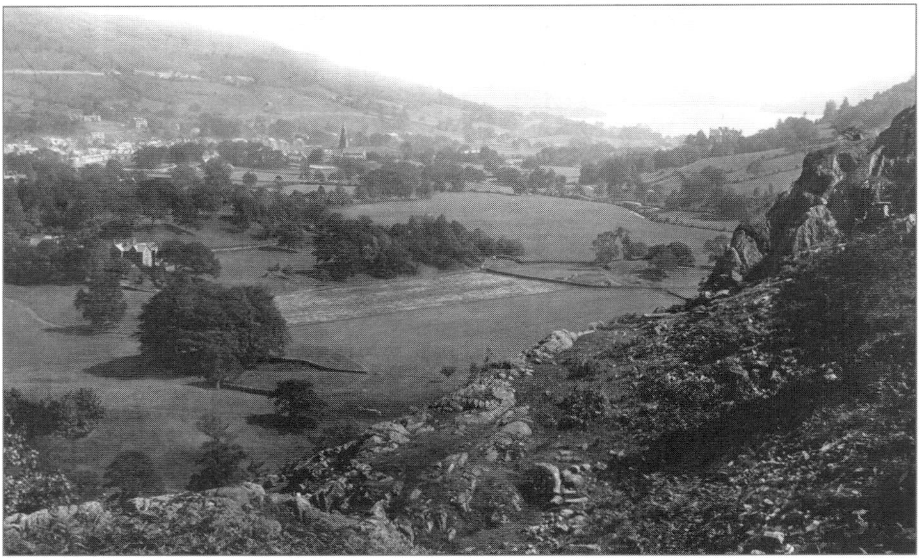

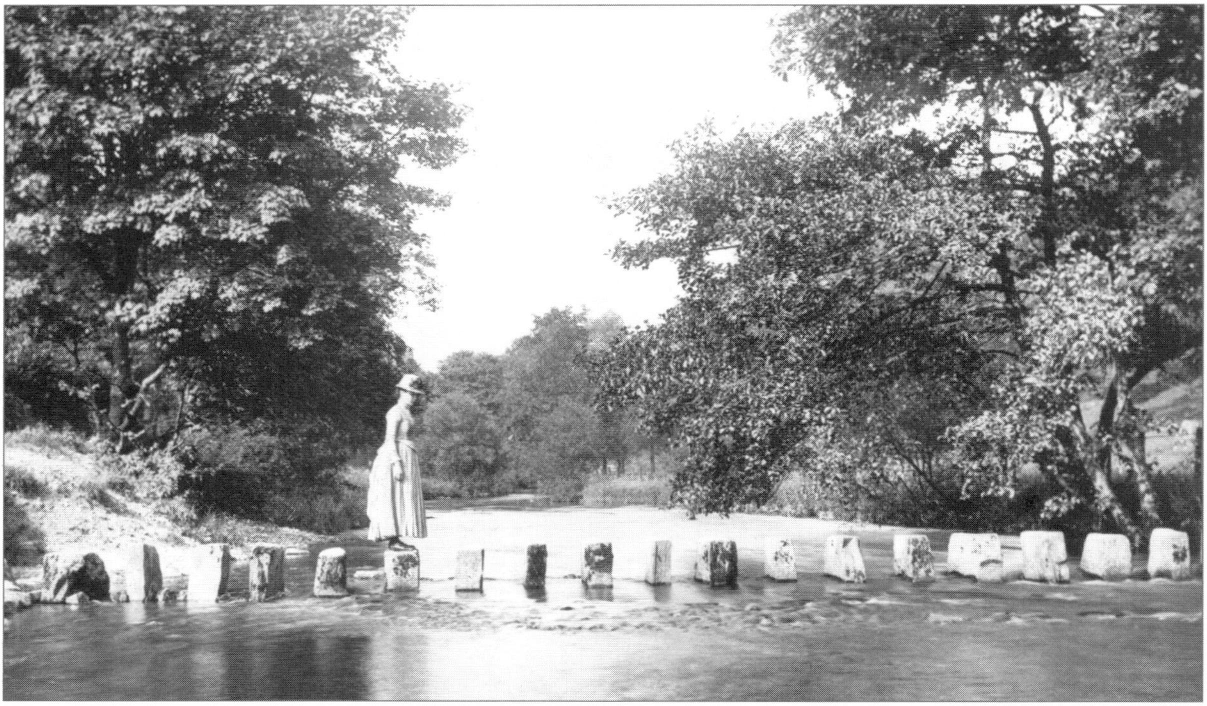

AMBLESIDE, *The Stepping Stones 1888* 20484

A short distance to the west of the town centre, the stepping stones have long provided a foot crossing of the River Rothay, at least for those with good balance; they link Ambleside with properties on the Under Loughrigg road and with a track up Loughrigg itself. Despite the impediment of Victorian dress, the young lady appears to be confident; in any case, if the worst happens, the water level is comparatively low!

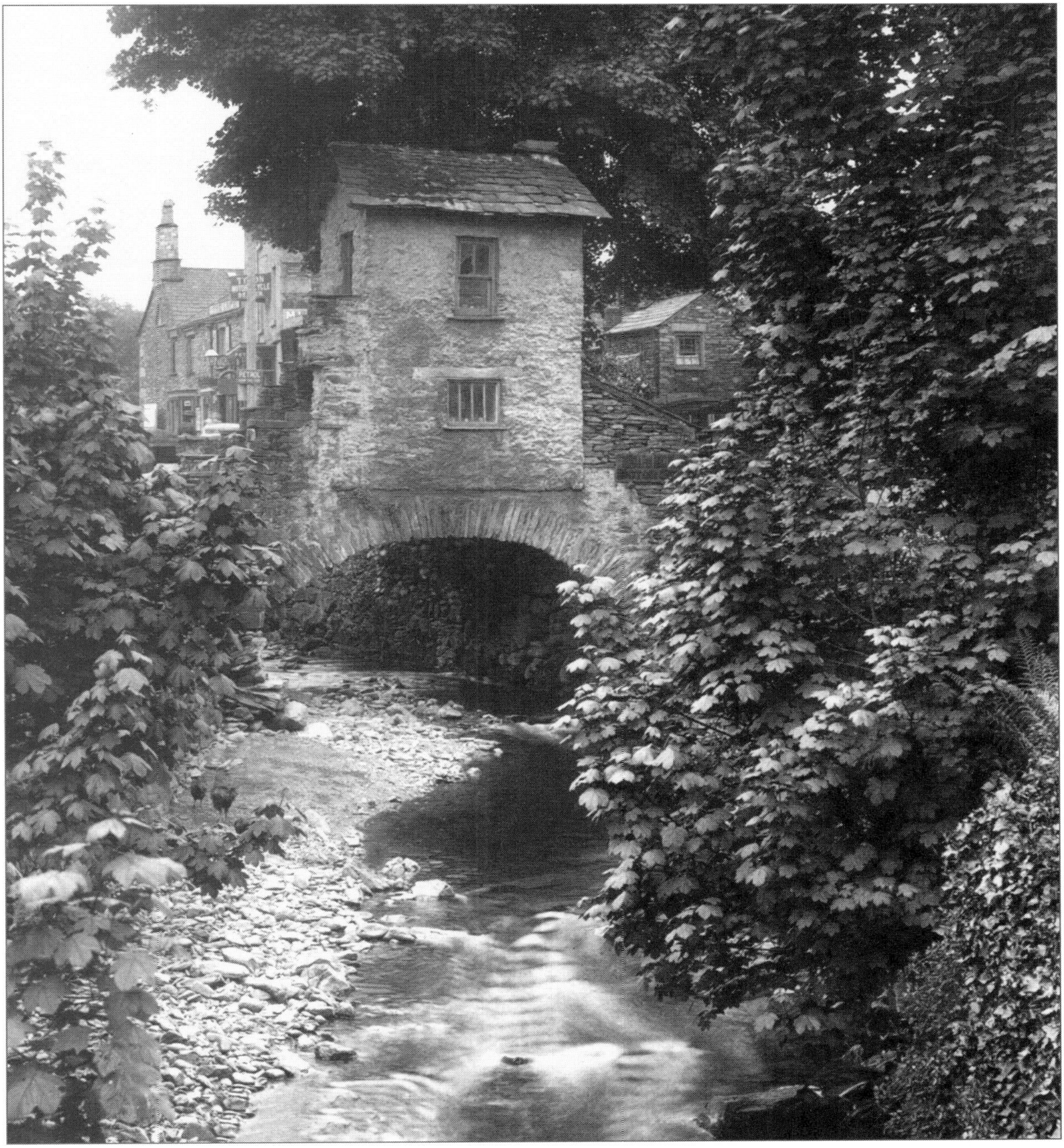

AMBLESIDE, *The Bridge House 1912* 64306

Straddling Stock Ghyll, which runs by the side of the main road, this curious little structure is probably the best-known feature of Ambleside. It is claimed by some to have been built over water to avoid having to pay land-based rates. The reality is more down to earth. It was a store building used in conjunction with the former Ambleside Hall; it was occupied for a time as a family home, and is now owned and used by the National Trust as a shop/visitor attraction.

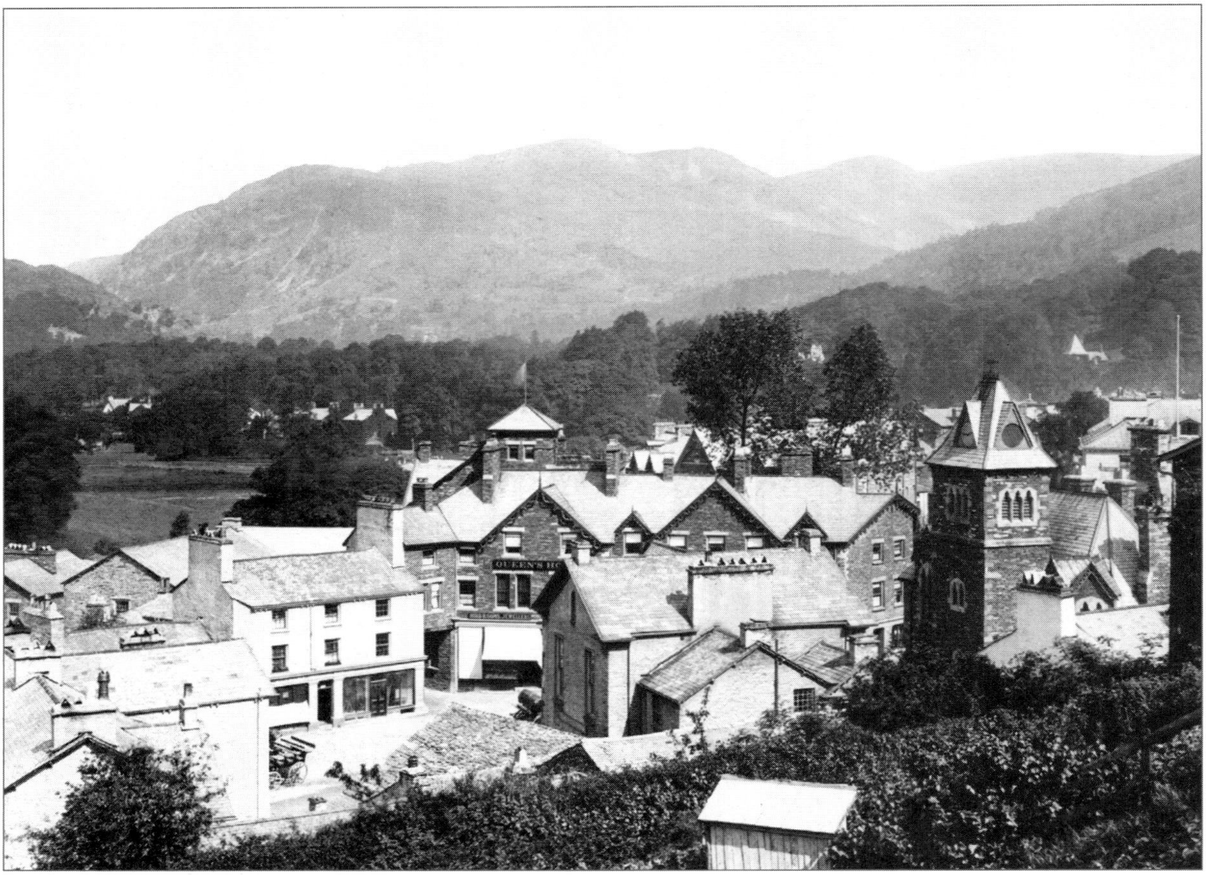

AMBLESIDE
From the Gale 1886 18672

Here we have a fine overview of the town centre against a backdrop of the Fairfield Horseshoe group of mountains. The large signboard leaves no doubt about the Queen's Hotel, dominant in the Market Square (centre), whilst Hird and Sons, jewellers, occupy part of the ground floor of the same building. The solidly constructed tower to the right is part of the Market Hall of 1863. To the left of the Market Hall is the back of the former Court House.

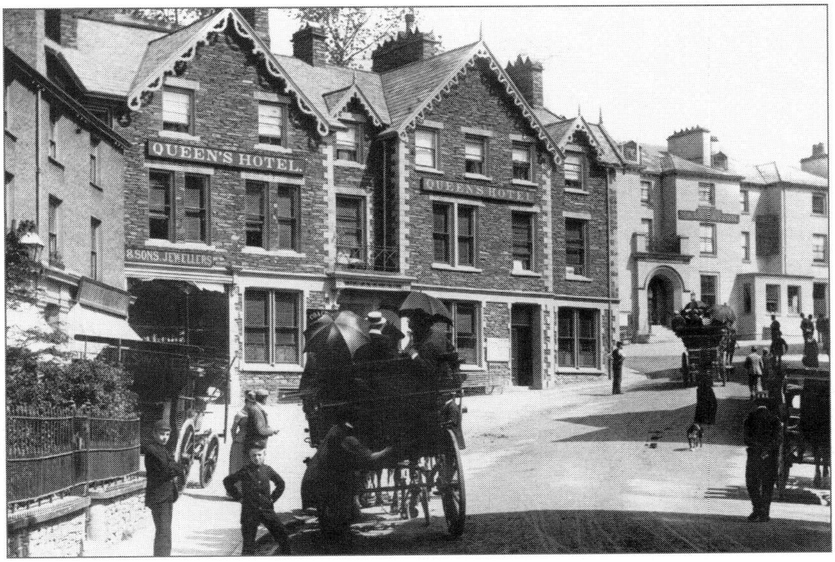

AMBLESIDE
The Queen's Hotel 1892
30484

A lively scene in the Market Square. Silver tea and coffee pots are evident in the window of the jeweller's shop. Beyond is the Salutation, a coaching inn of 1656. One of the horse-drawn coaches has an 'Ullswater' board, presumably showing its destination. Even today, climbing to the Kirkstone Pass from Ambleside en route to Ullswater is a long, hard slog. The young boy in the foreground seems to be proud of his uniformed status, whilst the use of dark umbrellas by travellers as sun protection is obviously common practice.

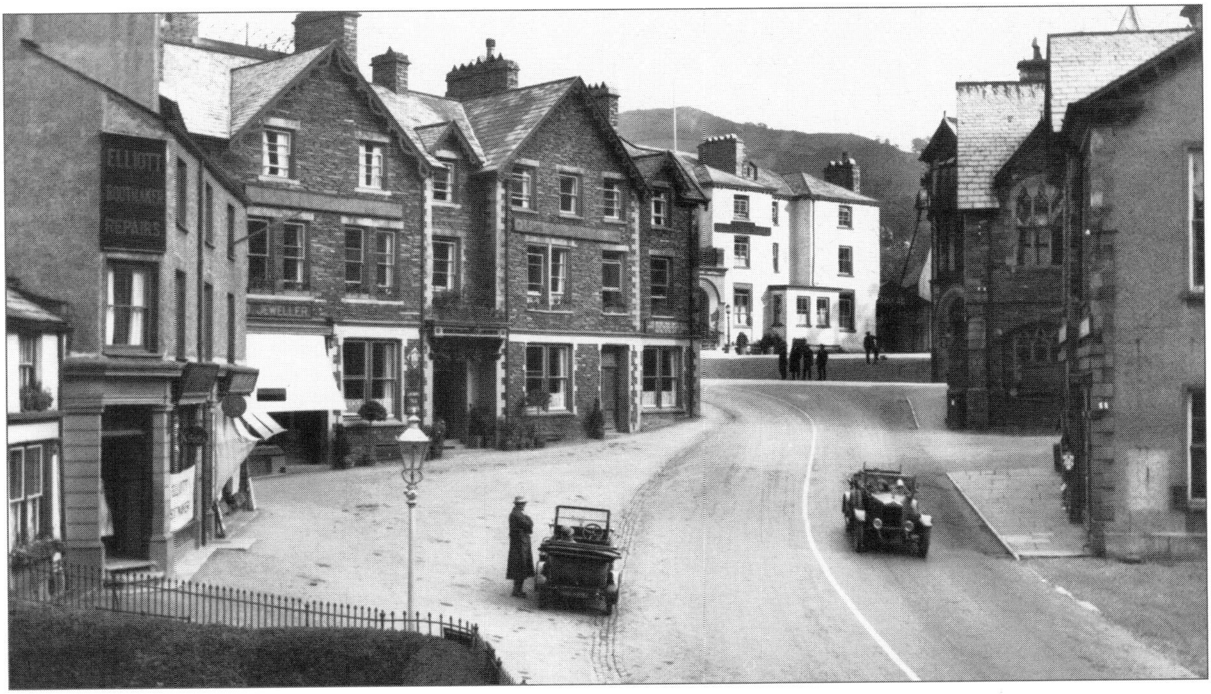

AMBLESIDE, *Market Square 1926* 79173

Now in the motor age, the Square is less animated. The Queen's Hotel has lost its dominant sign, but the jeweller's shop is still functioning. The board by the entrance to the Queen's building is offering 'luncheons, teas and garage'. Apart from losing its 'coaches' sign and acquiring a garage, the Salutation is little changed. Noteworthy is Elliott's shop, 'Bootmaker, Repairs' (left), since occupied by several generations of the present-day Tyson family, mountain boot specialists. We can see the front of the former Market Hall of 1863 on the right.

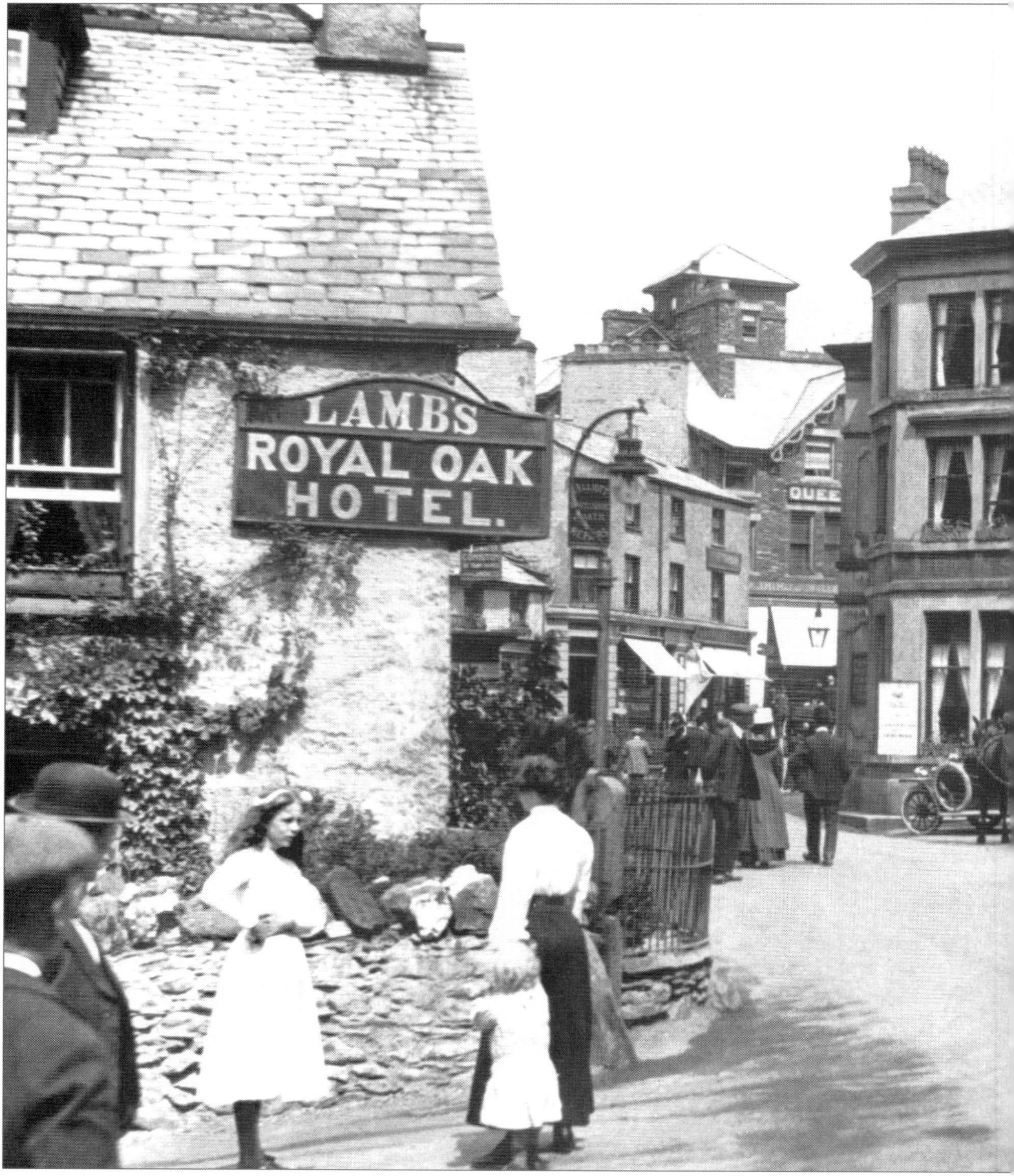
LAMB'S
ROYAL OAK
HOTEL.

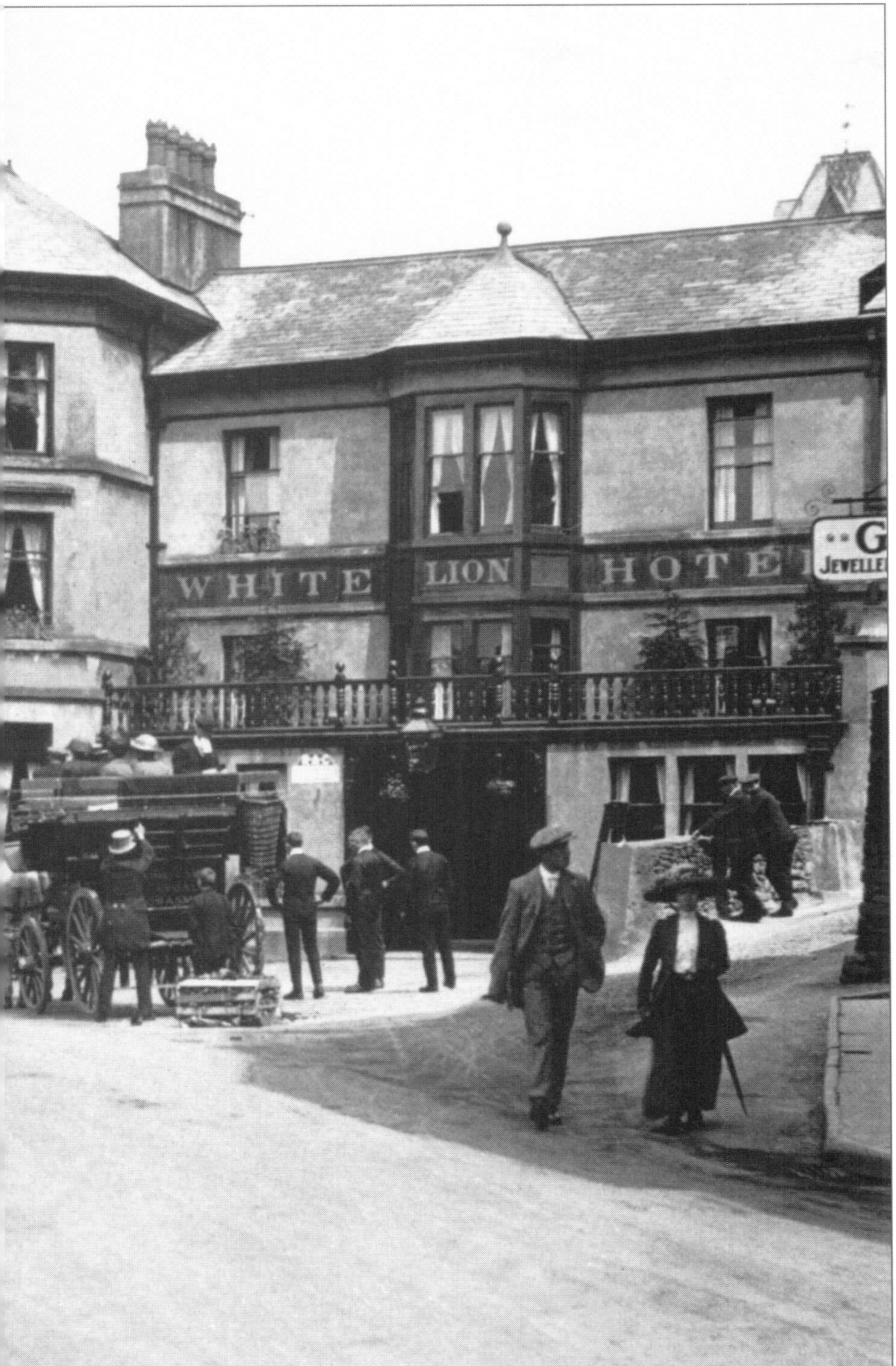

AMBLESIDE
The White Lion and the Royal Oak Hotels 1912 64303

As we move further down the main street, no less than three hotels are now in view: the Queen's peering round the corner (centre left), the impressive White Lion and the more humble Royal Oak. At a time when motor cars were beginning to mingle with the horse-drawn vehicles, it was obviously considered still to be safe to wander in the middle of the street.

▼ **AMBLESIDE,** *Rothay Bridge 1888* 20483

This simple but well-proportioned bridge spans the River Rothay on the western fringe of Ambleside. Behind the centre of the bridge, Gilbert Scott's spire of St Mary's parish church stands out from the fell side. Inside the church is a large mural of the traditional rush-bearing procession painted by Gordon Ransom in 1944, and also a piece by the celebrated local sculptress, Josefina de Vasconcellos.

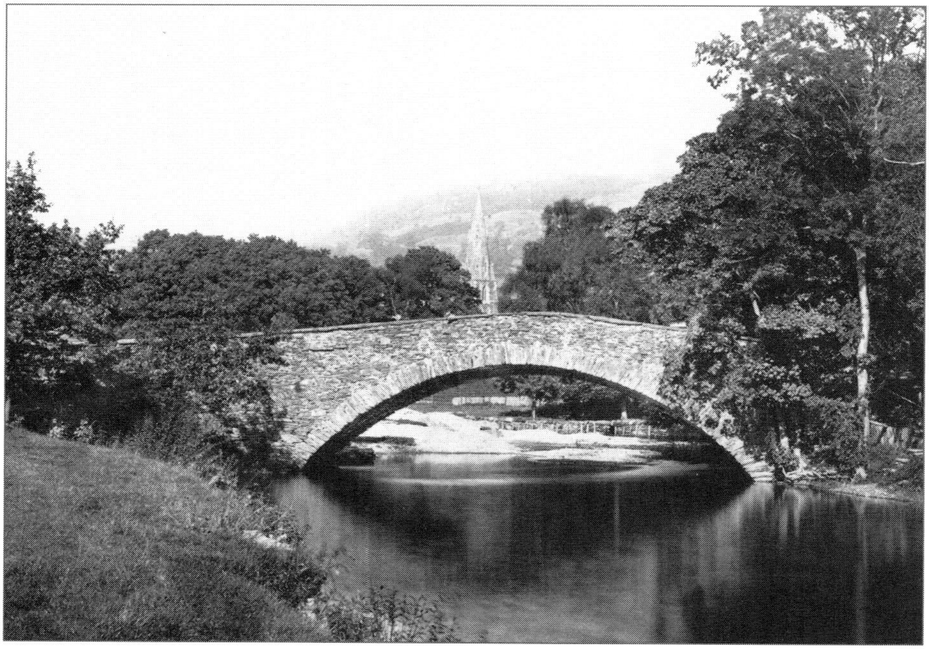

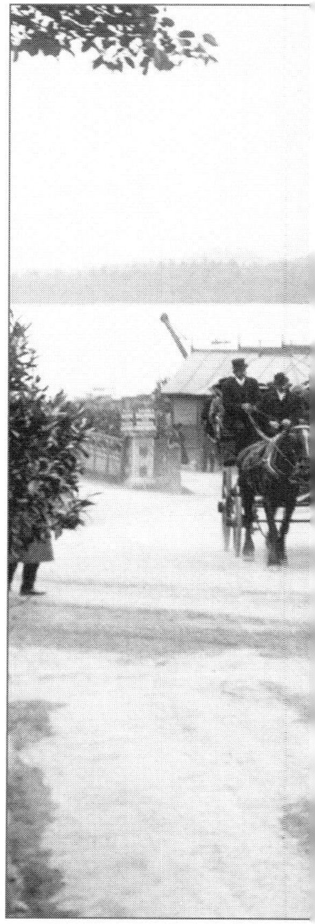

► **AMBLESIDE**
Windermere from Loughrigg 1912 64311

This classic view of England's largest lake was taken from the south end of Loughrigg. Ambleside town is round the corner to the left. The steamer terminal at Waterhead (left) had been fully developed well before the time of this photograph, and the large buildings to the right of the pier, now a Youth Hostel, had more recently been constructed. The River Brathay meanders across the meagre flat land before entering the lake. Immediately on its left bank is the site of the successive Roman forts known as Galava.

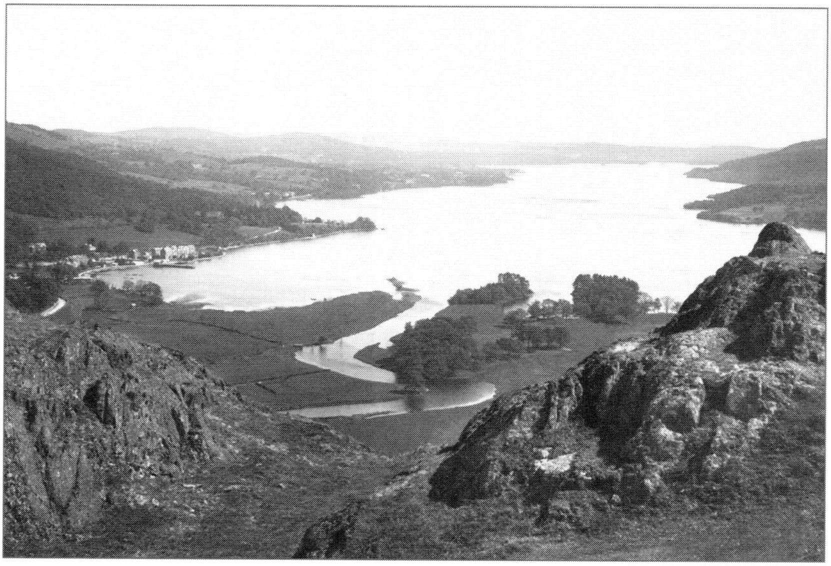

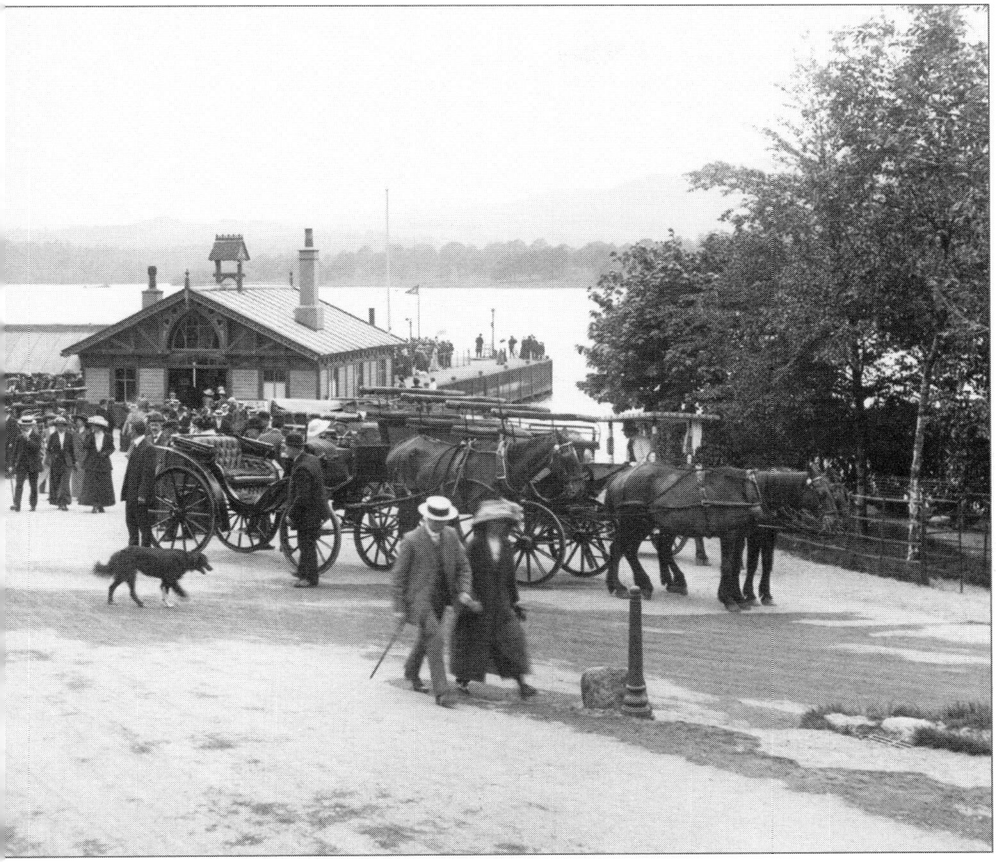

◄ **WINDERMERE**
Above Waterhead 1912 64319

The steamer terminal at Waterhead, one mile south of Ambleside, has changed little over the years. The hustle and bustle suggests the recent arrival of a steamer bringing passengers from Lakeside and Bowness; part of the funnel and a flag are visible behind the pier buildings. Carriages are taking some of the passengers on to Ambleside, but one couple are clearly setting out briskly on foot.

► **WINDERMERE**
The Waterhead Hotel 1887 20463

The Waterhead Hotel sits tightly in the angle between the main A591 road and the minor road which skirts the head of the lake before bearing right towards Ambleside. The coach and pair has plenty of passengers; they are either heading for Coniston or Hawkshead via Rothay Bridge (see No 20483), or going to Ambleside town centre by the longer route via Borrans Road.

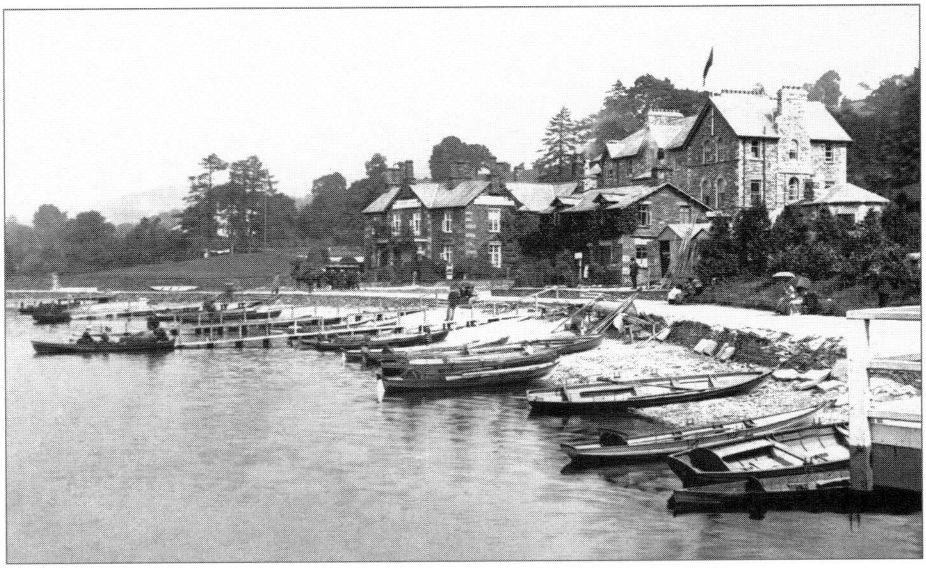

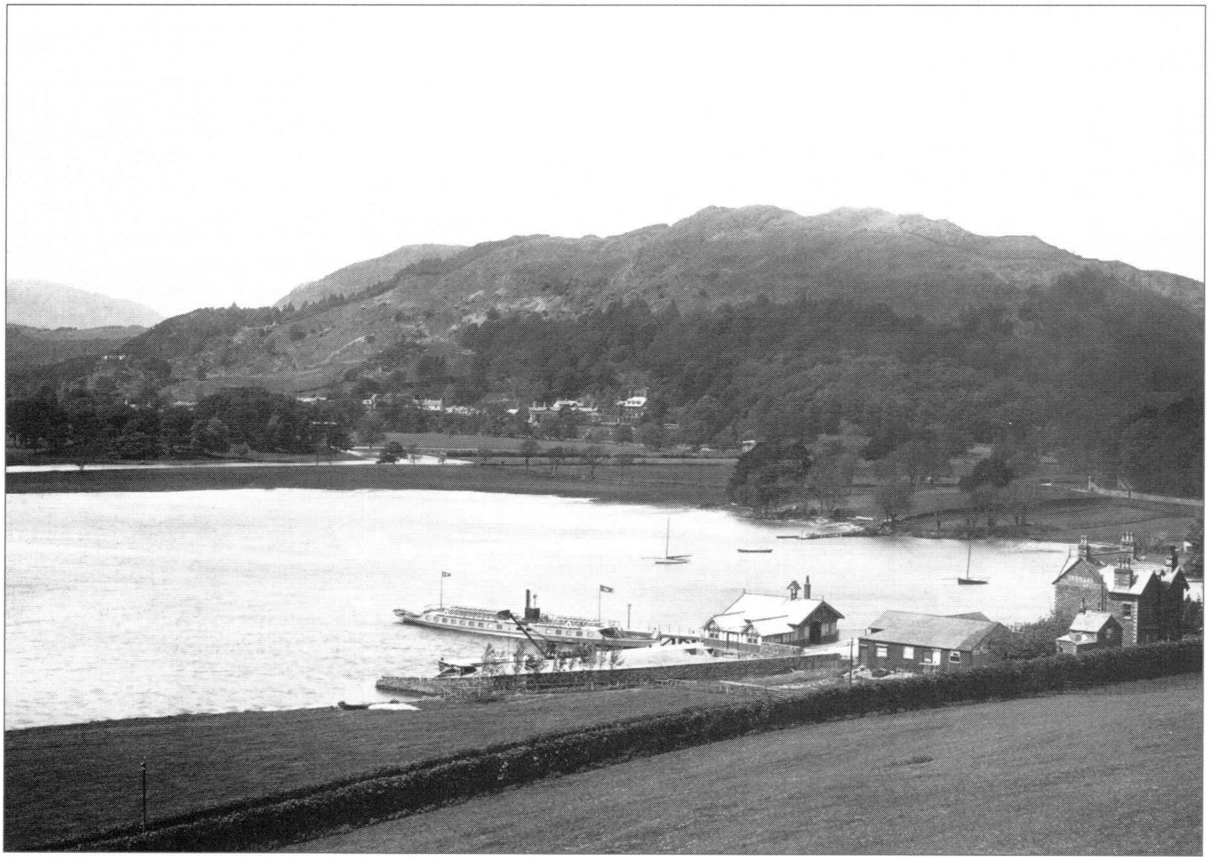

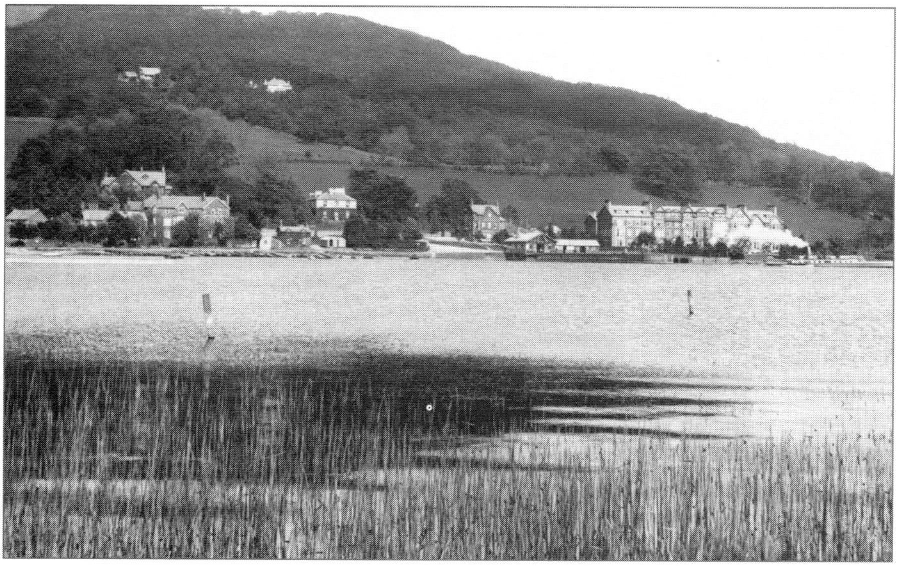

◀ **WINDERMERE**
Waterhead 1912 64313

From the opposite side of the lake, the turn of the century development to the right of the steamer pier now dominates the scene. To the left of the picture is the Waterhead Hotel, set against the backdrop of the lower slopes of Ambleside's own mountain, Wansfell Pike. On the extreme right a lake steamer has just departed, heading for Bowness.

WINDERMERE
Above Waterhead
1892 30477

Here we see the boat station, originally built in 1845, at the head of the lake, taken from the hillside above. This picture pre-dates the construction of the large buildings by the shore, now the youth hostel. One of the lake steamers sits at the pier, whilst the County Refreshment Rooms are boldly advertised on the stone building to the right. Across the end of the lake, the hamlet of Clappersgate sits below the bulk of Loughrigg.

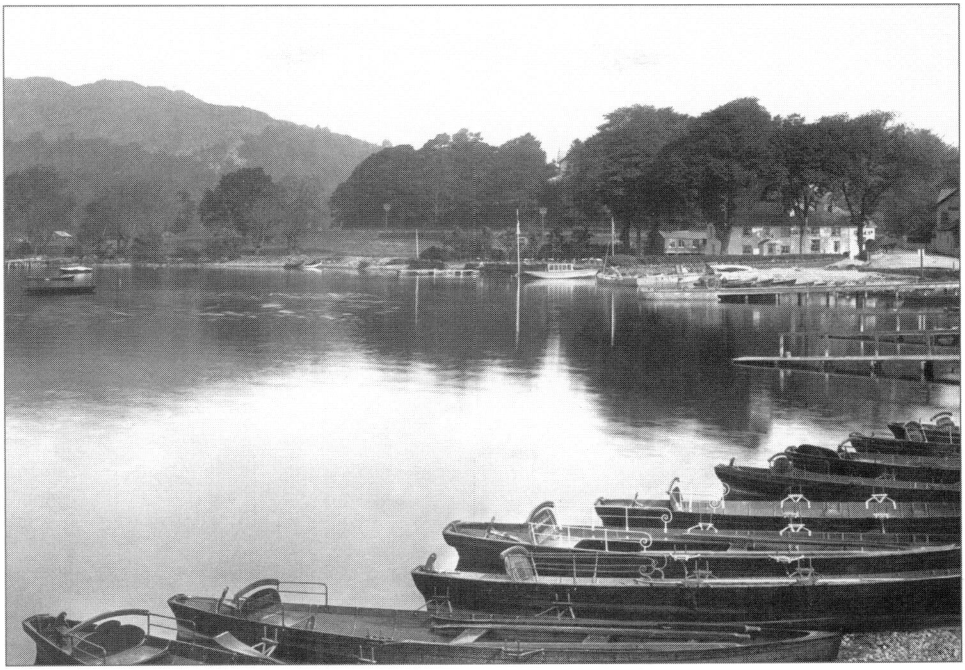

WINDERMERE, *Waterhead 1912* 64316

From the steamer pier side of the lake, this viewpoint emphasises the enduring importance of tourism to boating on the lake. The solid clinker-built rowing boats have been available for hire here since the mid 19th century. The Wateredge Hotel, sitting by the lake shore (background right), has grown considerably since 1912. Loughrigg is the hill closing off the scene to the left.

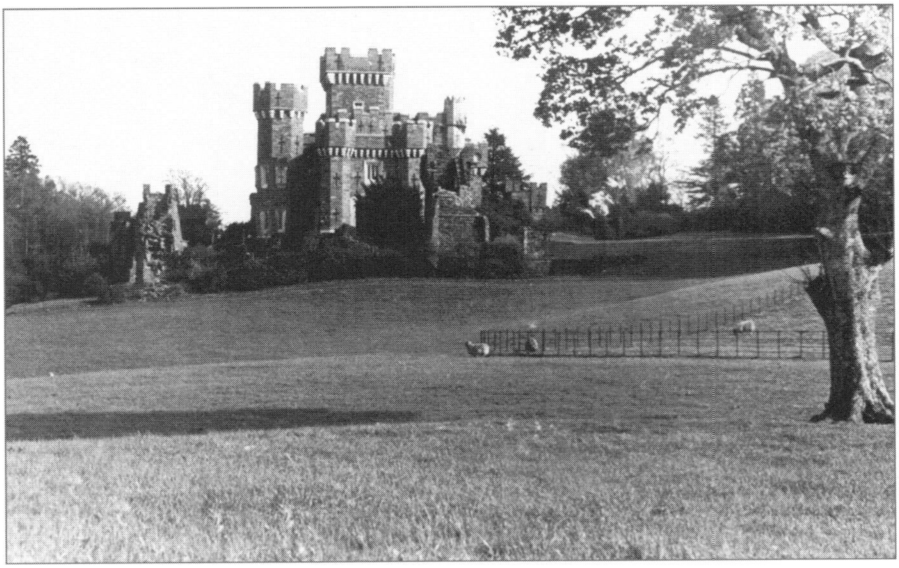

AMBLESIDE
Wray Castle 1955
A46135

Described as a 'neo-Gothic monstrosity', Wray Castle was built for an eccentric Liverpool surgeon, James Dawson, in 1840-47. Once used as a holiday home by the sixteen-year-old Beatrix Potter and her family, the castle was later acquired by the National Trust, and has for many years been used as a training centre for marine communications.

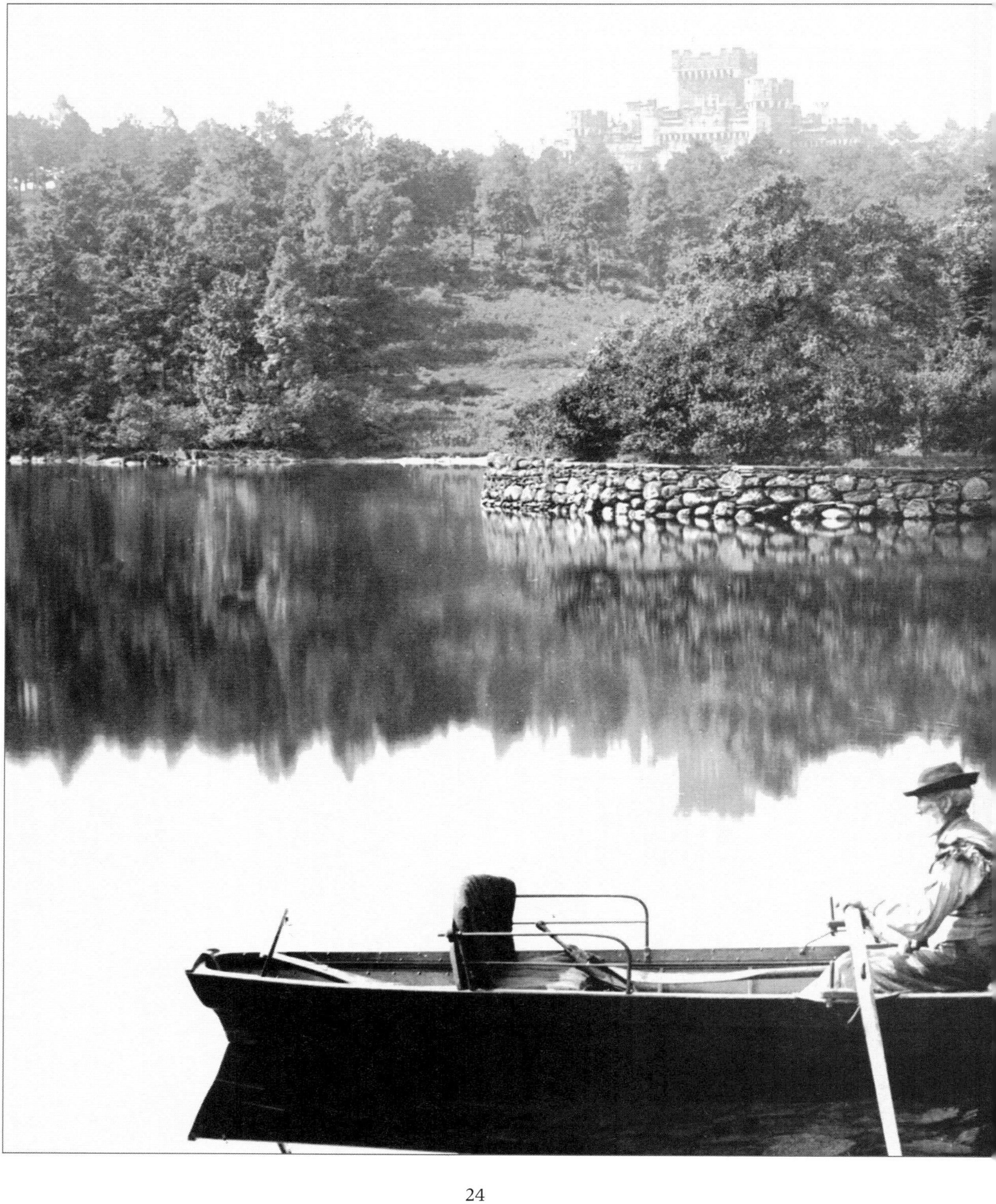

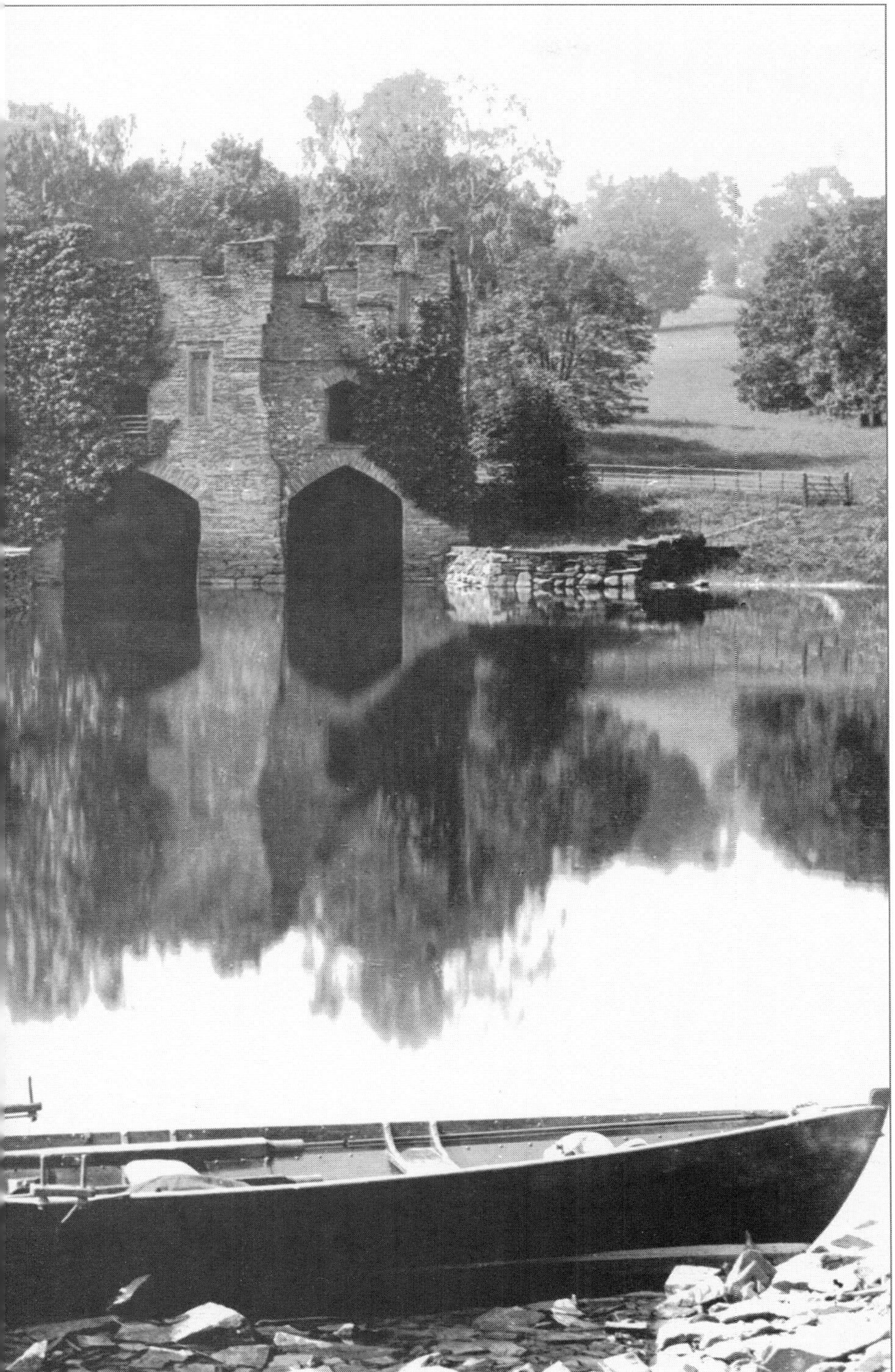

WINDERMERE
Wray Castle and the Boathouse 1886 18665

A lone elderly oarsman reflects on life on the still waters of the little bay below Wray Castle and its impressive ornate boathouse. The substantial boat is typical of many used on Windermere both for traditional char fishing and for hire to visitors. Raised on its knoll above Watbarrow Point, the castle has a fairy-tale appearance.

SKELWITH BRIDGE
Skelwith Force
1888 20488

The great surging waterfall (the word 'force' is derived from the Old Norse 'foss') at Skelwith has been a great visitor attraction since Victorian times. The force is not very high, but it generates immense power; some of the water was formerly conducted in a large pipe to workshops a short distance downstream where locally quarried slate was split and dressed for building and other uses.

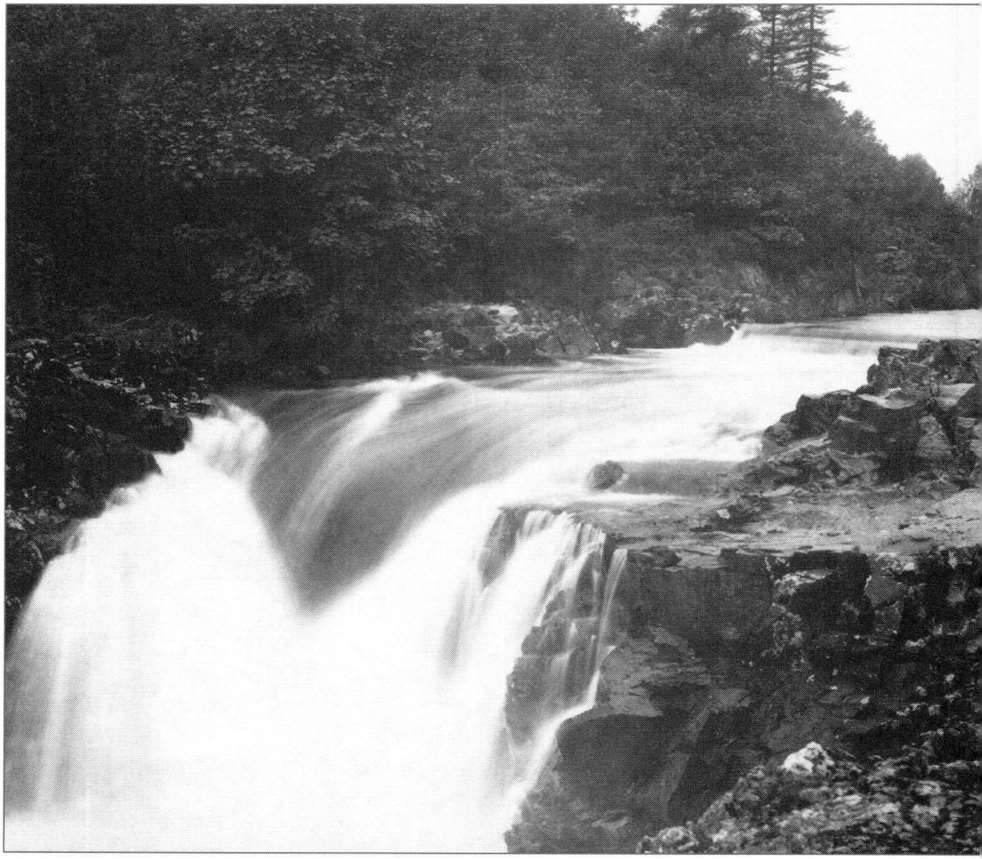

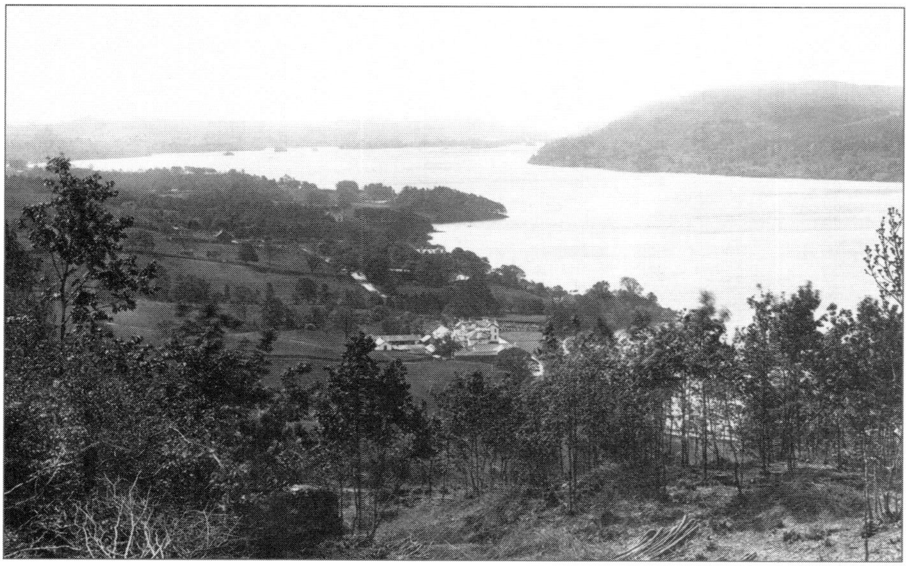

WINDERMERE
From above Lowood
1892 30474

This sweeping view of much of the northern half of the lake was taken from the hillside above the Lowood Hotel. On the far side of the lake the extensive late 18th-century planting of larches and other trees by the Curwen family clothes the Claiffe Heights hillside. Belle Isle, home of the family for many years, is just visible.

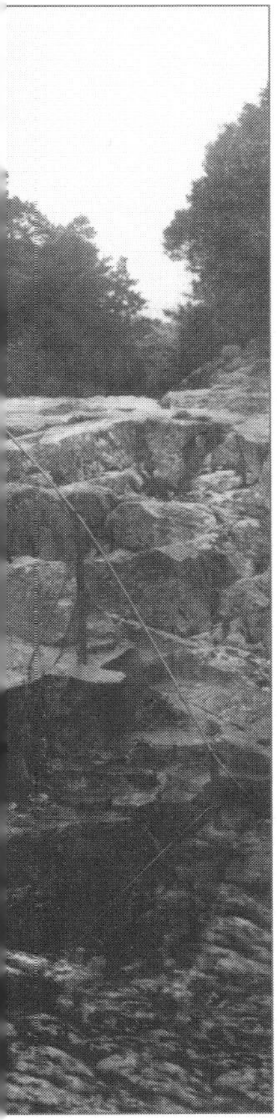

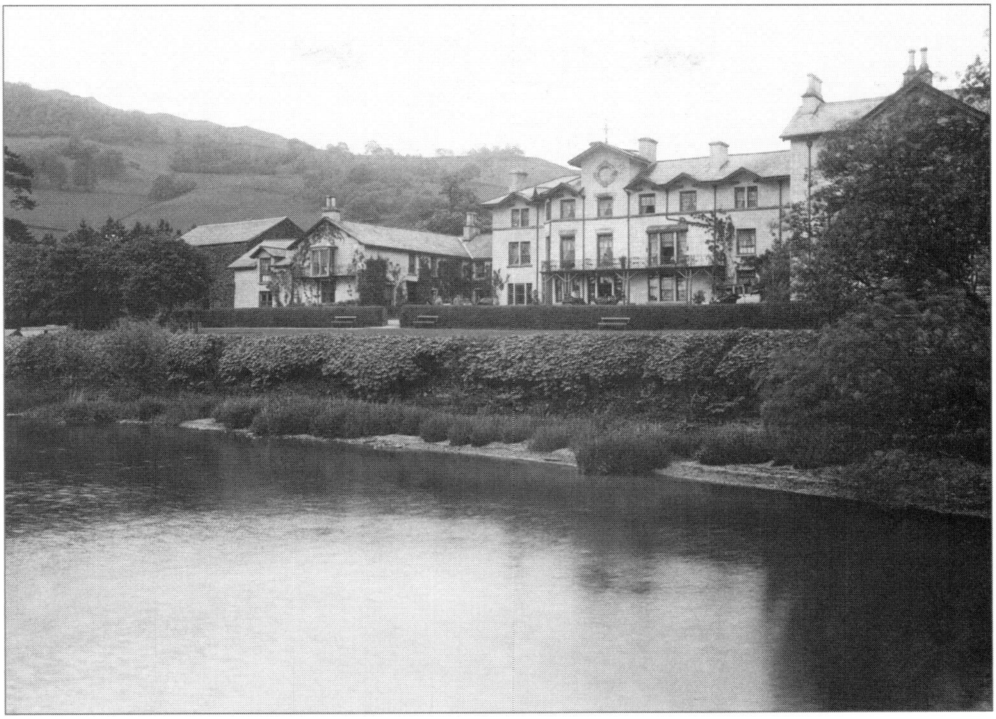

▲ **WINDERMERE,** *The Lowood Hotel 1912* 64327

Here we see the front view of the already spacious Lowood Hotel, with a horse and carriage waiting by the main door. These were tranquil times, evidenced by the deserted A591 passing between lake and hotel.

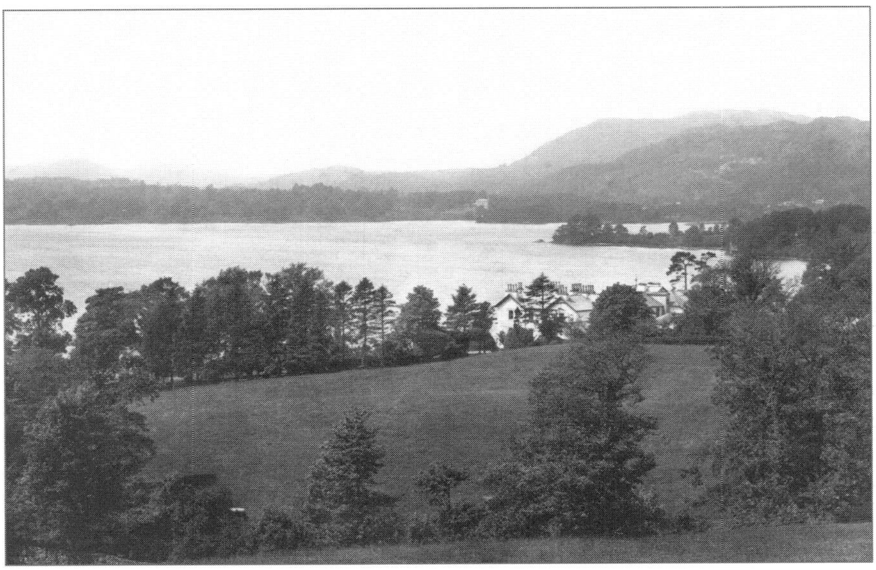

◀ **WINDERMERE**
From above Lowood 1892 30473

This is a slightly earlier view over the rooftops of the hotel complex, with some of the buildings of Clappersgate visible below Loughrigg. For many years the Lowood was one of several hotels owned by the locally-based speedboat ace Norman Buckley (no relation of the author) and his family.

WINDERMERE, *From Calgarth 1887* 20470

This view looks across White Cross Bay to the northern end of the lake. On the shore to the right a factory for the construction of Sunderland flying boats was established during World War II. The site is now a caravan park. The number on the rowing boat is evidence of the 19th-century regulation of boating on the lake. The 1881 Census recorded Thomas Walker, whose name is painted on the boat, as a boat builder, resident at Crown Villas, Bowness.

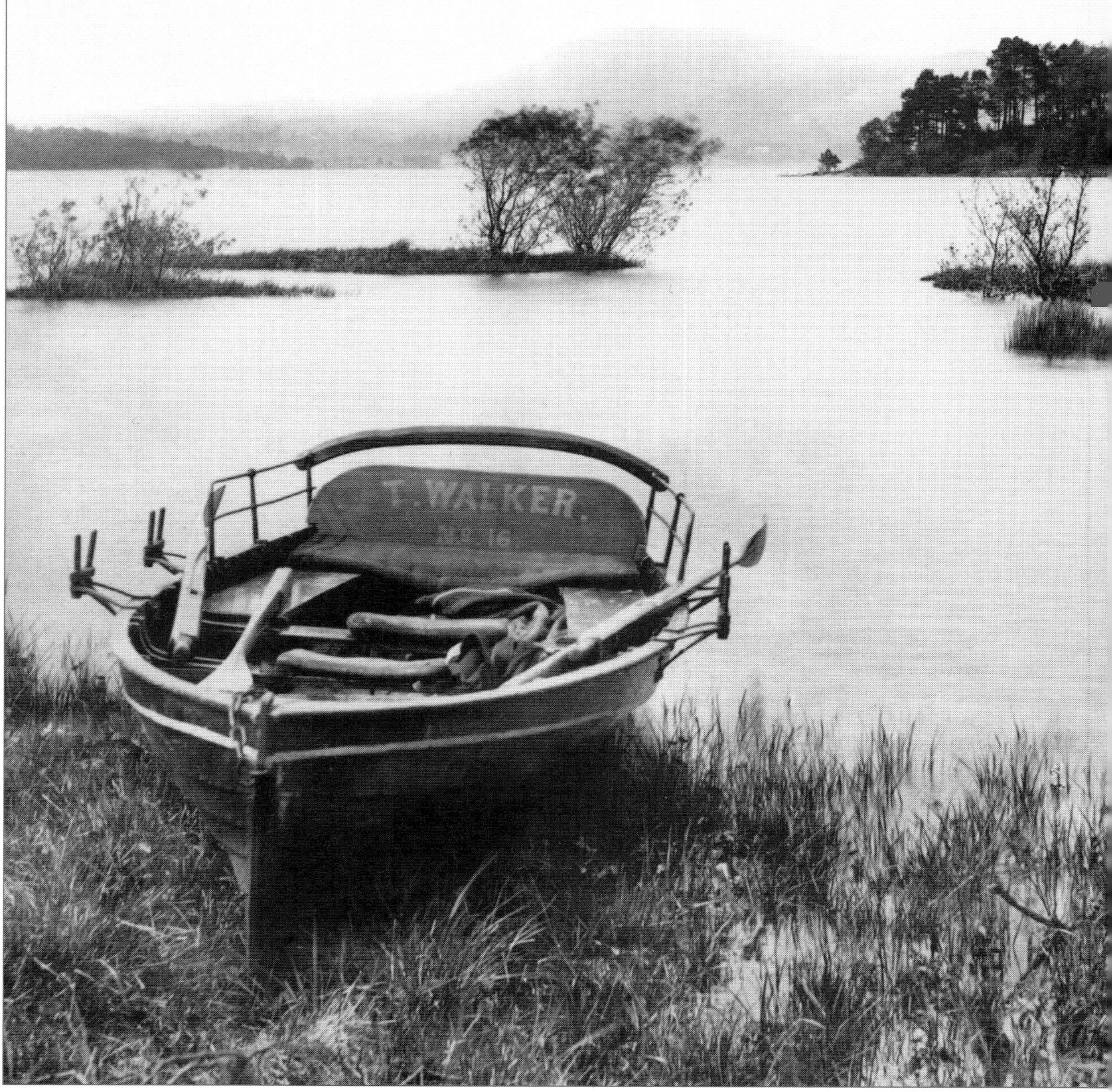

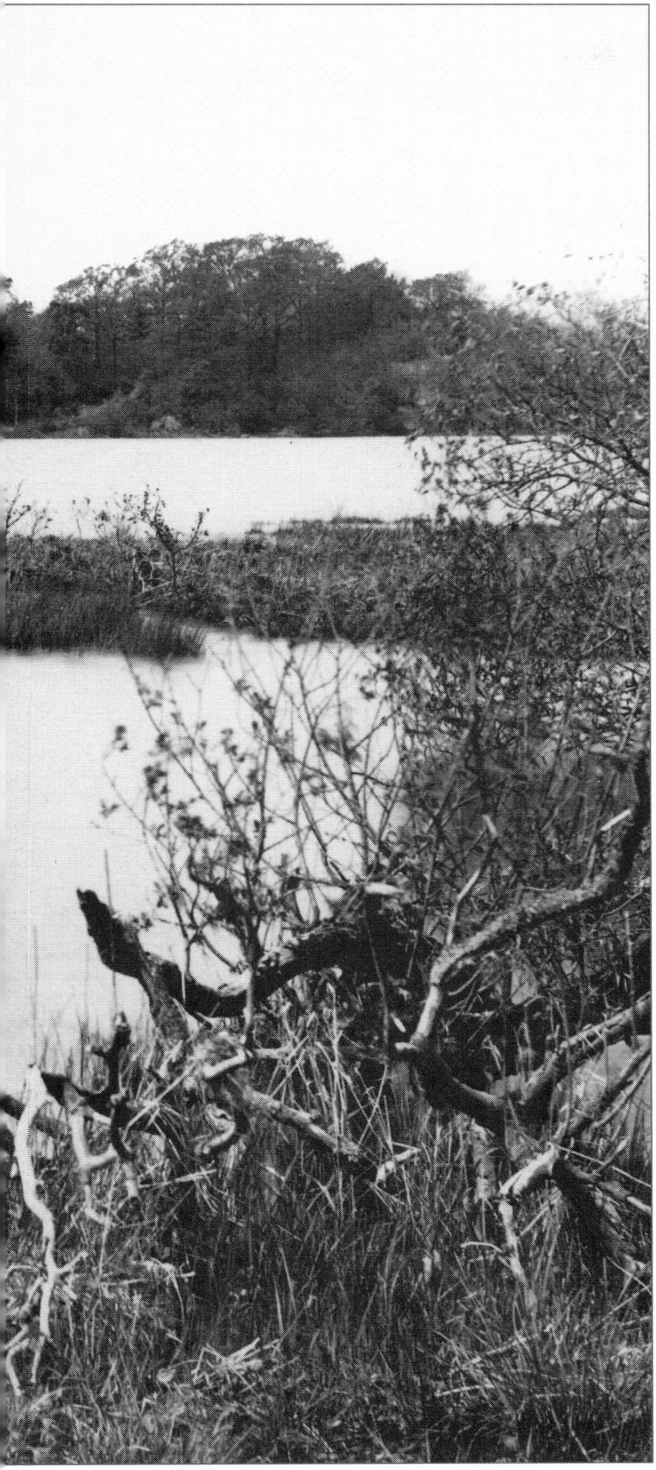

BOWNESS-ON-WINDERMERE

THE oldest remaining settlement on the lake is the cluster of dwellings, inns and shops around St Martin's church, Bowness, which from the 17th century was a community of boatmen and fishermen. As in the case of nearby Windermere village, after the arrival of the Kendal and Windermere railway in 1847, the building of hotels such as the Old England and the Hydro and fine houses such as Belsfield proceeded apace, giving Bowness its present Victorian appearance.

Mass tourism flourished from the latter part of the 19th century. A considerable boat station, with a steamer pier and moorings for both private and hire boats, was developed on the shore of the lake. The wide Promenade and the road around the Glebe were added early in the 20th century. Many shops and cafés, largely to attract holiday visitors, were built on both sides of Crag Brow, the road which rises steeply towards Windermere village. Excursion trains from many northern towns and cities brought the crowds to the lake, via both Windermere station (up to 17 trains a day at summer weekends) and the terminus built at Lakeside in 1868 by the Furness Railway. On Whit Monday 1883 it was estimated that there were 10,000 day trippers. Most will have visited Bowness by one means or another.

WINDERMERE
From Miller Ground 1926 79185

This is the boating area at Miller Ground, with its jetty and traditional Windermere rowing boats. In previous centuries a foot ferry service crossed the lake from Miller Ground to Belle Grange on the western shore. Just off this picture to the right, an early 17th-century cottage still stands, but now without the bell which was used to summon the ferryman.

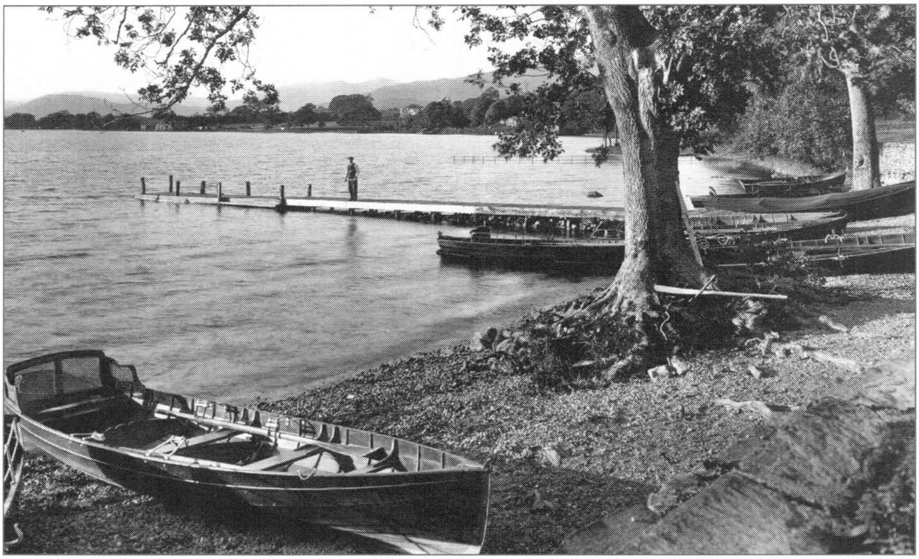

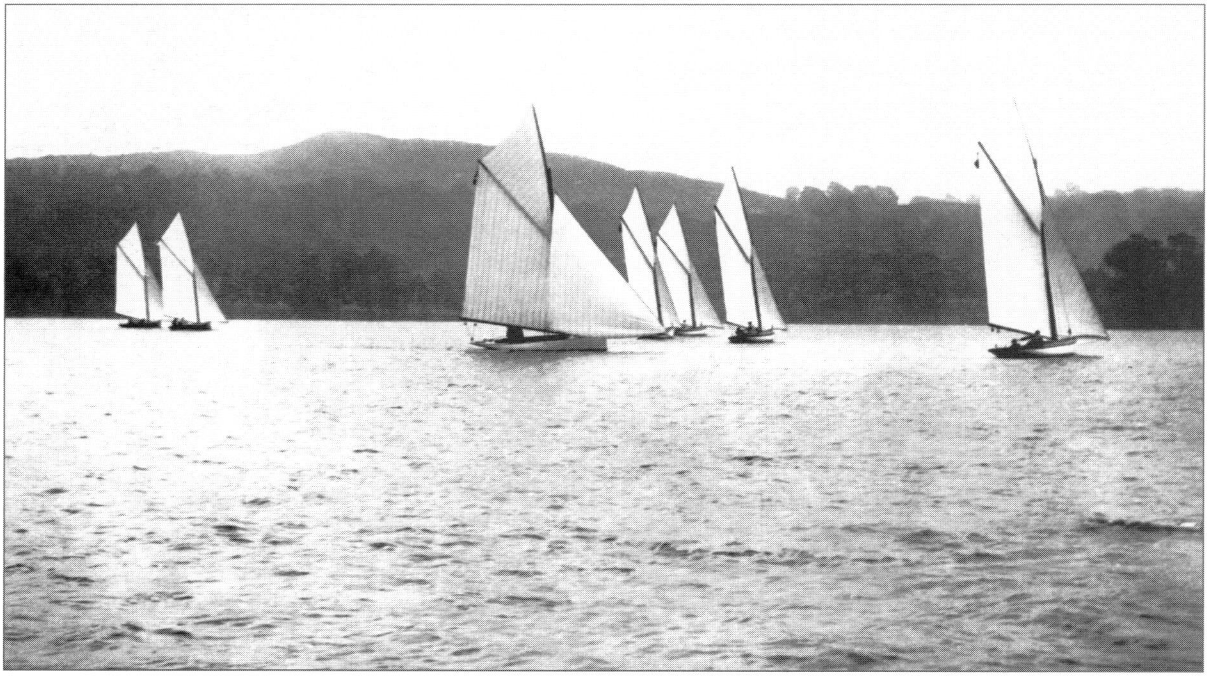

BOWNESS-ON-WINDERMERE, *Sailing Boats 1896* 38804

Almost certainly a race or regatta is in progress, as the distinctive boats of the Royal Windermere Yacht Club pose gracefully against the wooded shoreline. Sailing was one of the favourite pastimes of the wealthy late 19th-century 'off-comers' who built houses close to the shore of the lake. The club was formed in 1860 as the Windermere Sailing Club, initially using a room in the Old England Hotel as headquarters. A Royal Warrant was granted in 1887. The boats were built to a high (and expensive) specification, the original 22ft class later being supplemented by the more affordable and manageable 17ft class.

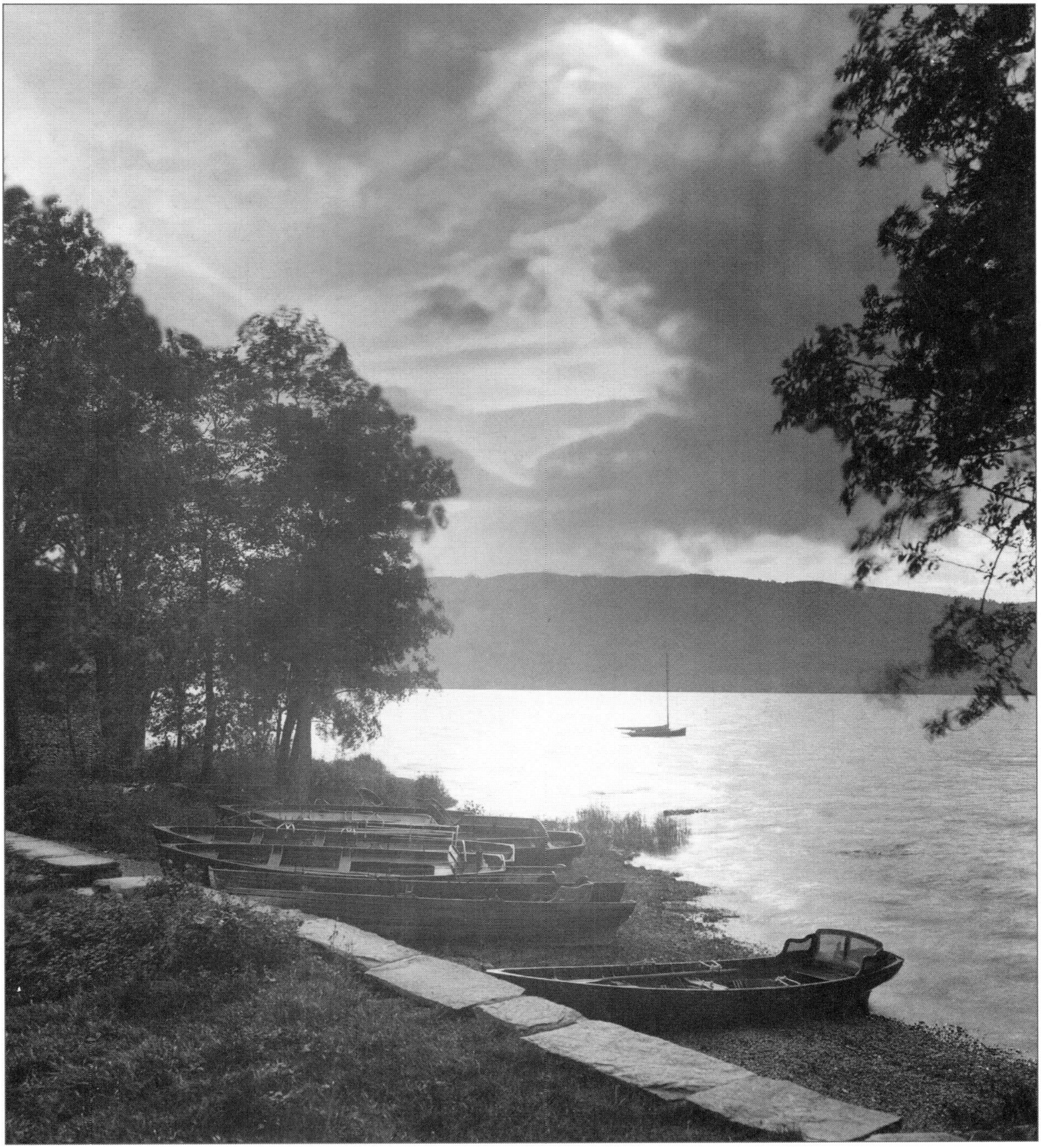

WINDERMERE, *Sunset 1926* 79186

From the area of Miller Ground, sunsets have always been a much-admired Windermere feature, with shafts of silver/copper light escaping from heavy clouds and crossing the water from Claiffe Heights to the near shore. The solitary boat is well placed in this radiant beam.

BOWNESS-ON-WINDERMERE, *The Boat Station c1880* 13305

This is the corner of the Bowness boating area which is used by rowing boats for hire, following the onset of mass tourism from the mid 19th century. Particularly distinctive is the row of 'cushion huts' used by the various boat owners, so called because their primary purpose was for storage of the cushions from the boats when not in use. Oars are stacked against the fronts of the huts.

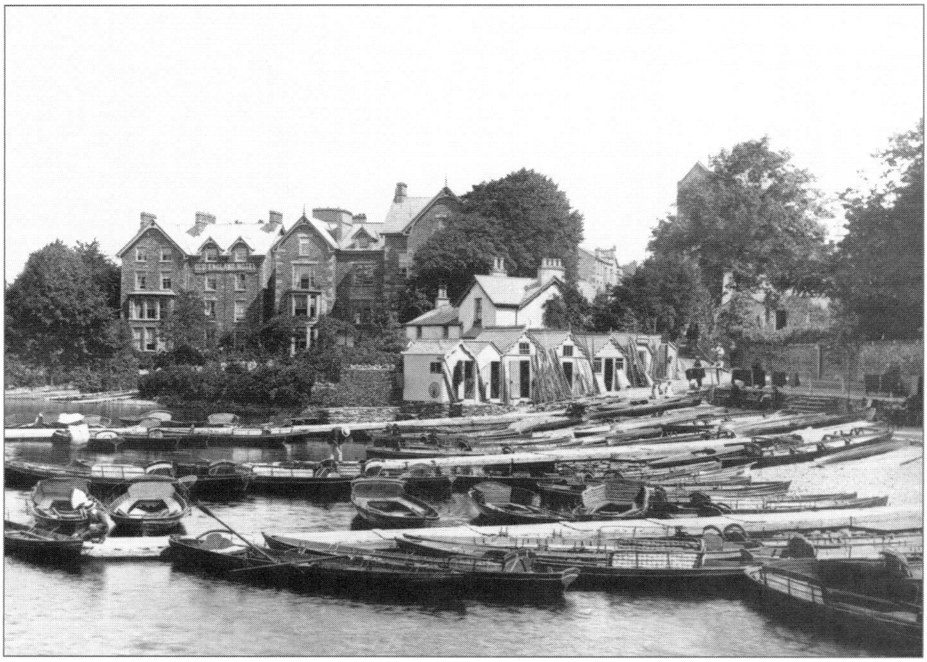

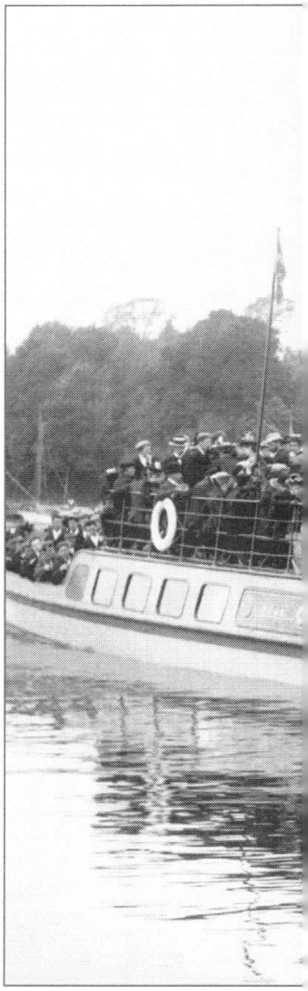

BOWNESS-ON-WINDERMERE
The Pier 1887 20450

One of the very early paddle-driven steamers approaches Bowness pier, the plume from its funnel being strongly indicative of a coal-fired steam boiler. The exposed position of the helmsman, open to all weathers, is also very typical of Victorian practice. The Old England Hotel (right), constructed by the local Pattinson family building company in 1859 following the opening of the railway to Windermere in 1847, forms part of the backdrop.

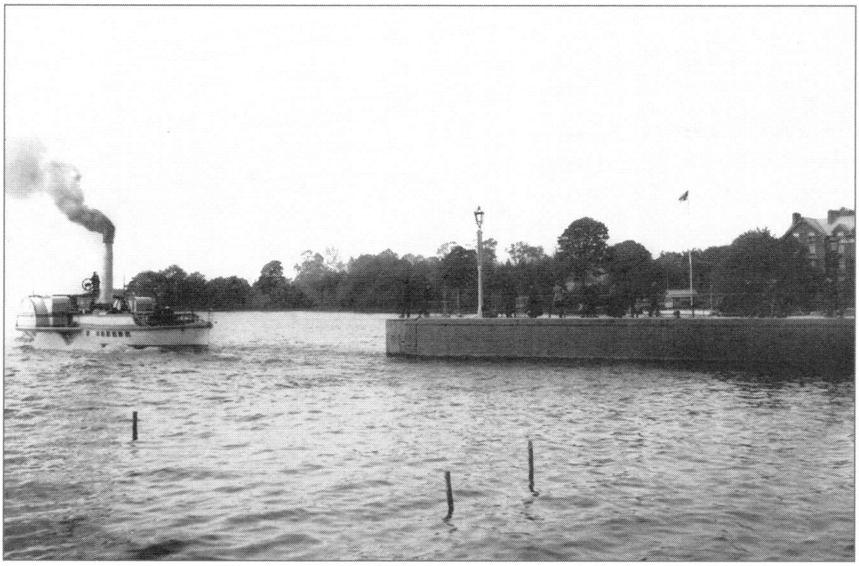

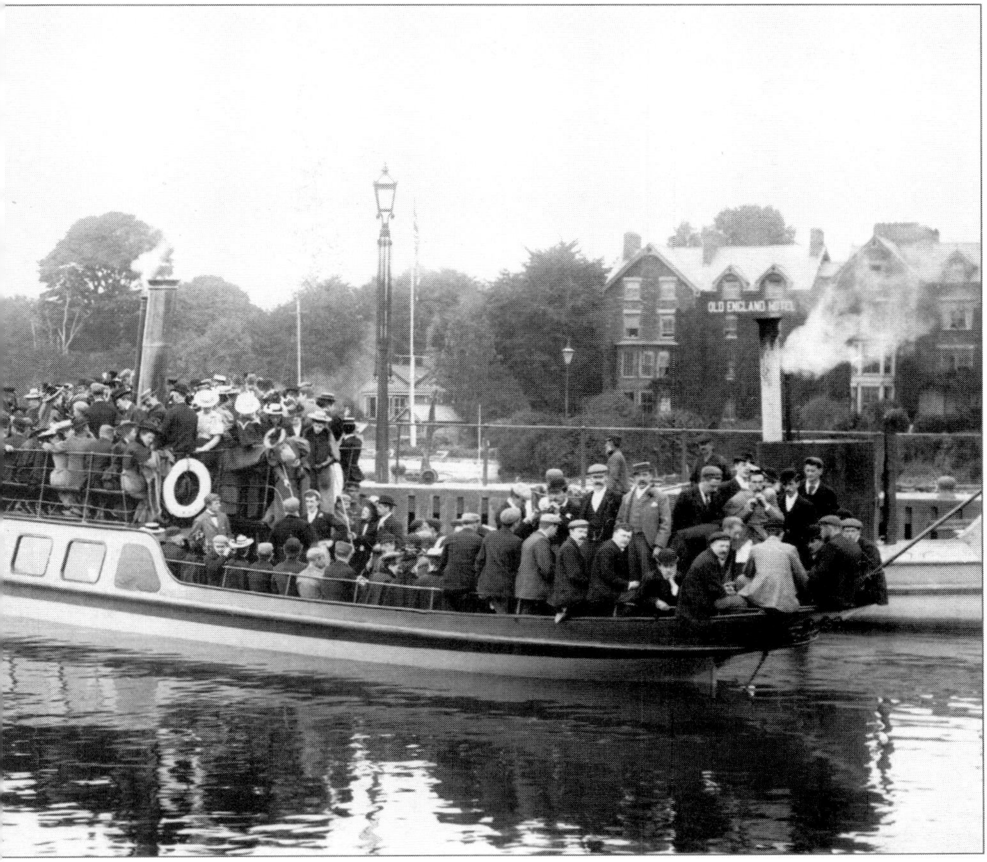

◄ **BOWNESS-ON-WINDERMERE**
The Pleasure Steamer 'Teal' 1896 38795

The overloaded state of the steamer has every appearance of a Bank Holiday trip. The 'Teal', the 'Swan', the 'Cygnet' and the 'Tern' were very similar screw-driven steamers, launched on the lake between the years 1869 and 1891. The 'Teal' was launched in 1878, and worked until 1927. Socially, there appears to be some distinction between the boater-hatted mixed sexes on the upper deck and the dour cloth-capped men packed into (and overhanging!) the stern.

► **BOWNESS-ON-WINDERMERE**
The Boat Station 1896
38794

We are obviously well into the age of mass tourism. This photograph shows one of the late Victorian screw-driven steamers by the end of the pier. Observing this remarkably packed mass of presumably happy humanity are the occupants of a private steam launch and people in rowing boats. The two boys in the foreground seem to be more interested in setting up an oar than in the comings or goings of the steamer.

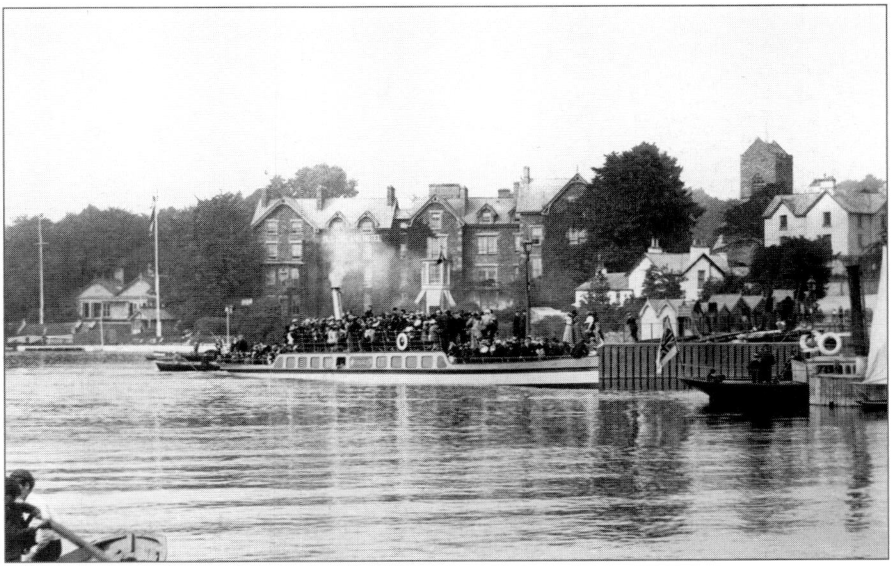

BOWNESS-ON-WINDERMERE
The Boat Station 1896 38793

This is another of the fine series of Bowness Bay pictures of 1896, this time taken from a viewpoint a little further to the south, allowing a wider view of most of the boat station, including the steamer pier and its associated buildings. At the end of the pier crowds of people are waiting to board one of the steamers.

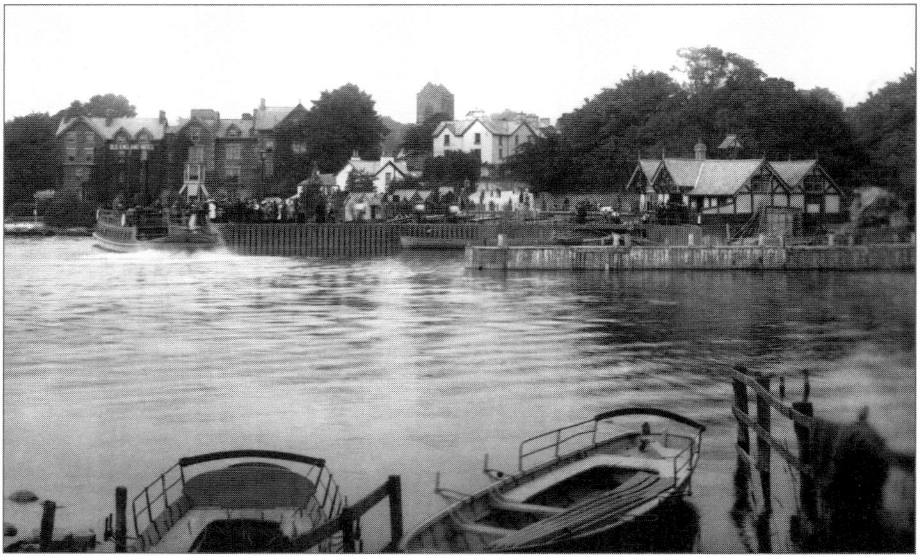

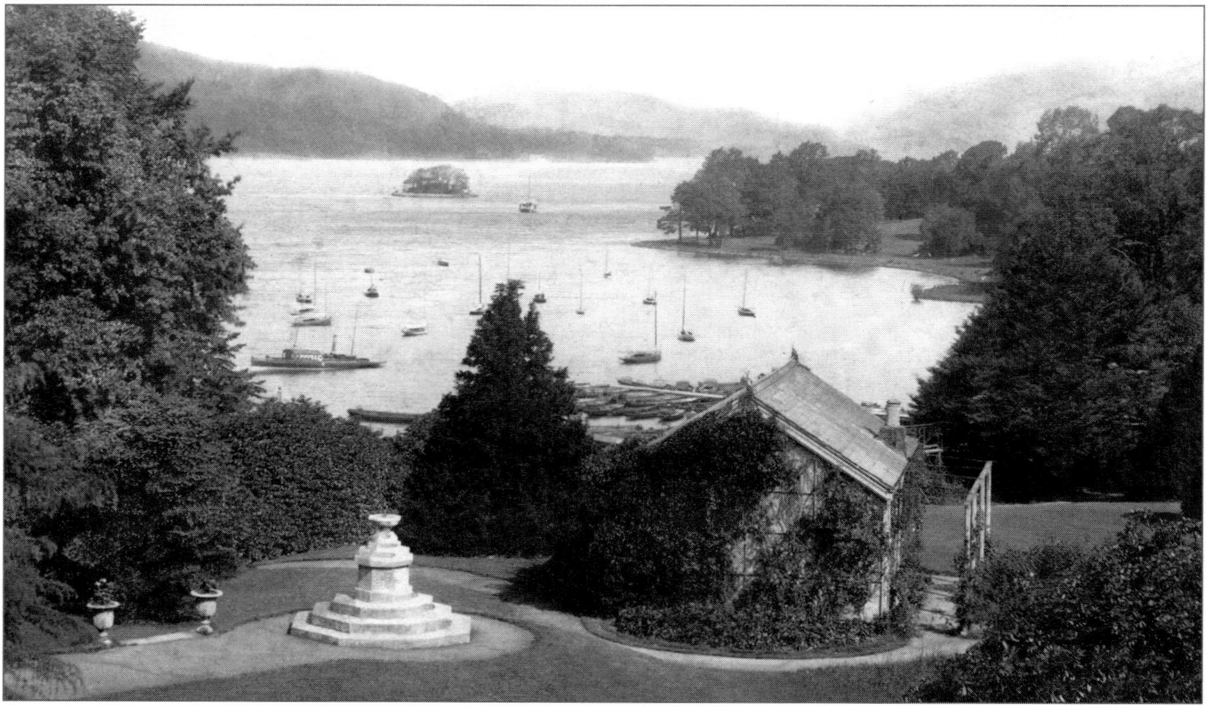

BOWNESS-ON-WINDERMERE, *The View from the Belsfield Hotel 1896* 38798

The sloping gardens below the Belsfield Hotel provide the viewpoint for this Windermere scene. The boat station is immediately below, with clustered rowing boats for hire. A steam launch passes by. Bowness Bay opens out into the north basin of the lake; Hen Holme island is backed by wooded Claiffe Heights and the mountains around Langdale. The building in the foreground and the gardens have changed little over the years since 1896.

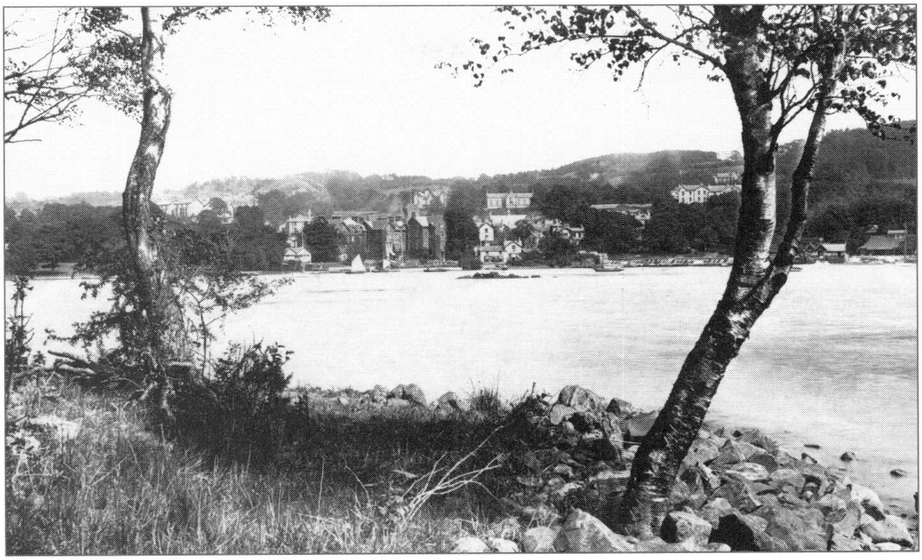

BOWNESS-ON-WINDERMERE
From the Island 1893 31945

This unusual view of Bowness was taken from the shore of the privately owned Belle Island. Behind the waterfront, we can see buildings on the land rising towards Windermere village. By 1893 the two settlements had grown towards each other almost to the point of the merger which exists today.

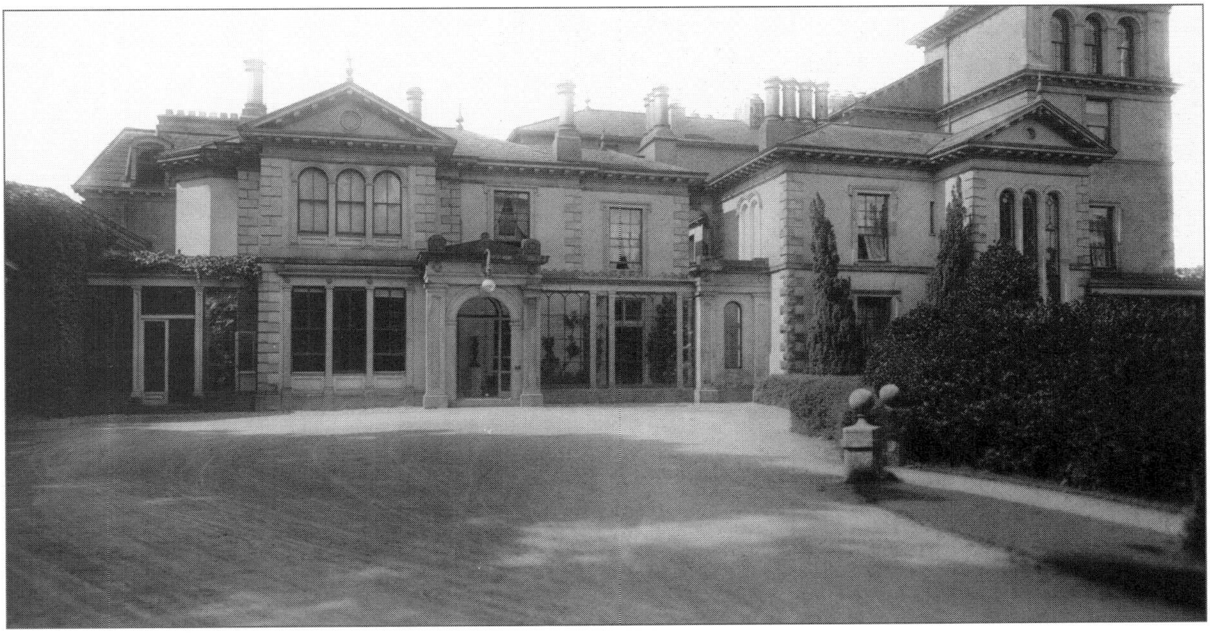

BOWNESS-ON-WINDERMERE, *The Belsfield Hotel 1896* 38797

This elegant Italianate structure was built in 1845-1848 as a home for Countess de Sternberg. In 1869 it was acquired by the legendary H W Schneider, the iron and steel magnate of Barrow-in-Furness. Each morning the great man would walk through his gardens to the boat station, where his fine steam yacht 'Esperance' was waiting at the jetty. Schneider was preceded by his butler carrying a silver tray with breakfast, which was to be consumed during the journey to Lakeside, where a private train (Schneider was a director of the Furness Railway) awaited to convey him on to Barrow. After Schneider's death in 1887, Belsfield was sold, soon becoming a hotel. Despite subsequent extensions, the building remains very recognisable.

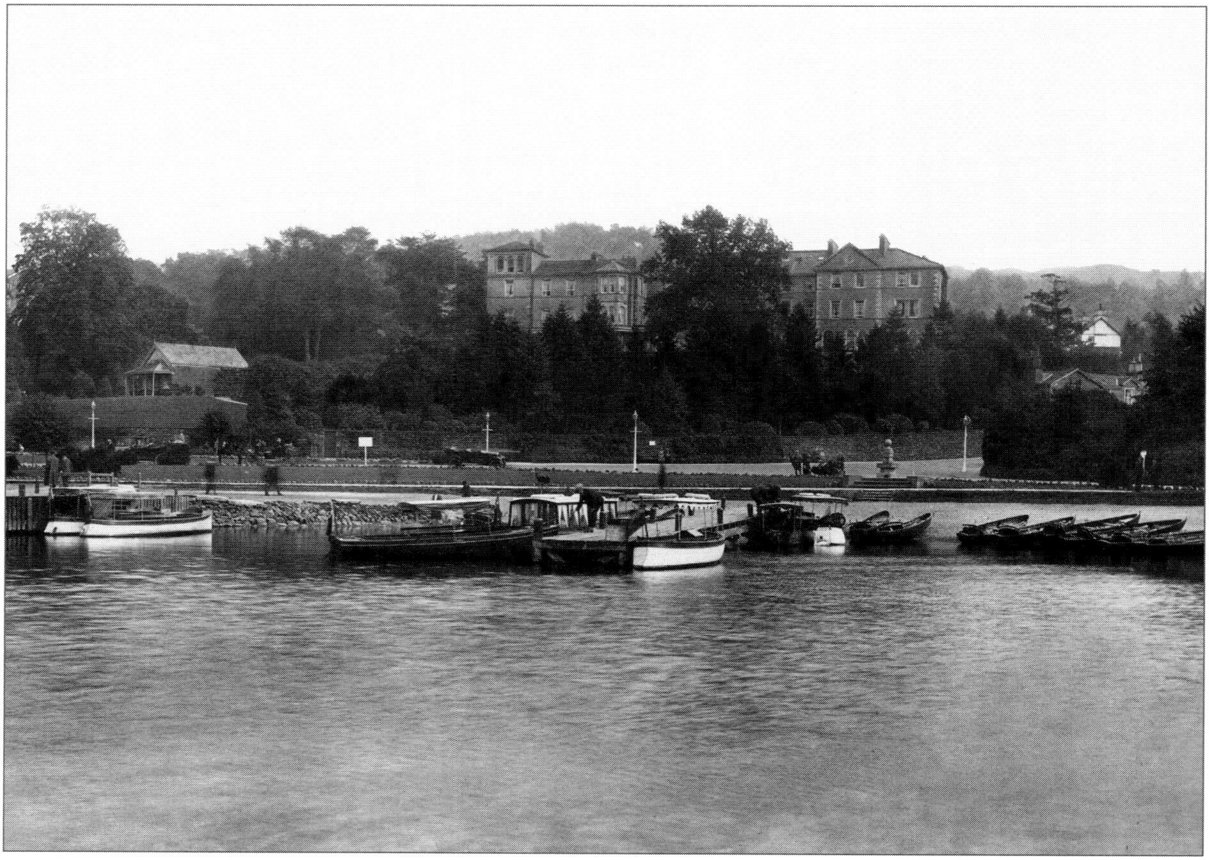

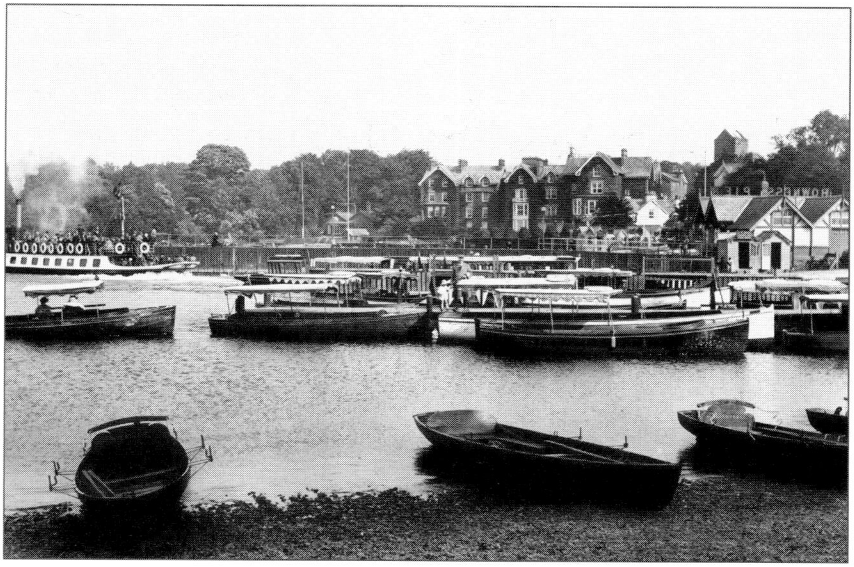

◀ **BOWNESS-ON-WINDERMERE**
The Old England Hotel 1925 77879

The well-filled departing steamer is one of the fleet constructed in the second half of the 19th century, still puffing happily on the timetabled service, but now supplemented by a considerable number of smaller motor launches, ideal for shorter excursions. The pier buildings now carry bold 'Bowness Pier' lettering on the roof (right), whilst J T Saul, advertising 'launches and boats for hire', has huts tacked on to the near end of the buildings.

◀ **BOWNESS-ON-WINDERMERE**
The Belsfield Hotel 1925 77883

This later picture of the Belsfield Hotel emphasises its commanding position above the lake. The third storey was added when Schneider's former home became a hotel. By 1925, the Promenade behind the boat station was fully developed; here it is being used by a variety of vehicles - a charabanc, a horse and trap, a motor car and an invalid carriage. Behind the horse and trap (left) we can just see the little gate used by Schneider en route to and from his steam yacht.

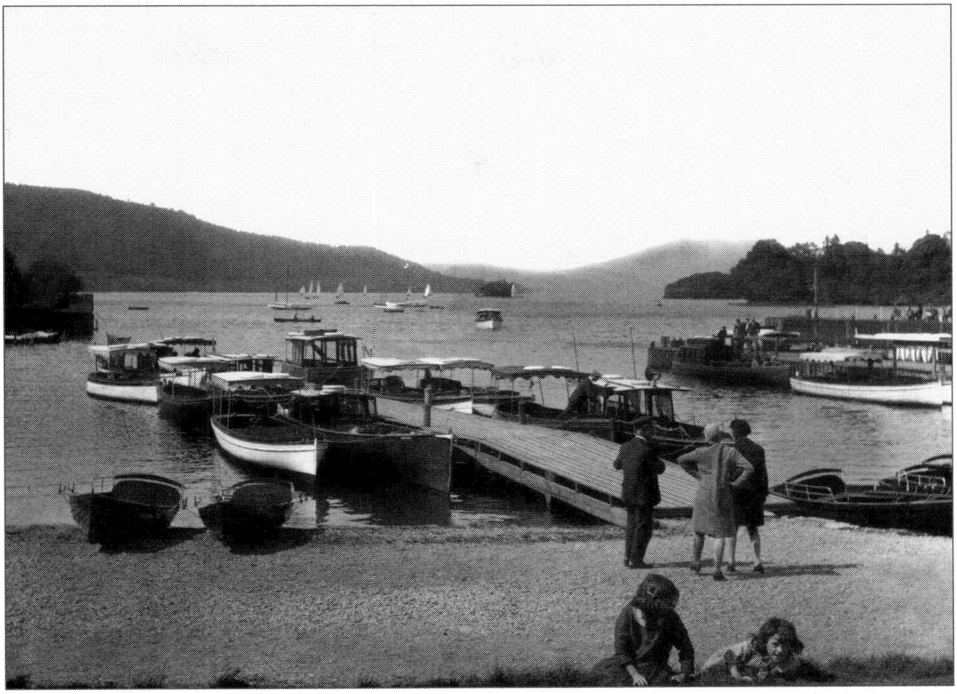

▲ **WINDERMERE,** *The Lake 1929* 82811

This slightly later view looks across what has become the motor launch area of the Bowness boat station. Prospective customers are apparently discussing excursion options with the uniformed boatman, whilst two little girls amuse themselves on the adjacent grass bank. One, at least, is watching the photographer with some suspicion.

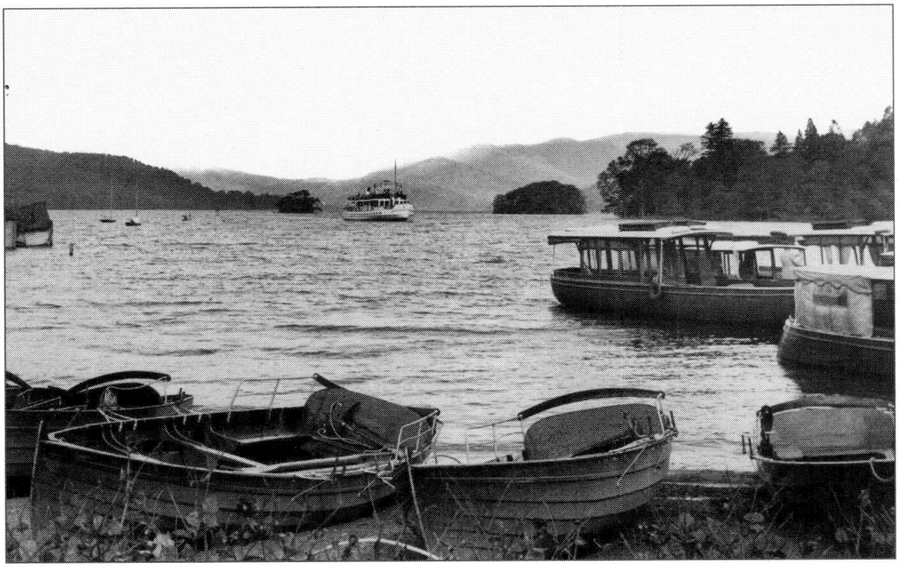

◀ **BOWNESS-ON-WINDERMERE**
The Arrival of the 'Teal' c1955 B166013

In this later picture, the 'Teal', a comparatively modern large boat, launched in 1936, approaches the steamer pier at Bowness. Both the 'Teal', and her sister ship the 'Swan', launched in 1938, are diesel-powered. The islands we can see are Hen Holme and the larger Lady Holme. The latter was the site of an ancient chantry, and is now owned by the National Trust.

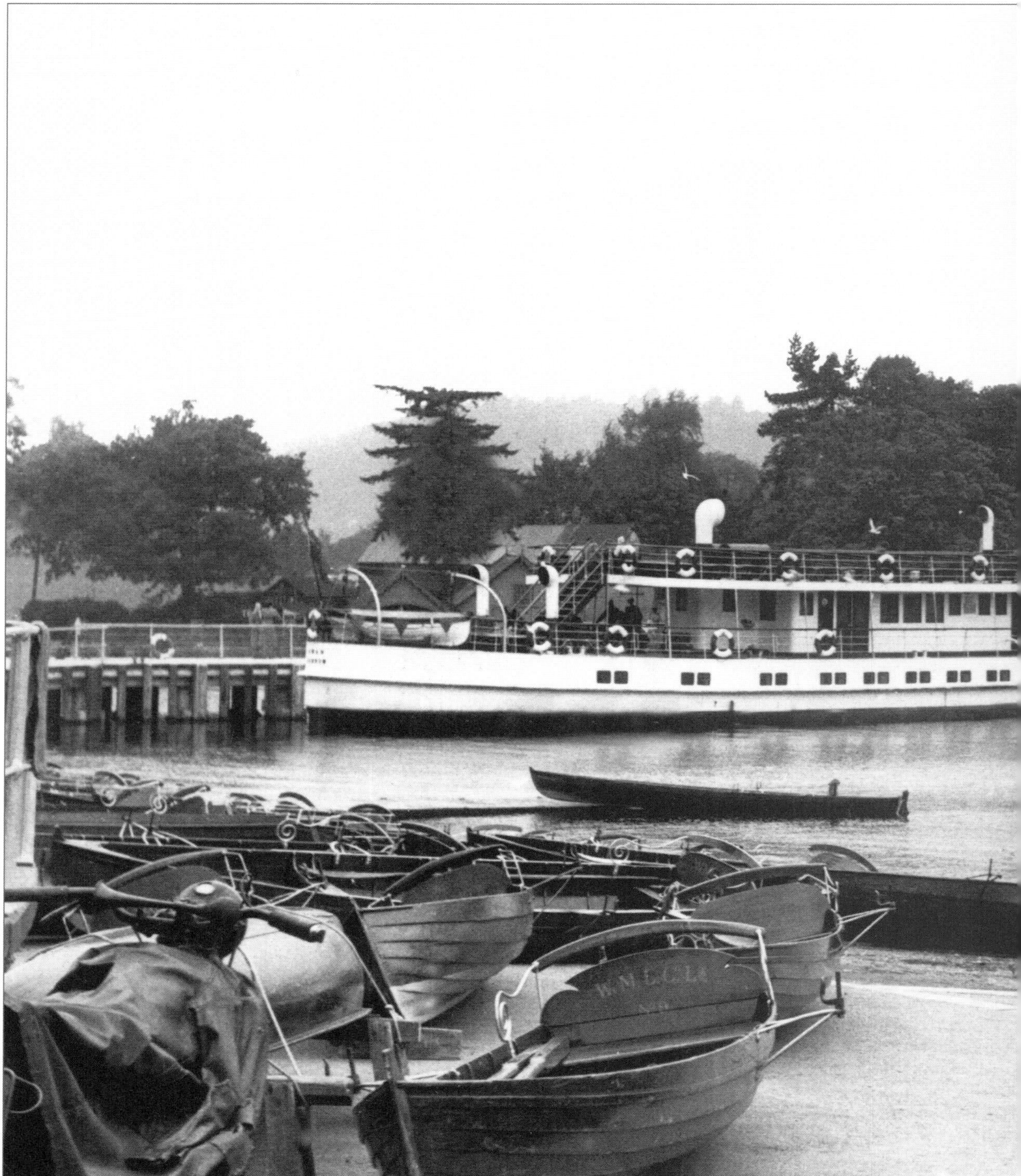

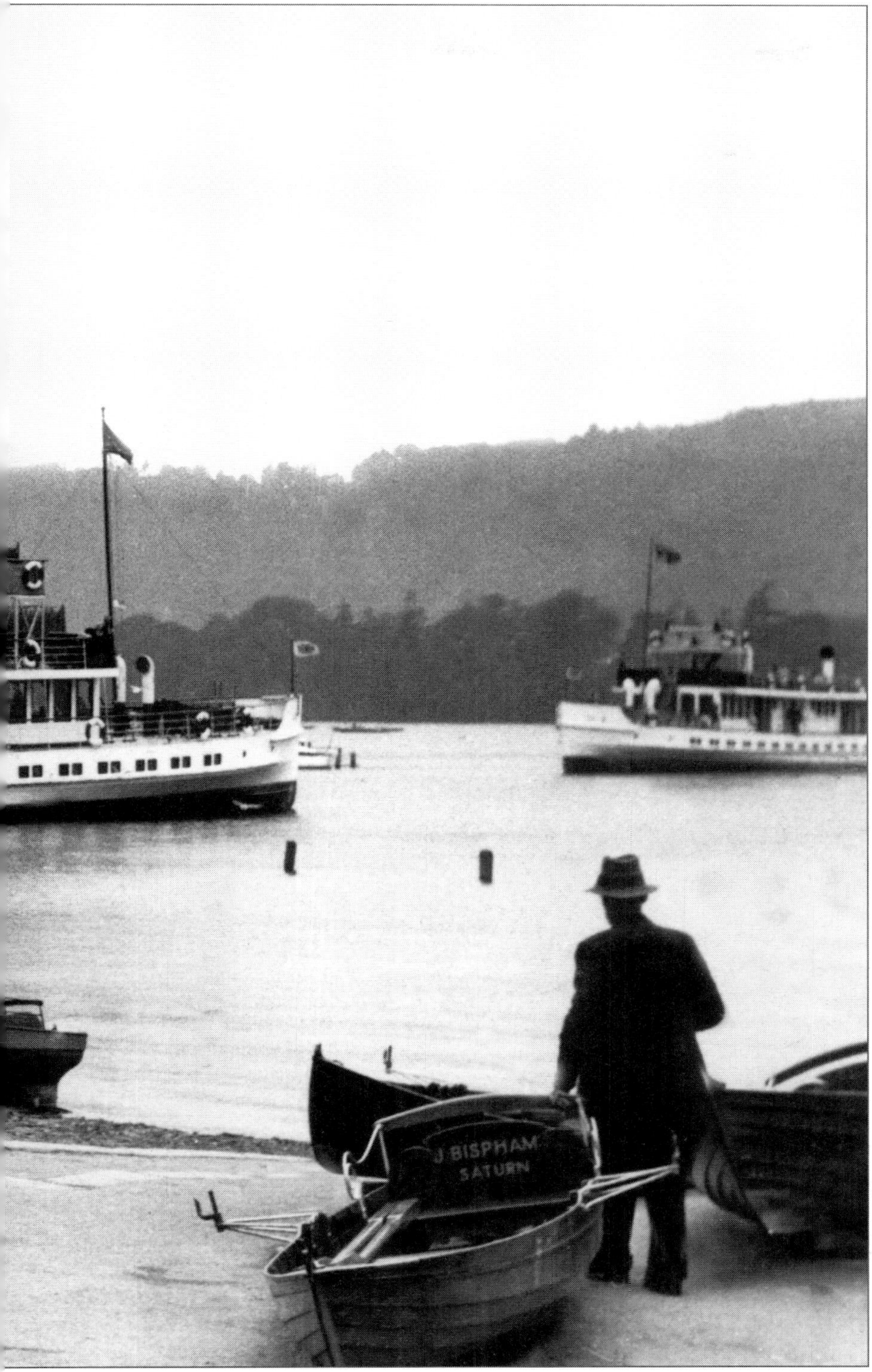

BOWNESS-ON-WINDERMERE
The Pier c1955 B166019

We can see the large boats of the 1930s, the 'Teal' and the 'Swan', each taking the name of one of the Victorian steamers, in this post-World War II scene by Bowness pier. There are surprisingly few passengers, and the helmsmen remain almost as unprotected from the weather as were their Victorian predecessors. The same boats are still working, but their wheelhouses have since been enclosed.

WINDERMERE
From Biskey Howe 1887 20439

The rocky knoll of Biskey Howe, rising abruptly above the built-up area of Bowness, has long been a favourite viewpoint – from here a large proportion of the lake is visible. Here, the old core of the village, clustered around St Martin's parish church, backed by Belle Isle and Claiffe Heights, is being admired by three elegantly dressed ladies.

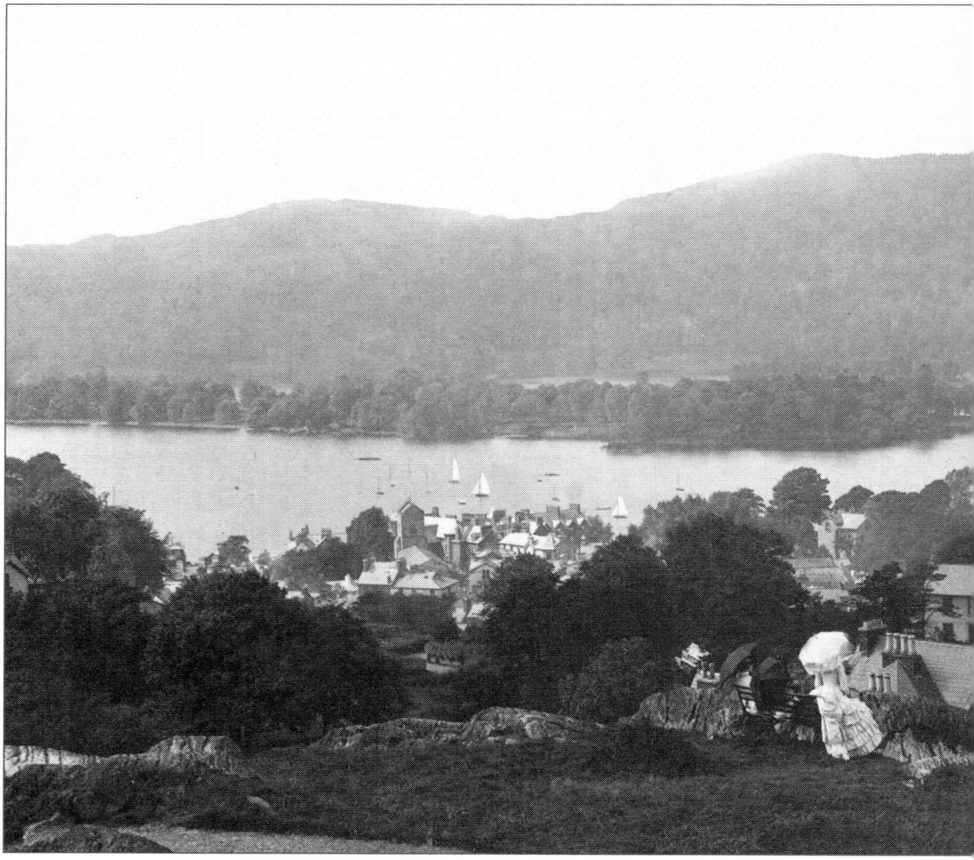

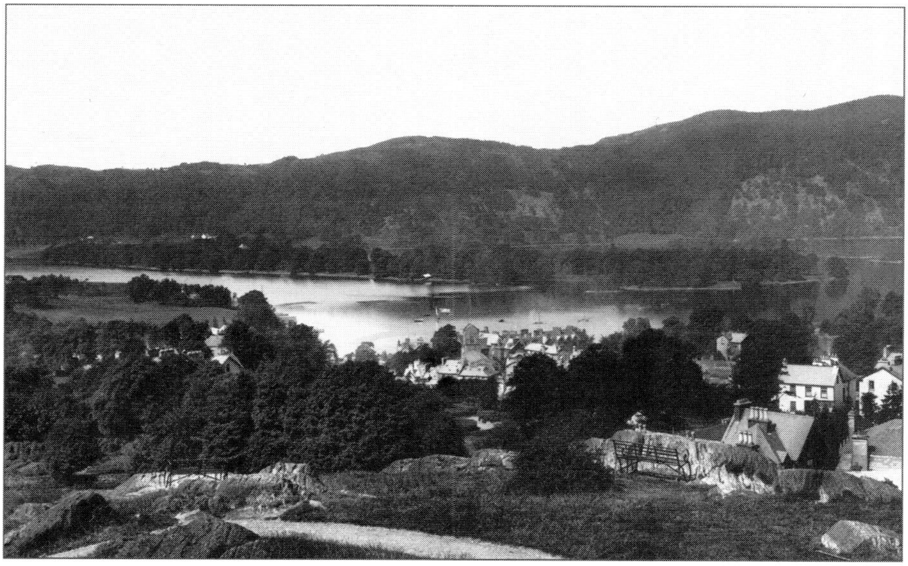

BOWNESS-ON-WINDERMERE
Belle Island 1893 31936

Apart from the absence of the elegant ladies, the classic view from Biskey Howe remains unchanged. The plentiful seats and the well-made path are evidence of the Victorian recognition of the value of the viewpoint. With changes only in detail, and considerable growth of trees and shrubs, it remains much the same today.

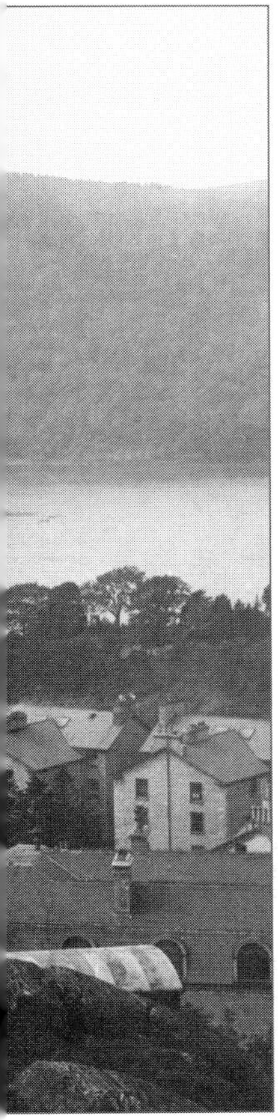

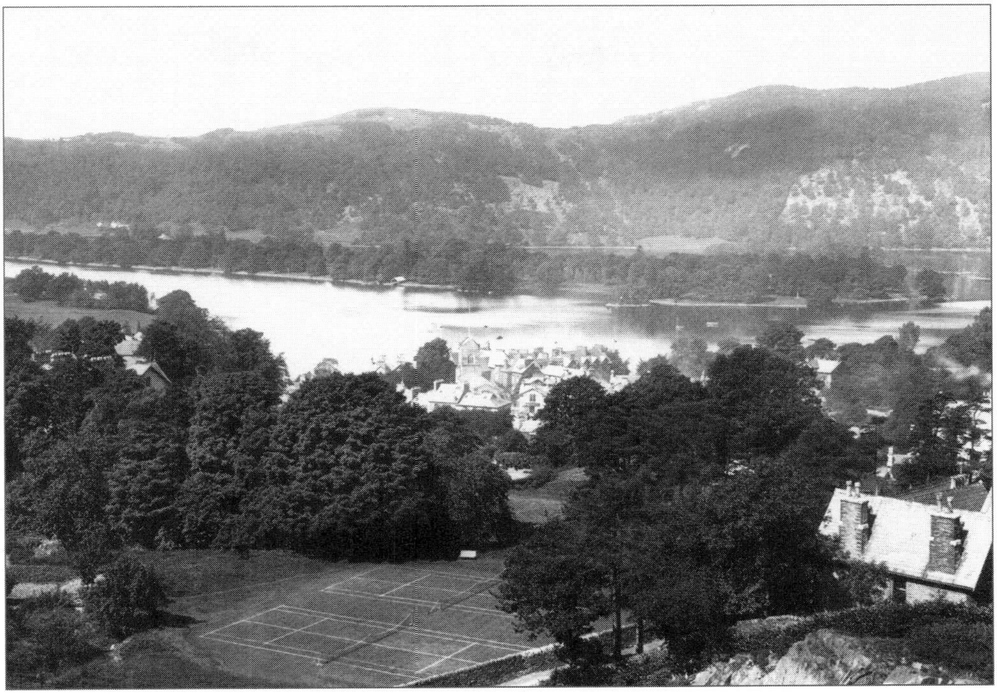

▲ **BOWNESS-ON-WINDERMERE,** *Belle Island 1893* 31937

Taken from high ground close to the Biskey Howe viewpoint, this scene includes tennis courts at the foot of the knoll. The heavily wooded Belle Isle and Claiffe Heights bear witness to the zeal of Thomas Curwen in planting huge numbers of larch and other trees following his purchase of the land a century earlier.

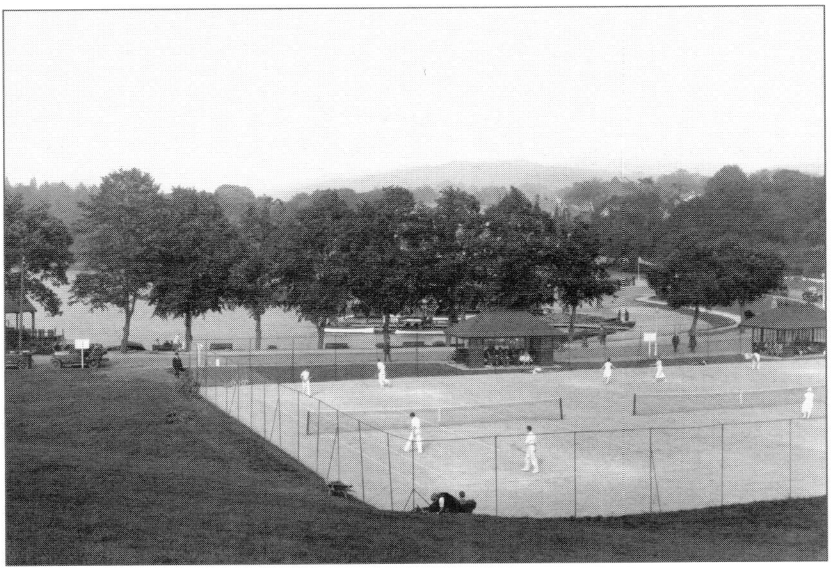

◄ **BOWNESS-ON-WINDERMERE**
The Tennis Courts 1925
77889

Here we have a summer scene showing part of the Glebe area behind the Promenade. People in the shelters watch the play on the three public tennis courts. Unlike the players on the same courts today, the dress for the game is immaculate. Just two motor cars are parked by what is now a very congested roadside. Until the development of the Promenade for tourism purposes early in the 20th century, the area of the tennis courts was occupied by the Bowness Council's sewage settlement tanks.

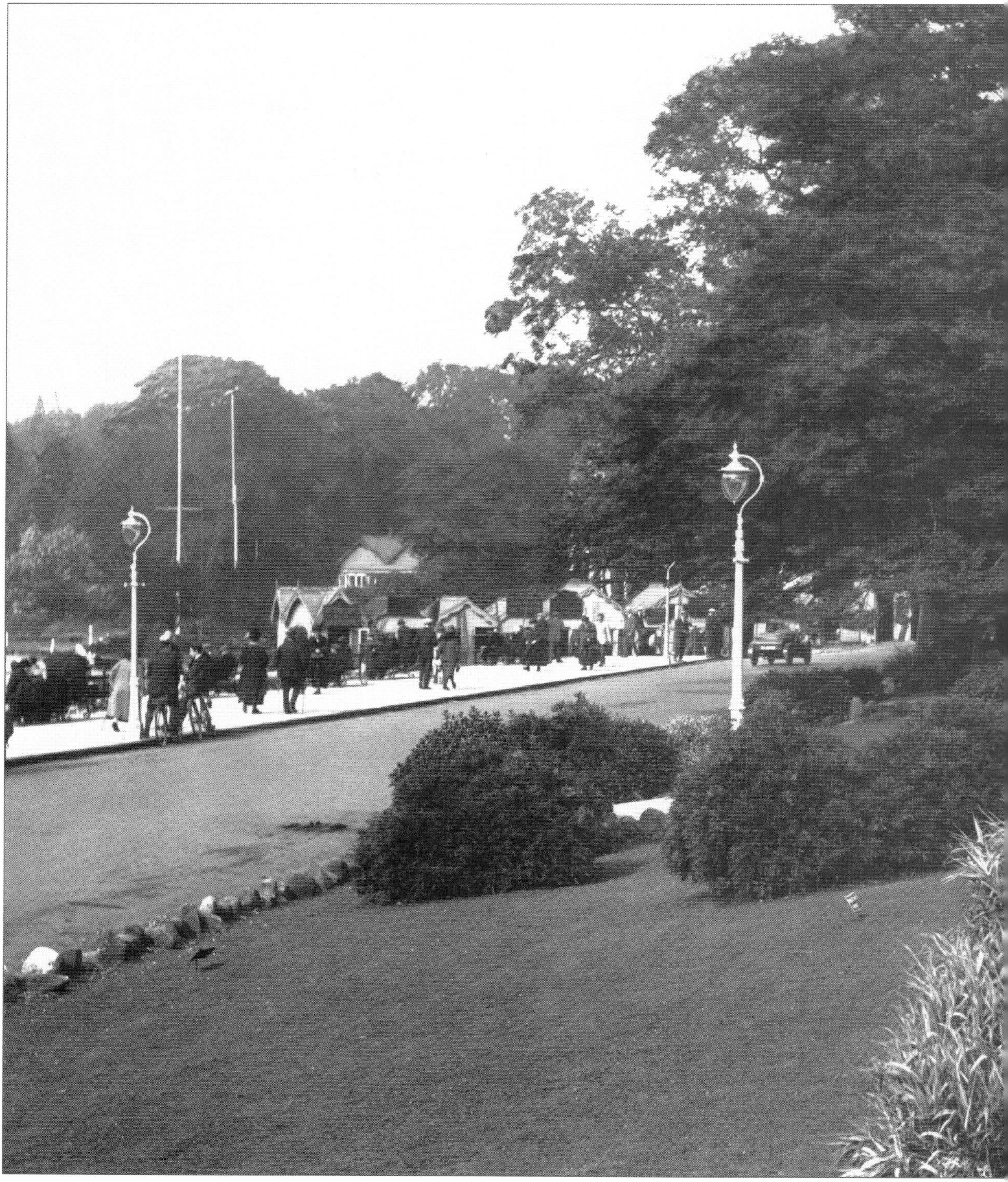

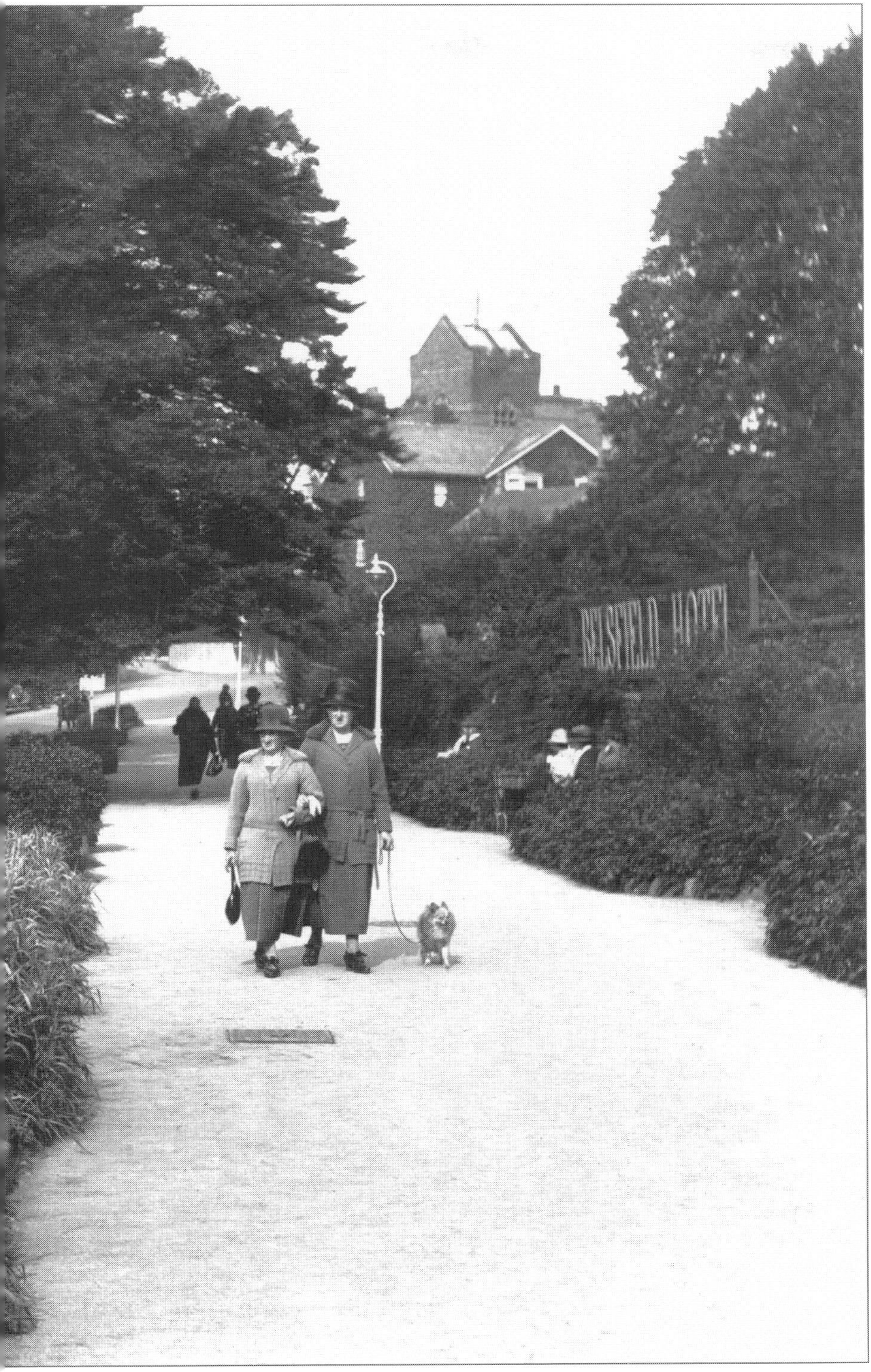

BOWNESS-ON-WINDERMERE
The Promenade 1925
77886

The spacious Promenade created around 1912 is here shown to advantage. We can see the back of the boat station, with 'cushion huts' peeping out behind the strolling crowds, whilst to the right 'Schneider's gate' is flanked by the bold 'Belsfield Hotel' sign. Over the ensuing years this has become 'The Belsfield', and the attractive street lights have been replaced by utilitarian columns. Despite the apparent sunshine, the amply-clothed women in the foreground are obviously leaving nothing to chance!

▶ **BOWNESS-ON-WINDERMERE**
The Church, Interior 1887 20455

The restoration work of 1870 included the plastering and decoration of the arcade piers and internal walls with Victorian patterns and verses, resulting in a light and airy interior. The verses on the spandrels are, however, older – they date from c1600. The great east window we see here is largely of the 15th century; at least some of the glass is believed to have come from Cartmel Priory following the dissolution of the monasteries by King Henry VIII in the 16th century.

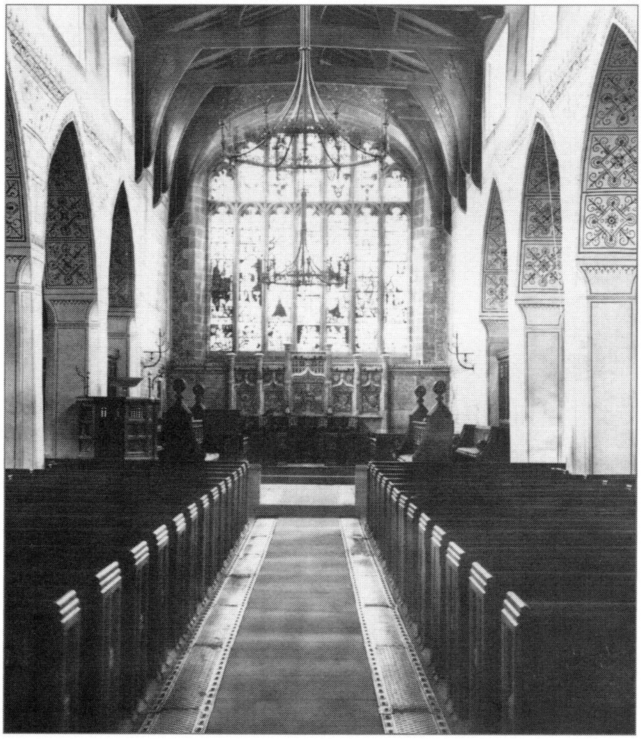

▼ **BOWNESS-ON-WINDERMERE**
The Church 1887 20454

Believed to be on the site of a Saxon church, the present building of St Martin's was consecrated in 1483. It forms the core of the old settlement of Bowness. It is seen here in pristine condition following the major renovations carried out by Pattinsons the builders in 1870, which included rebuilding the top of the tower to its unusual shape. This view of the church has changed little since 1887.

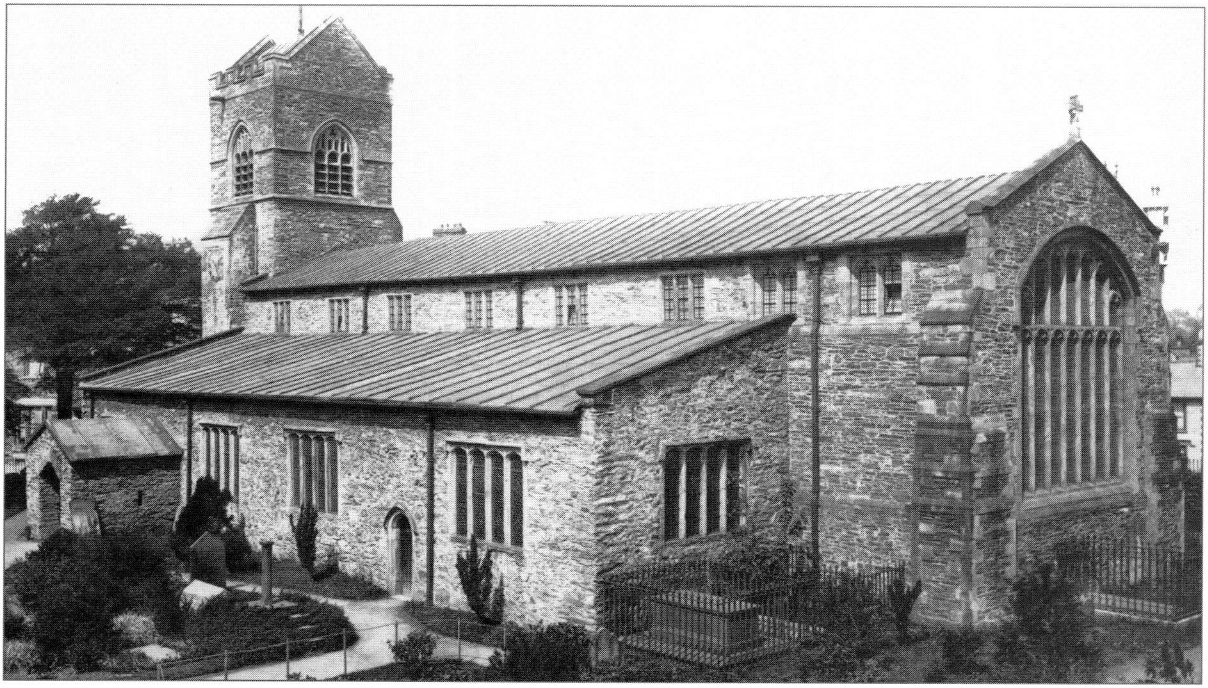

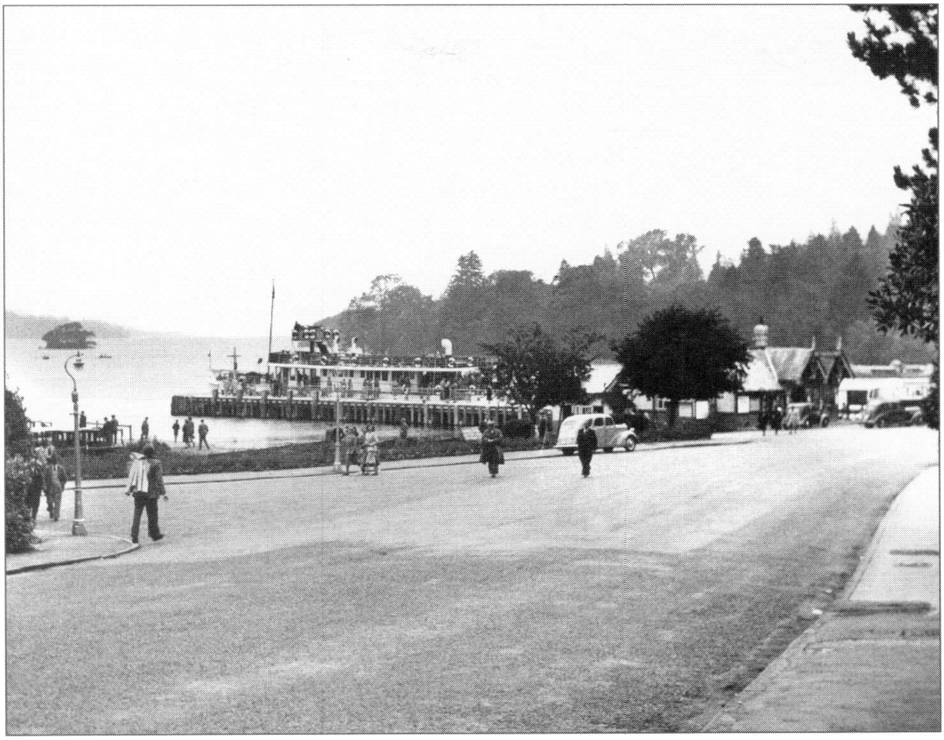

BOWNESS-ON-WINDERMERE
The Steamer Pier and the Promenade c1955
B166018

In this post-World War II photograph the Promenade is still unbelievably quiet, with just three apparently stationary motor cars in view. The 'Bowness Pier' sign has gone from the roof of the pier building. One of the large boats, either the 'Teal' or the 'Swan', sits at the far side of the pier.

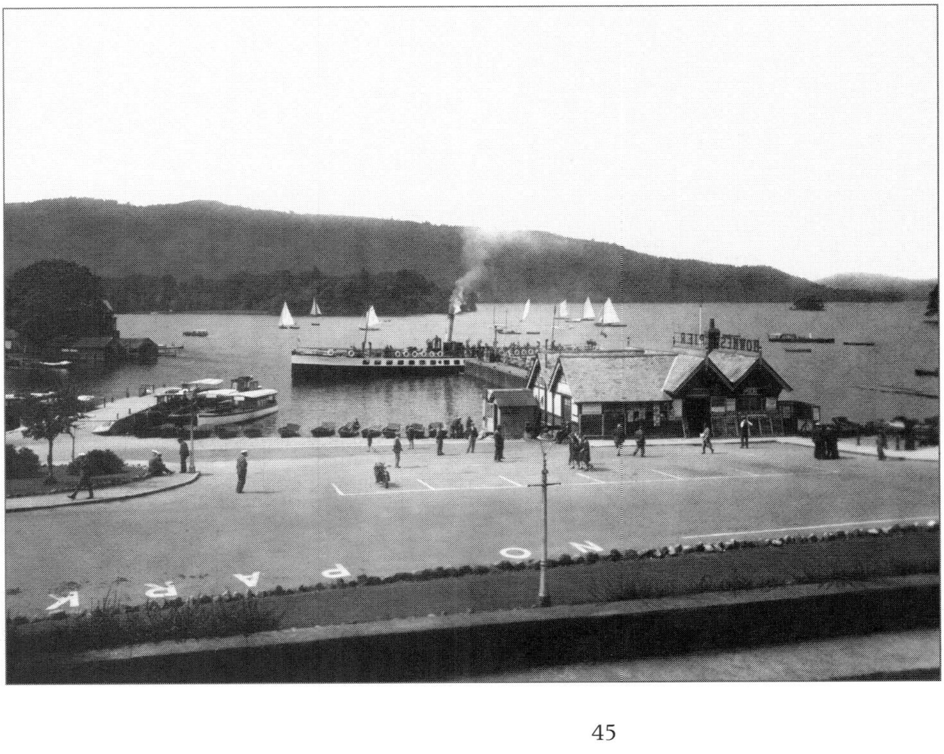

BOWNESS-ON-WINDERMERE
The Pier 1929
82809

The steamer 'Swift', launched in 1900 as the then largest boat on the lake, sits at the end of the pier, whilst a cluster of yachts, possibly racing, passes between the boat station and Belle Isle. Part of the pier building is occupied by the Central Café, with a display of postcards on the front wall.

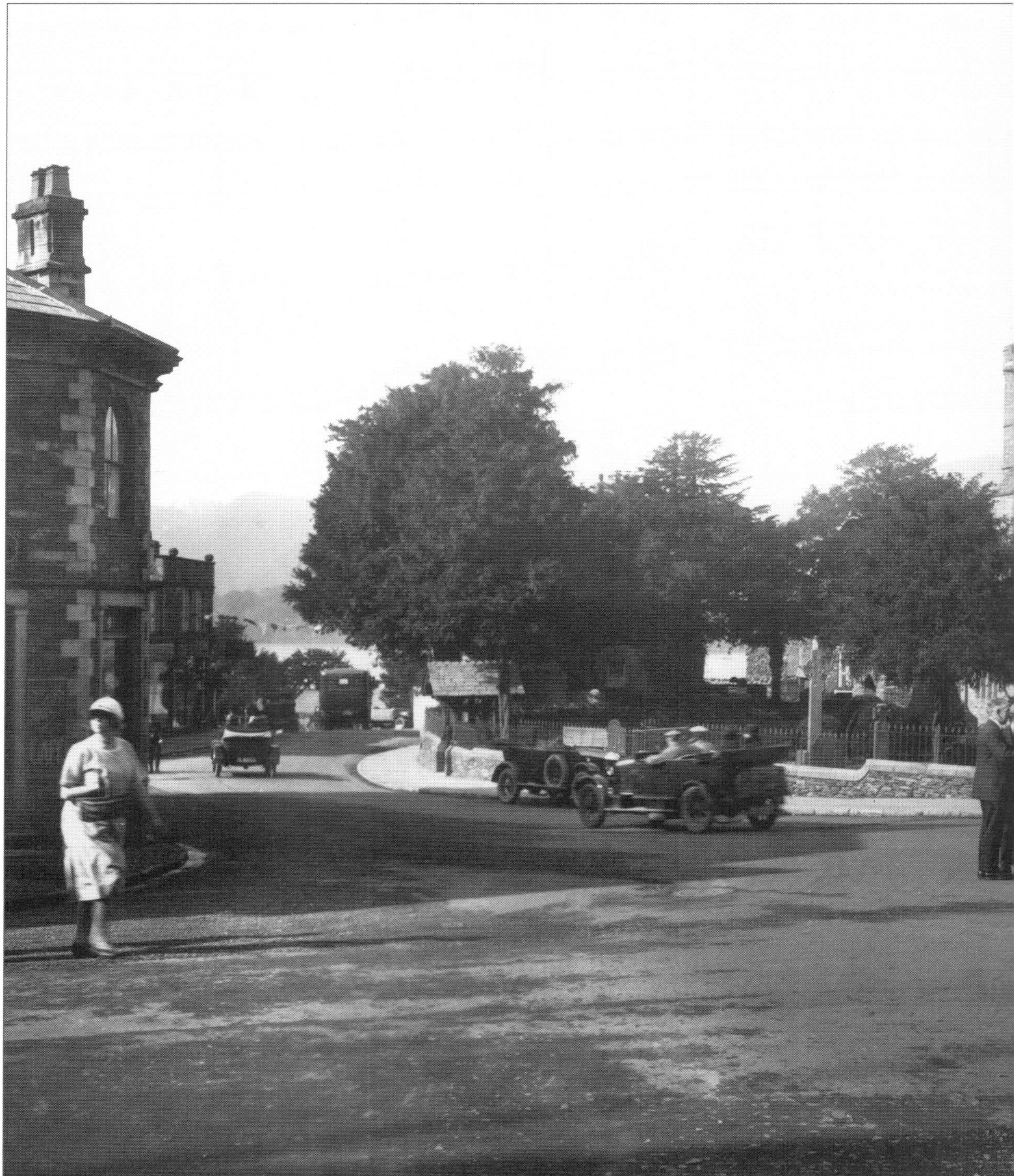

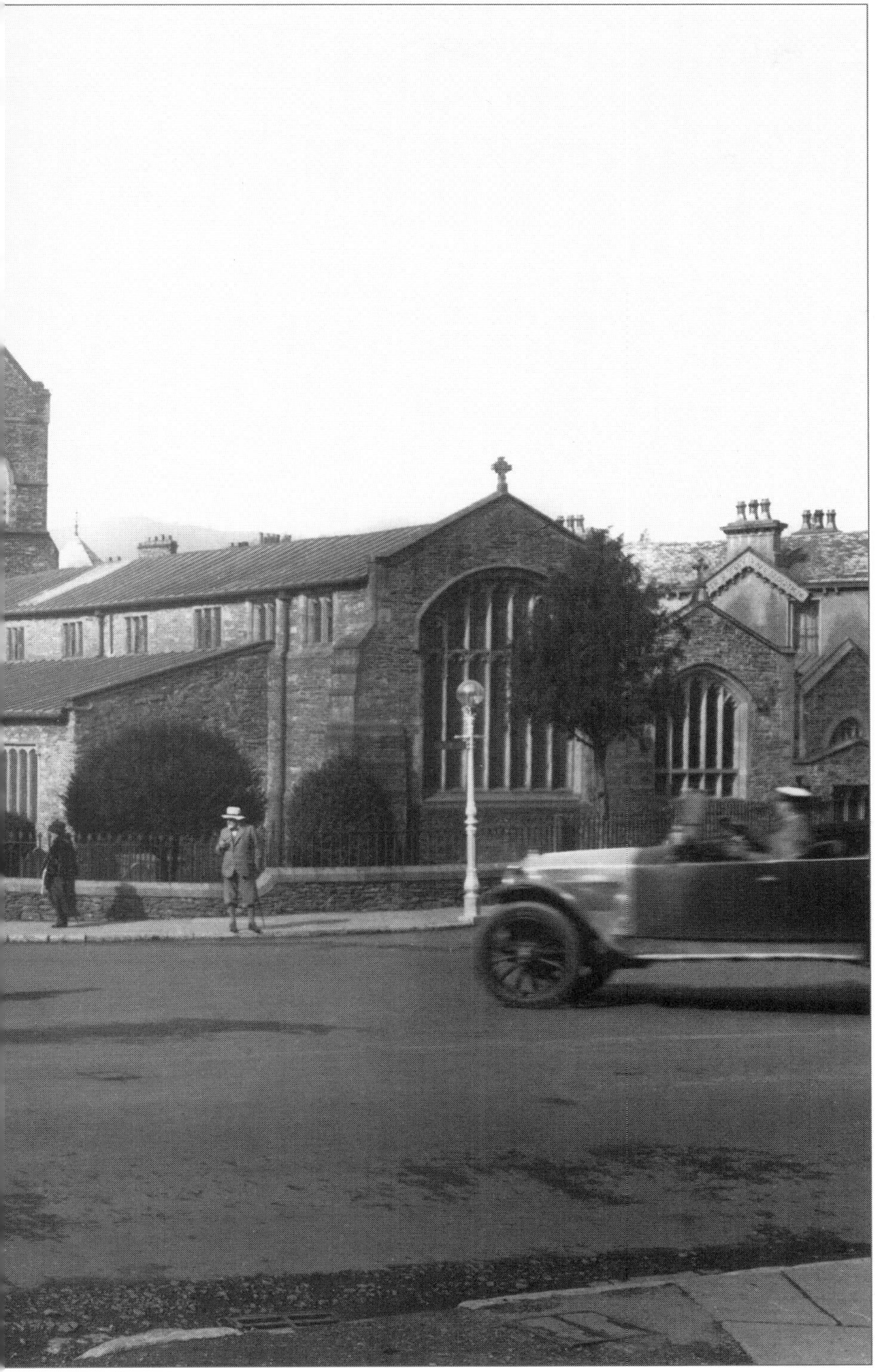

BOWNESS-ON-WINDERMERE
St Martin's Church 1925 77888

Here we see St Martin's Church after its 1870 renovation, in an apparently spacious setting but with the buildings of old Bowness tightly packed behind. Motor cars are now much in evidence, with various pedestrians rather anxiously taking care in crossing the road. The rear end of a large vehicle, probably an early motor bus, can be seen heading towards the lake (left).

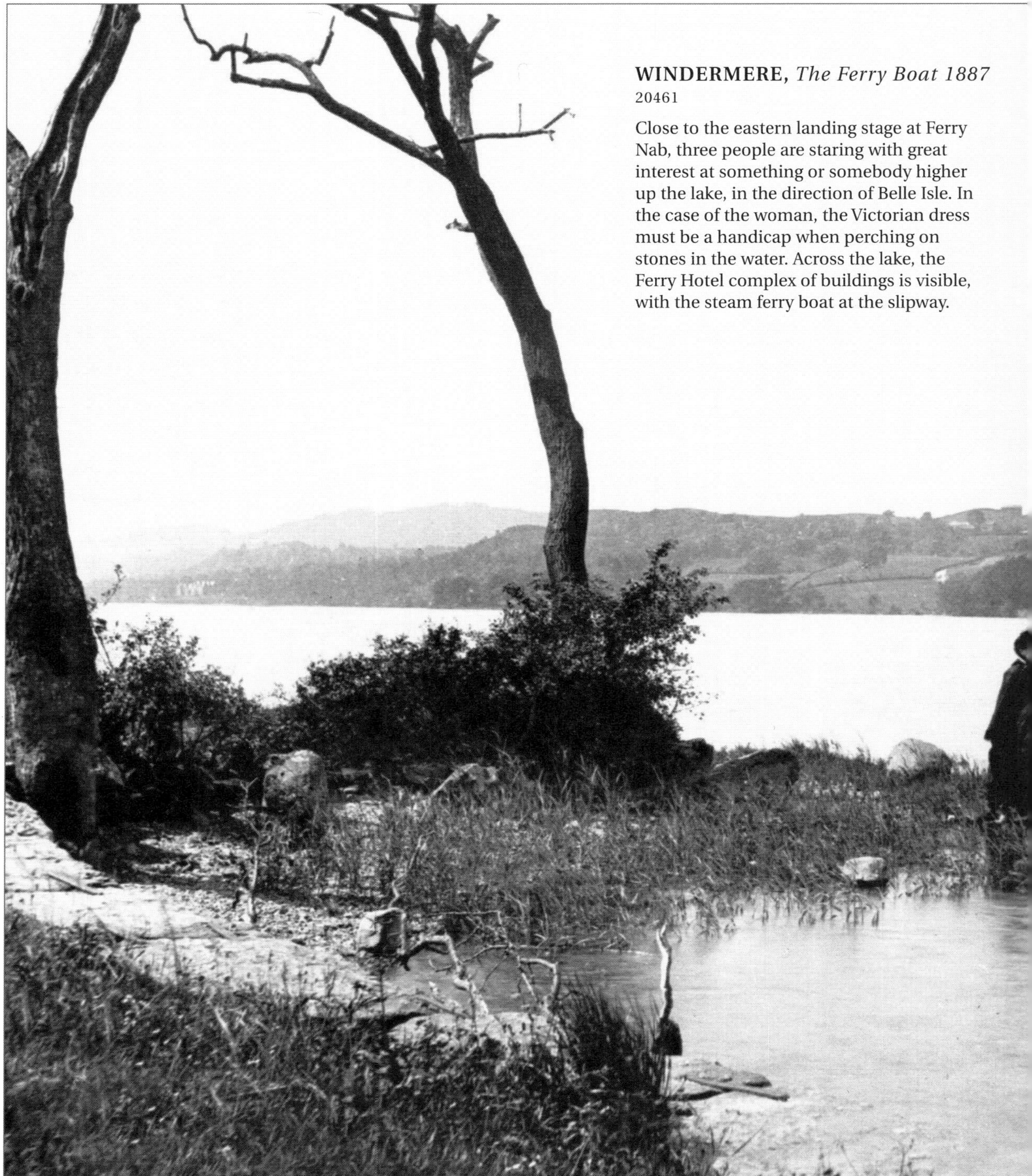

WINDERMERE, *The Ferry Boat 1887*
20461

Close to the eastern landing stage at Ferry Nab, three people are staring with great interest at something or somebody higher up the lake, in the direction of Belle Isle. In the case of the woman, the Victorian dress must be a handicap when perching on stones in the water. Across the lake, the Ferry Hotel complex of buildings is visible, with the steam ferry boat at the slipway.

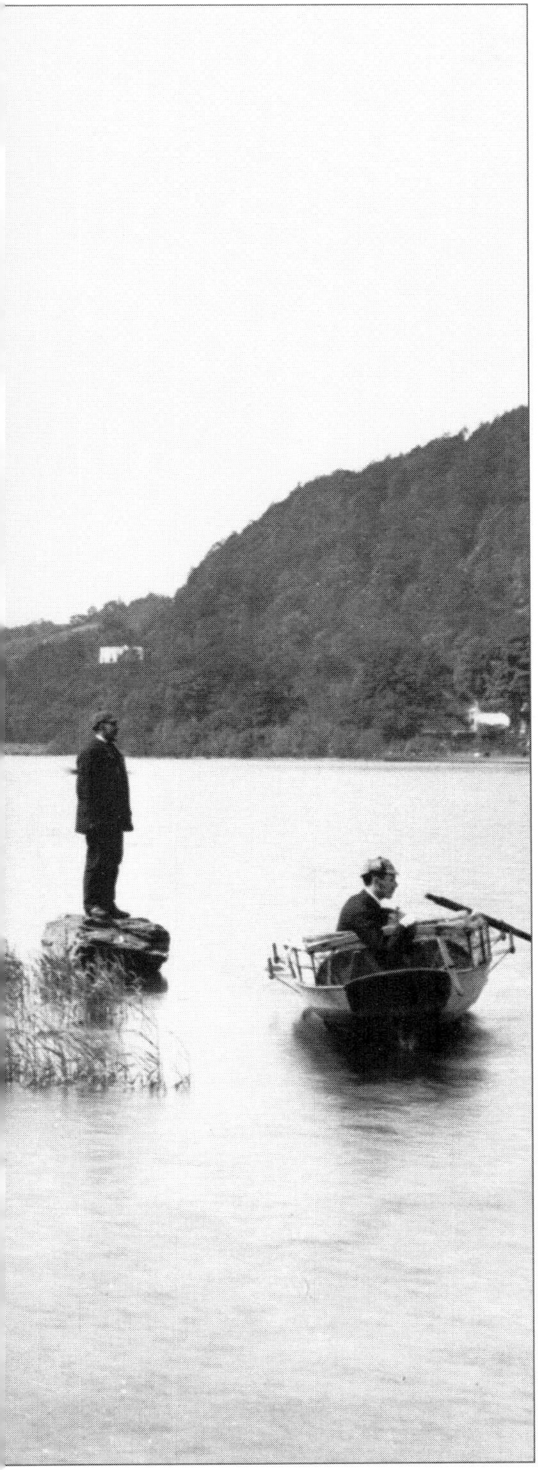

THE WINDERMERE FERRY

LOST in the mists of antiquity, the origins of the ferry across the narrowest part of the lake pre-date the first documentary reference of 1575, which refers to the passage of 'horses and men'. Although for centuries there was also a foot ferry across the lake from Miller Ground to Belle Grange, the crossing from Ferry Nab to the site of the former Ferry Inn has always been paramount as the obvious route from the old town of Kendal to the former market town of Hawkshead and beyond.

Over the centuries the vessels used in providing this vital link have changed a great deal. Until 1870, huge, wide, shallow rowing boats, propelled by great sweeps (oars), carried men and animals. The passengers usually helped with the oars. The 'Mary Anne' at the Windermere Steamboat Museum gives some idea of the type of craft used. In 1635, one of these boats capsized in stormy weather. The fact that no less than 47 persons and 11 horses, allegedly returning from a wedding party, were drowned gives some idea of the overloading which was probably not uncommon. The first steam ferry boat went into service in 1870, driven along chains (latterly hawsers) secured to each shore. Fully loaded, as we see in some of the following photographs, it could carry one large coach and horses or two smaller vehicles, plus a fair numbers of passengers on foot. With two coaches the horses would probably have to be unhitched. This boat was replaced by a larger vessel in 1915, which was itself replaced in 1954 by the 'Drake', which was steam-powered until its conversion to diesel propulsion in 1960. In 1990 the present 'Mallard', capable of carrying 18 average-sized motor vehicles, replaced the 'Drake'.

▼ **BOWNESS-ON-WINDERMERE,** *The Ferry 1893* 31948

The steam ferry boat of 1870 makes its presence felt as the smoke drifts across the woodland of Claiffe Heights; it has apparently just left the slipway beside the Ferry Hotel. The buildings are partially concealed behind the trees.

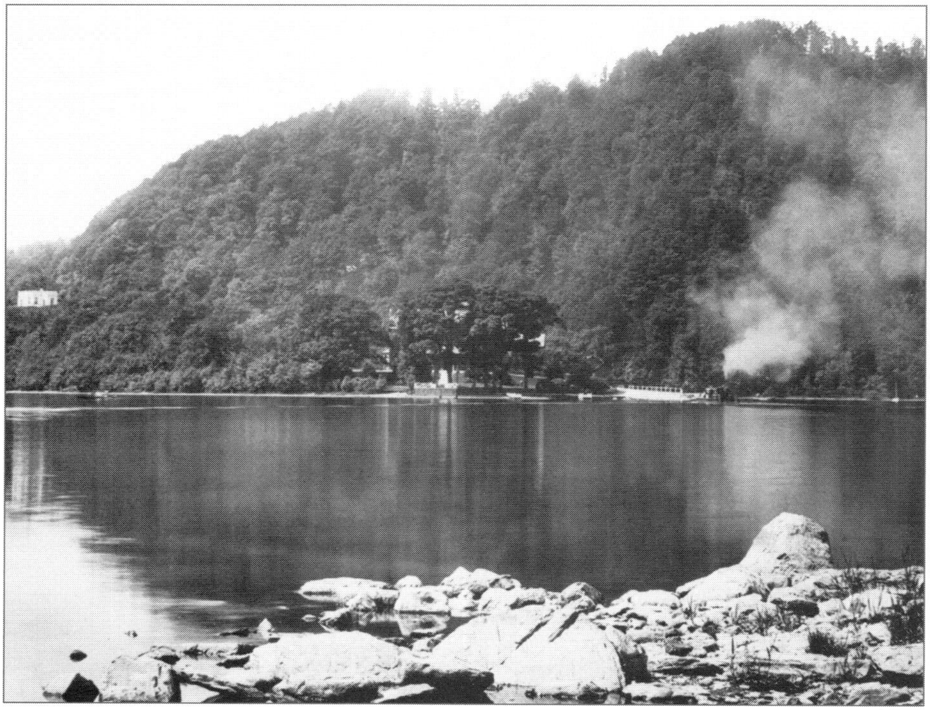

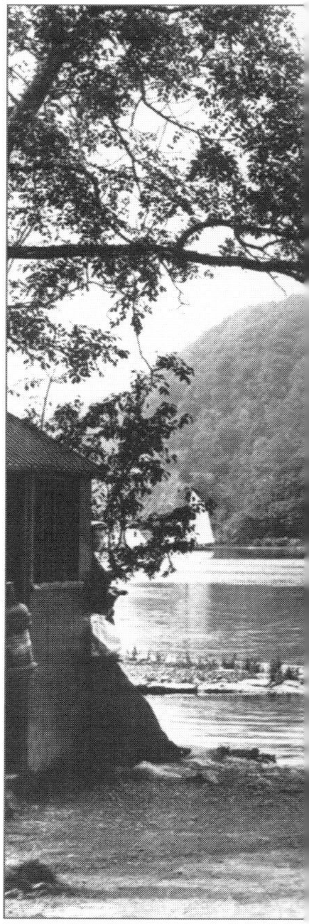

► **BOWNESS-ON-WINDERMERE**
Ferry Nab 1893 31947

The steam ferry boat of 1870 is seen at the Ferry Nab (Bowness) landing stage, with its route across the narrowest part of the lake to the Ferry Hotel at the foot of Claiffe Heights clearly apparent. This vessel was the first of the various ferries to be propelled along a fixed rope or chain.

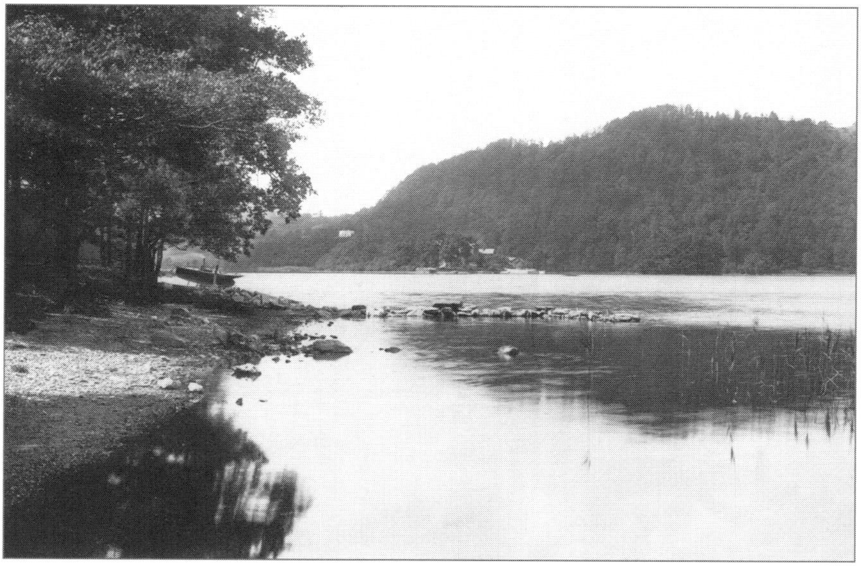

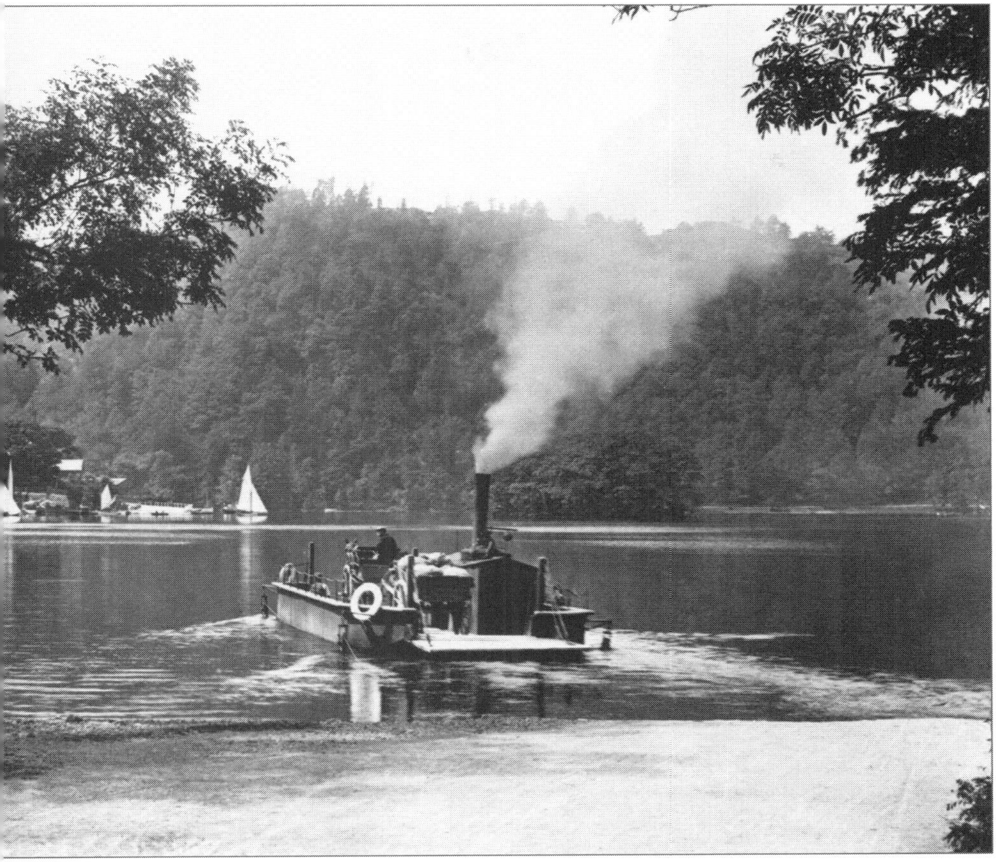

BOWNESS-ON-WINDERMERE, *The Ferry Boat 1896* 38802

The steam ferry leaves Ferry Nab with two horse-drawn vehicles on board, with the chain used in propulsion clearly visible. Due to occasional mishaps with this chain, it was later replaced by the present-day double hawser system. The shed-like superstructure of the boat houses the steam boiler. Quite unperturbed by the noise and wash created by the ferry, a long-skirted woman fishes with rod and line from a little promontory.

BOWNESS-ON-WINDERMERE *Ferry Nab 1893* 31940

As we look from the slipway on the Bowness side of the lake, we can see the coal-burning ferry boat at the Ferry Hotel, opposite. Beside the ferry, a plume of smoke gives away the presence of another steam boat, presumably a private launch, quite likely the one owned and operated by the hotel proprietor.

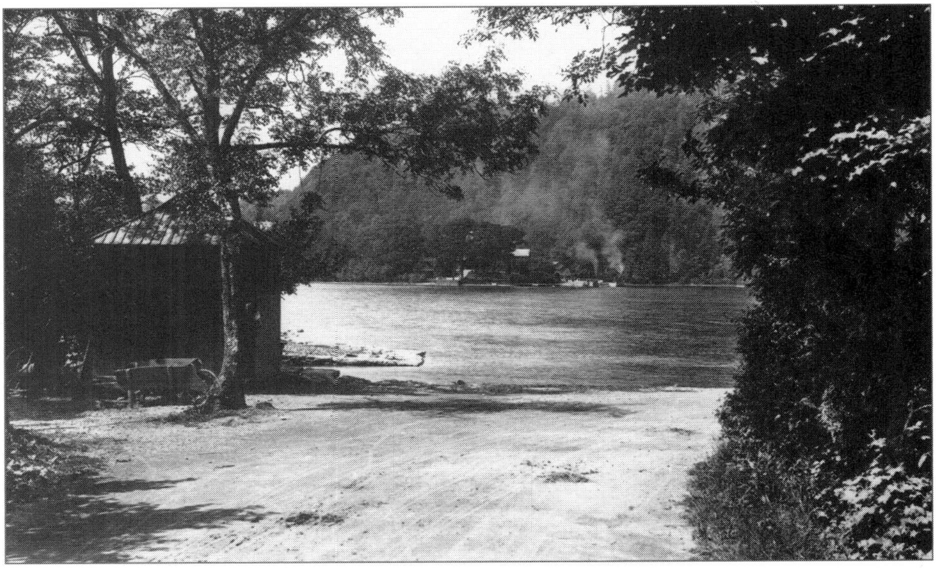

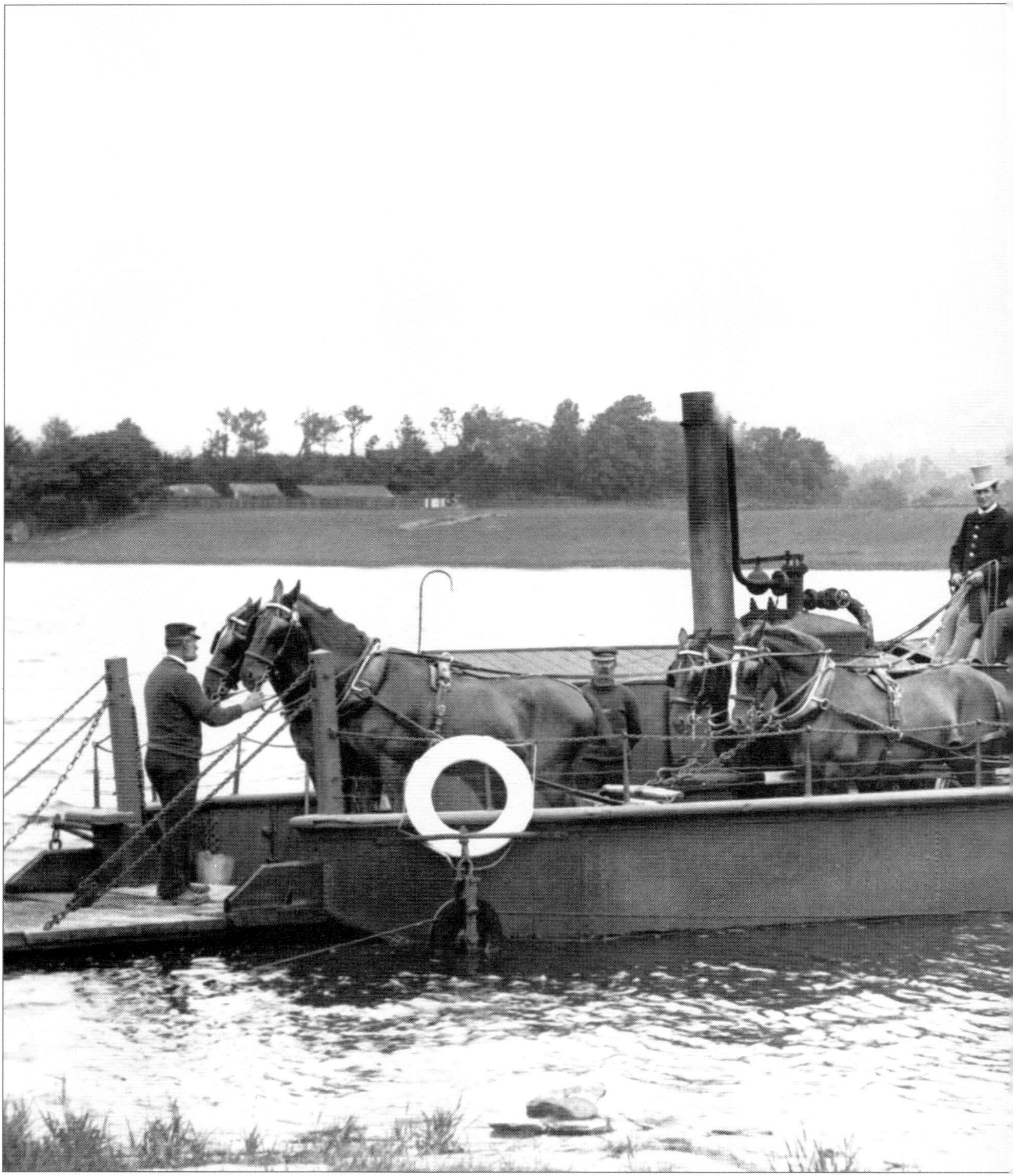

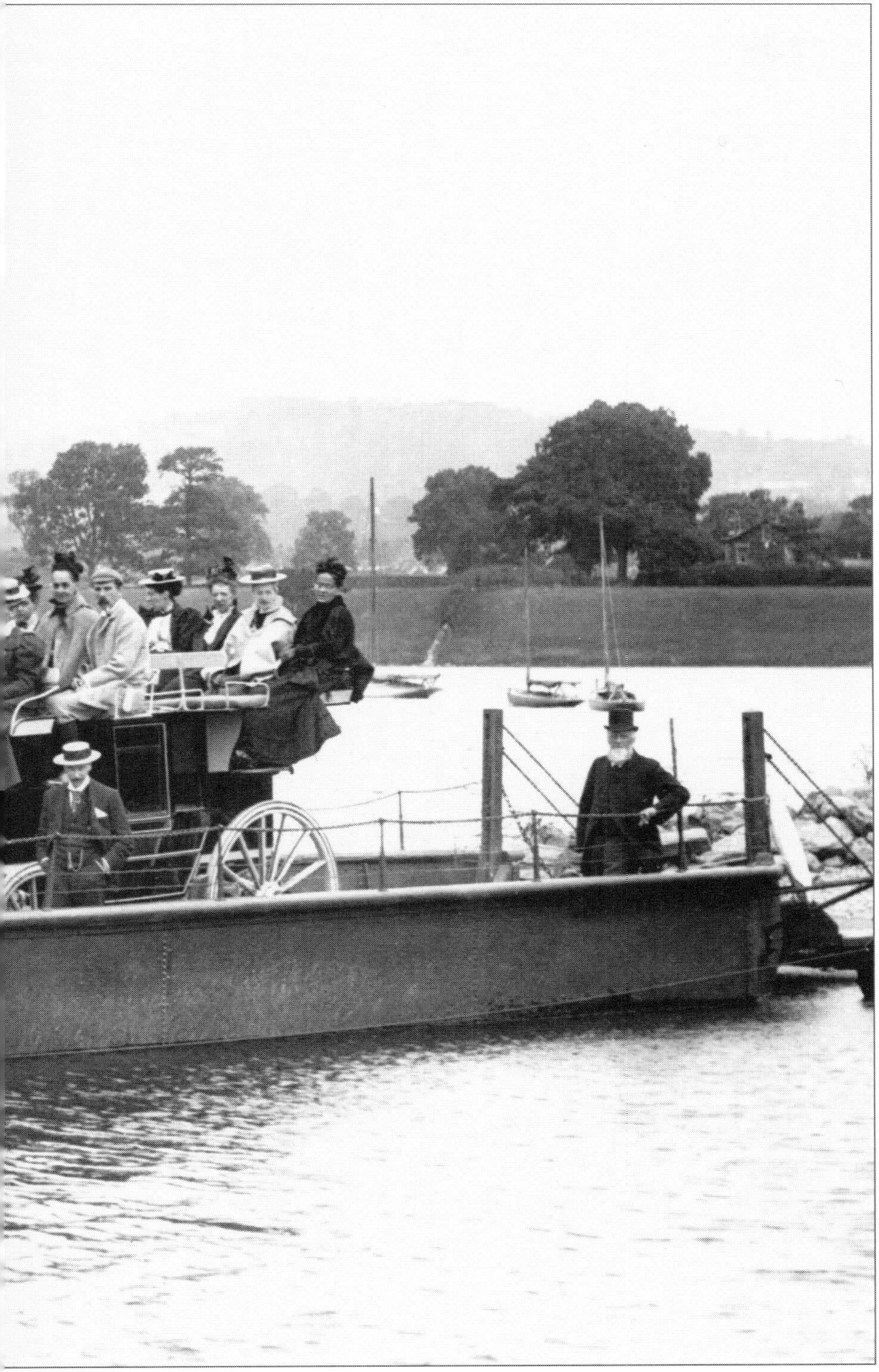

BOWNESS-ON-WINDERMERE
The Ferry Boat 1896
38800

This superb picture shows the late Victorian steam ferry boat at the Ferry Nab slipway. The boat is well filled by the substantial coach and four, heavily laden with passengers; the lead horses are being calmed by one of the ferrymen. All the passengers and crew have head coverings of one sort or another, including several examples of the then popular and appropriate boater.

BOWNESS-ON-WINDERMERE
The Ferry Hotel 1887 20459

The Ferry Hotel was constructed in 1879 as a replacement for the old Ferry Inn. The hotel has since closed, and in 1948 the cluster of buildings became the research establishment of the Freshwater Biology Research Association. At the quayside is the steam yacht 'Esperance', which was owned by the legendary H W Schneider before its purchase and use by the then Ferry Hotel proprietor. After some years of use by the Boy Scouts, the vessel has been restored; it is displayed at the Windermere Steam Boat Museum.

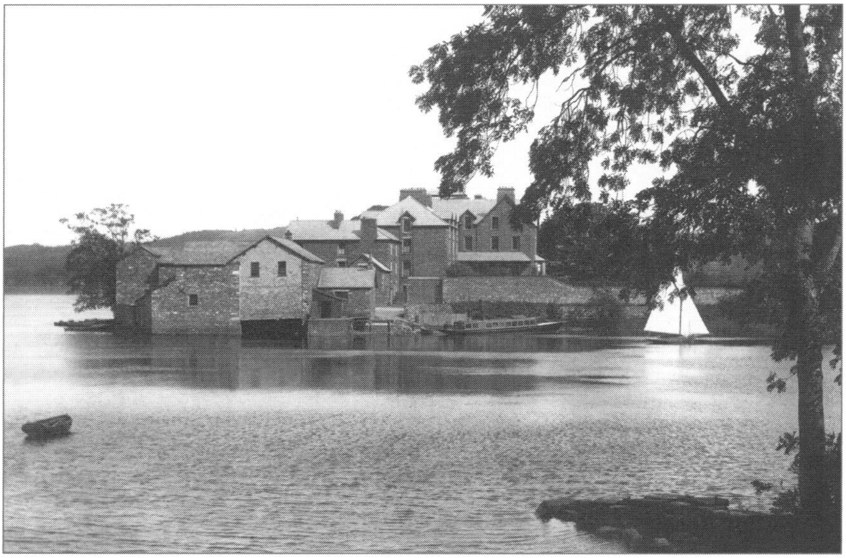

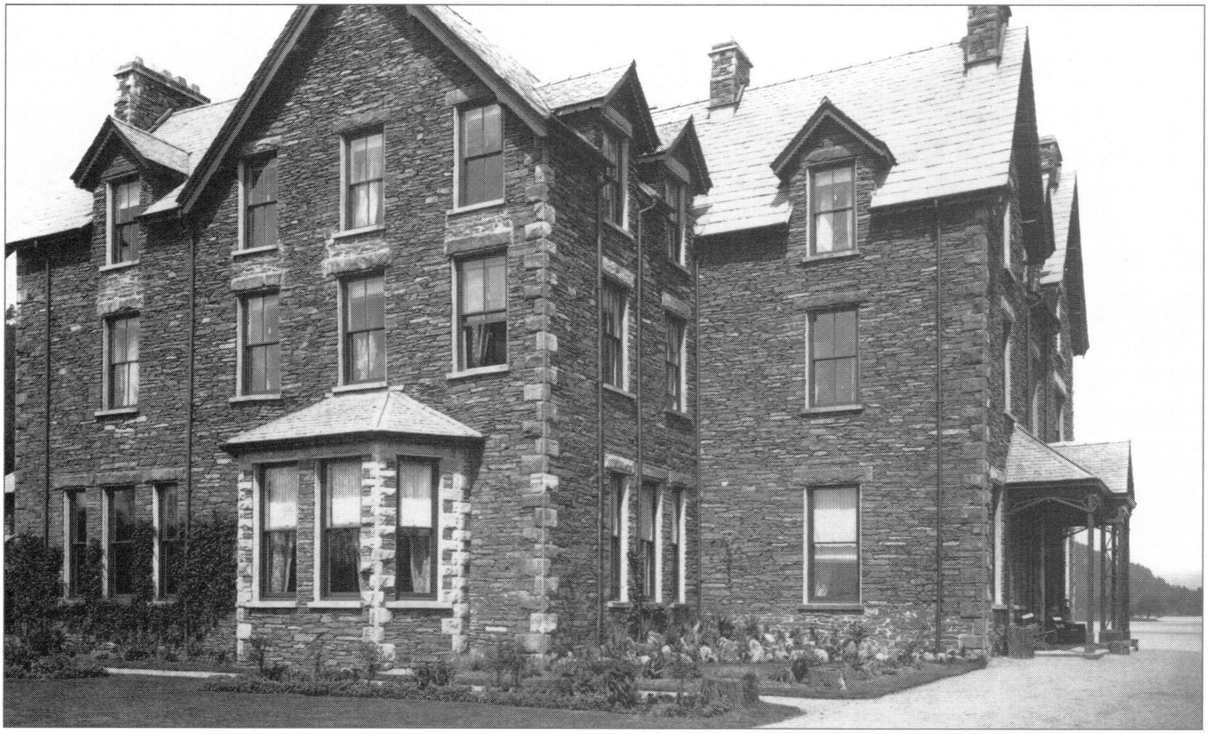

BOWNESS-ON-WINDERMERE, *The Ferry Hotel 1887* 20458

The substantial Ferry Hotel, traditionally constructed in local stone and slate, just a few years after it was built in 1879 to replace the old Ferry Inn. Despite its conversion to research laboratory use, the building remains much the same today, but now it has large visually unappealing additions at the rear.

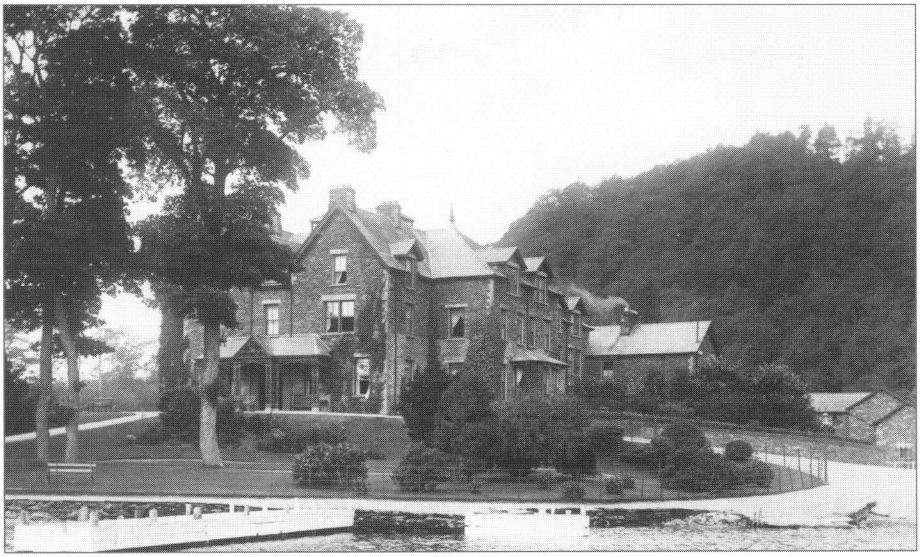

BOWNESS-ON-WINDERMERE
The Ferry Hotel 1896
38806

A few years after photograph 20458, this frontal view of the hotel may well have been taken from the ferry boat, close to the landing ramp. Although the building has changed very little over the ensuing years, the gardens are nowadays less attractive, and the jetty shown here has gone.

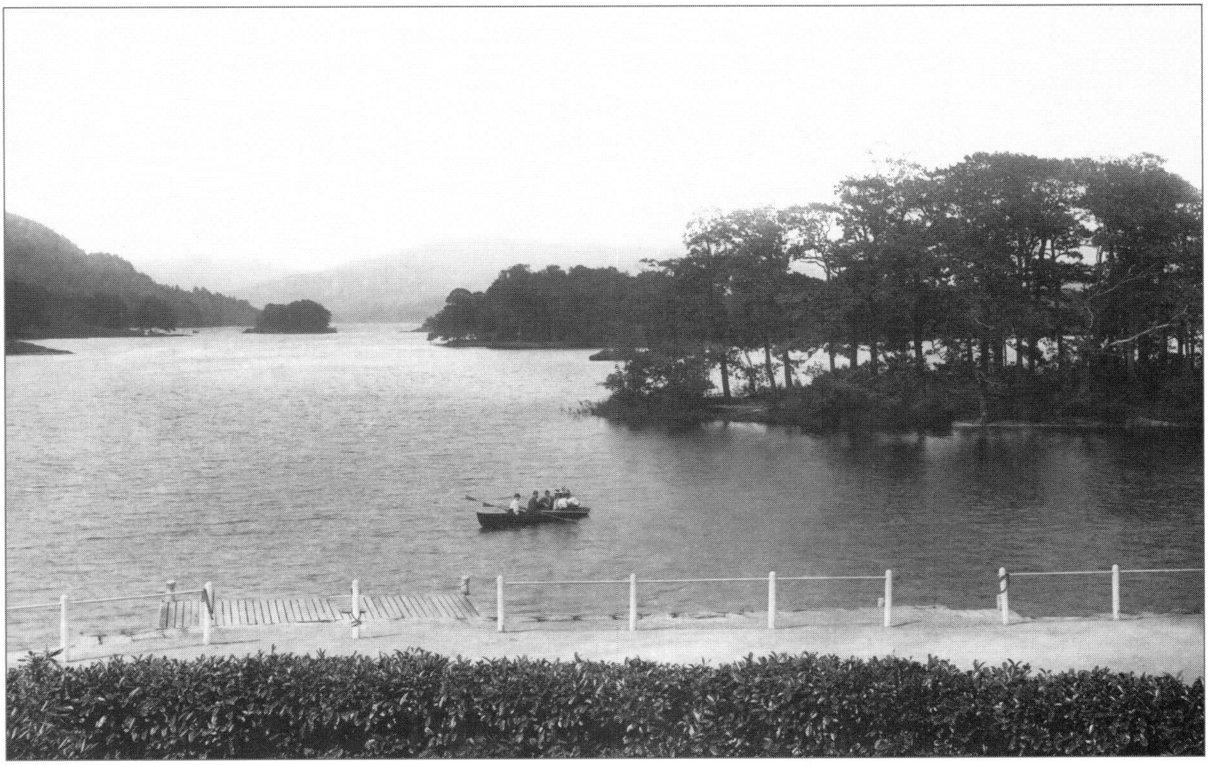

BOWNESS-ON-WINDERMERE, *The View from the Ferry Hotel 1896* 38808

A view along the north basin of the lake, including the islands of Belle Isle, Crow Holme, Maiden Holme and the two 'Lilies of the Valley'. A party of six or seven adults, the ladies dressed in summer attire, makes a full load for the rowing boat.

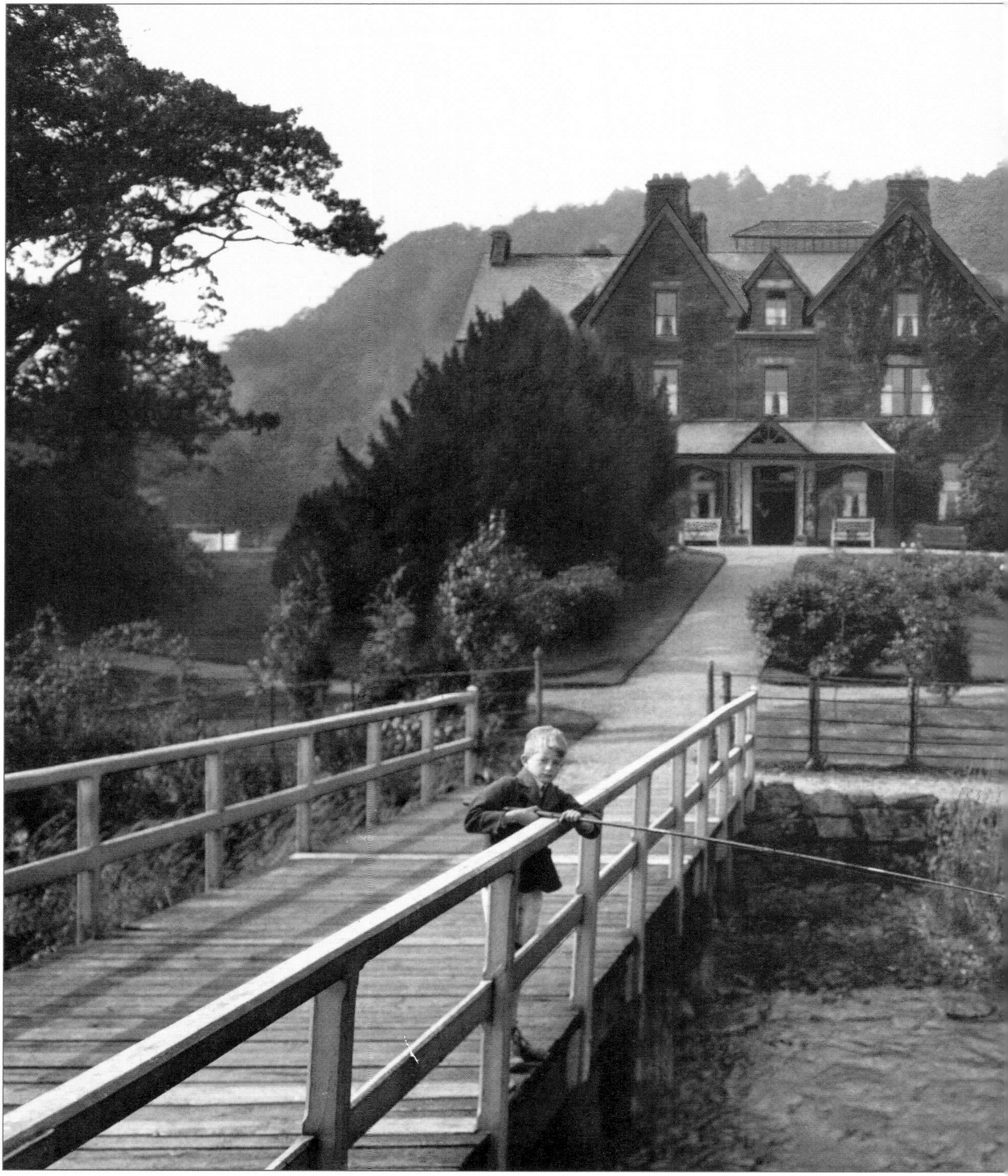

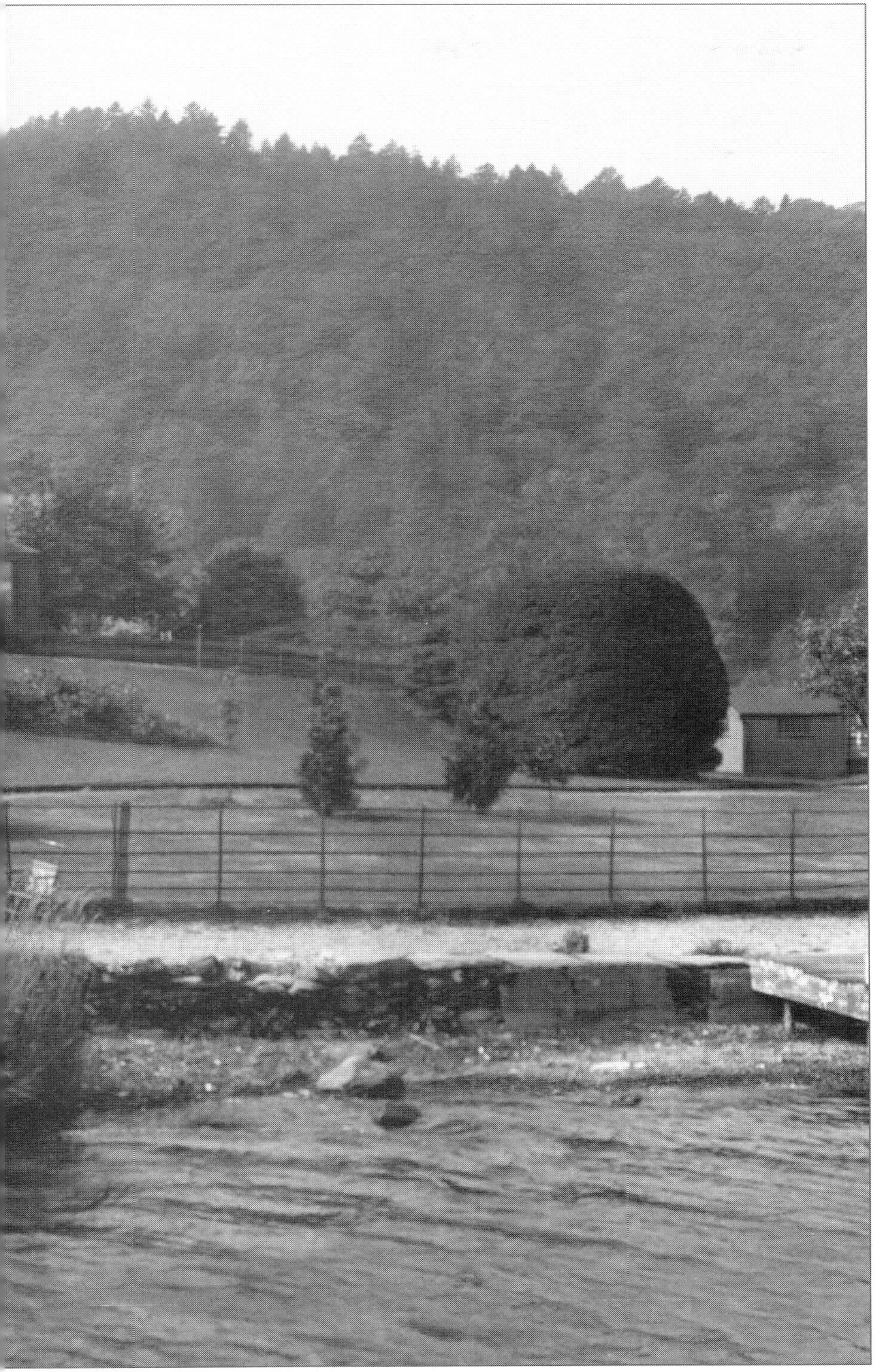

BOWNESS-ON-WINDERMERE
The Ferry Hotel 1925
77891

Now well into the 20th century, the hotel has acquired a growth of creeper over much of the fine stonework of its frontage. In the foreground the former short jetty is just visible on the right. The substantial wooden pier/jetty which dominates the foreground has since disappeared. From it the camera-wary boy is dangling his line in the water, probably hoping to catch the perch which have generally been plentiful in Windermere.

BOWNESS-ON-WINDERMERE
From Furness Fell 1887
20436

Furness Fell is now more generally referred to as Claiffe Heights. In view are Bowness village, Cockshot Point and the whole of Belle Isle (formerly Long Holme). This island, three-quarters of a mile in length and more than 30 acres in extent, was owned by Thomas English, who had the curious round house, the first dwelling in England to be built in this shape, erected in 1774. In 1781 John Christian Curwen bought the island and the adjacent land. He renamed it Belle Isle in honour of his wife Isabella, and set about planting 30,000 larches and many other trees. This planting included the screening of the house - its stark prominence had caused concern to early environmentalists.

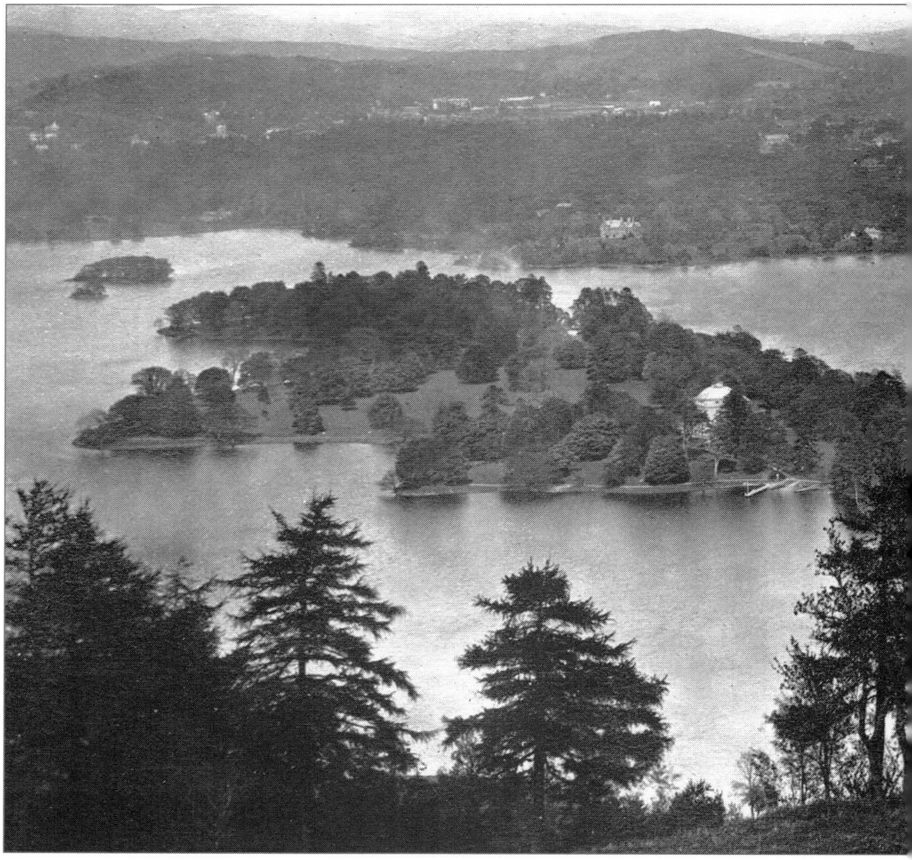

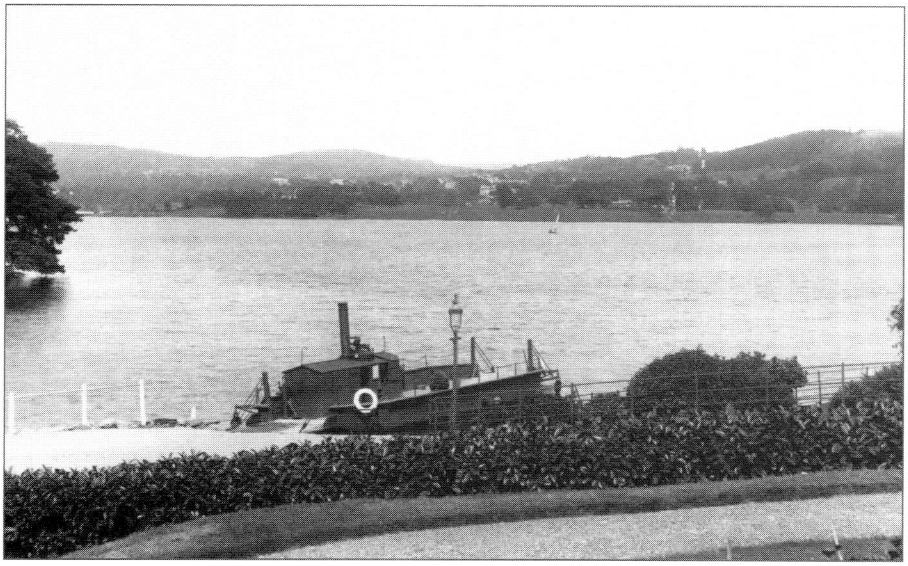

BOWNESS-ON-WINDERMERE
The View from the Ferry Hotel 1896
38809

In this photograph, the view is across the narrow portion of the lake towards Bowness, with Bowness Bay well to the left, behind the end of Crow Holme island. In the foreground the steam ferry sits at its ramp. Notice the lopsidedness of this boat when unloaded: this is due to the weight of the boiler installation.

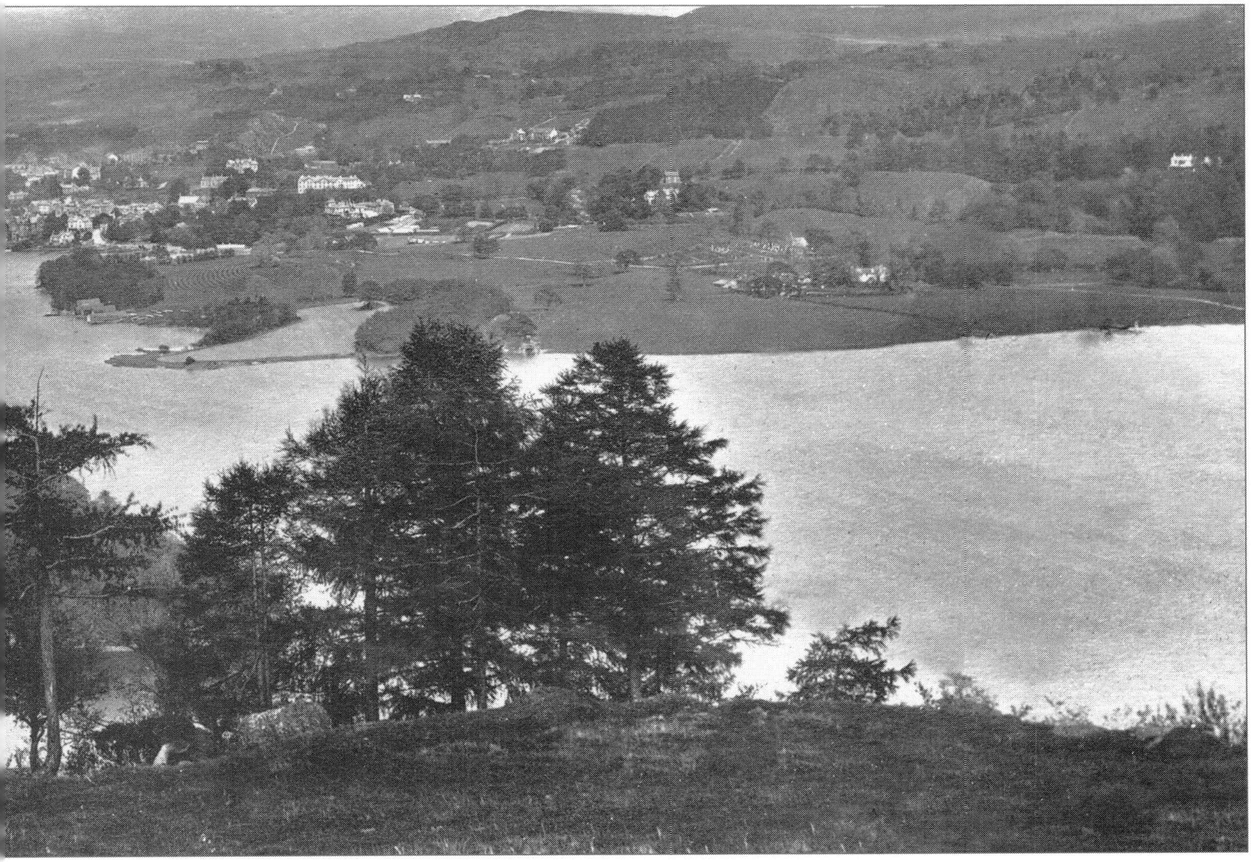

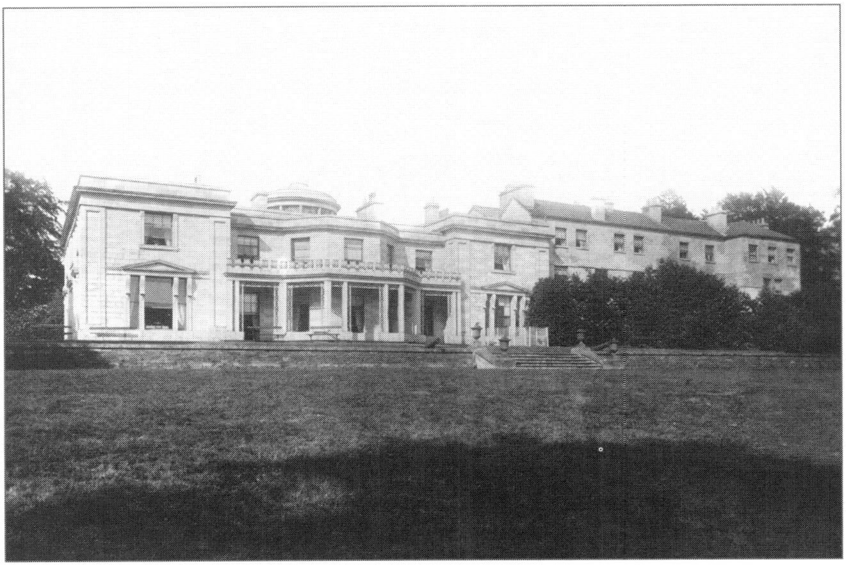

BOWNESS-ON-WINDERMERE
The Storrs Hall Hotel 1896
38799

Originally built in 1790 for Sir John Legard, Storrs Hall was purchased in 1806 by Col John Bolton, a local philanthropist, who from 1808-11 transformed it into the fine Georgian mansion we see here. Unfortunately, Bolton's wealth was based on Liverpool shipping, which included connections with the slave trade. After his death in 1837, the house passed to his nephew, and it was converted into a hotel after the latter's death in 1887.

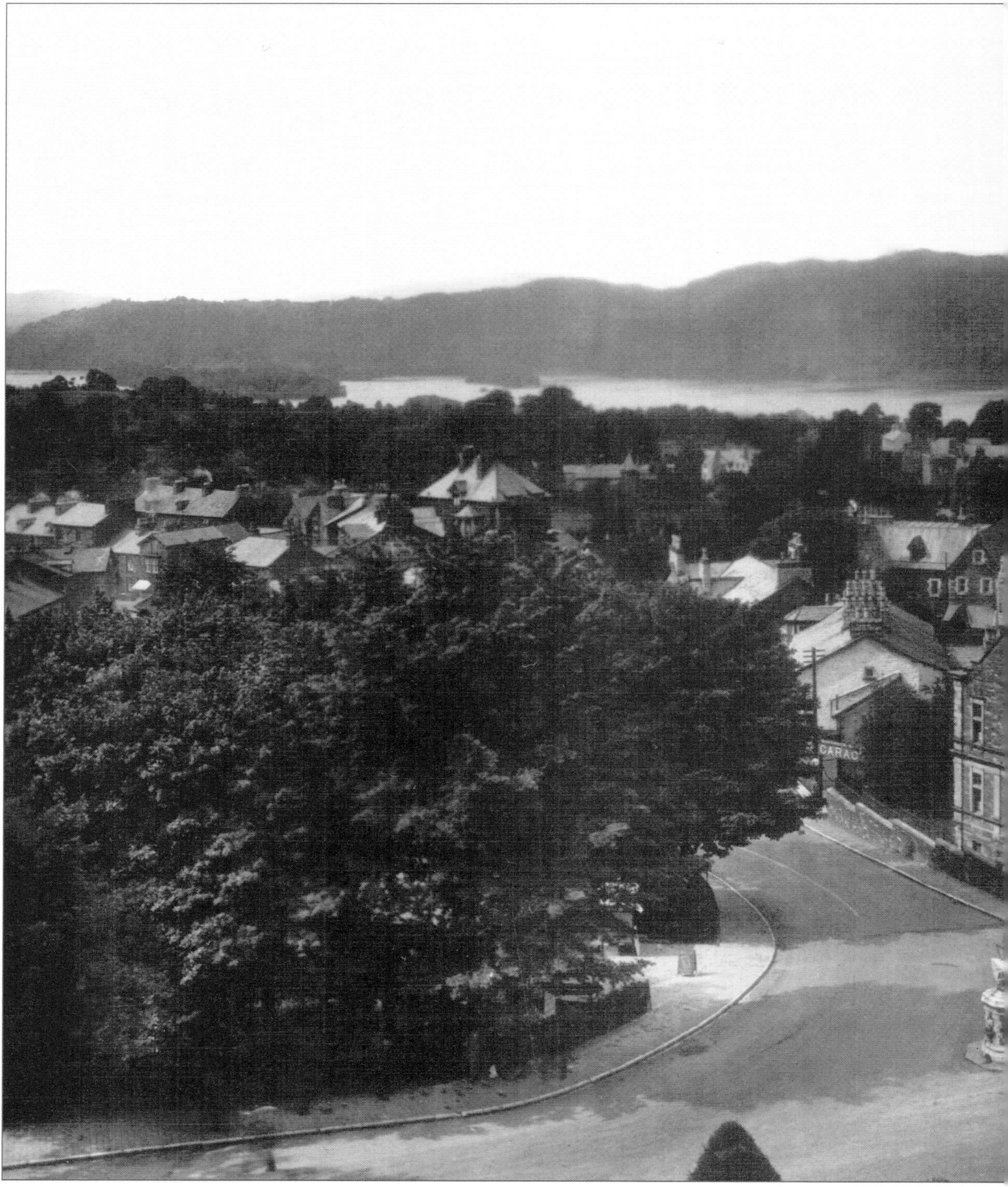

WINDERMERE VILLAGE

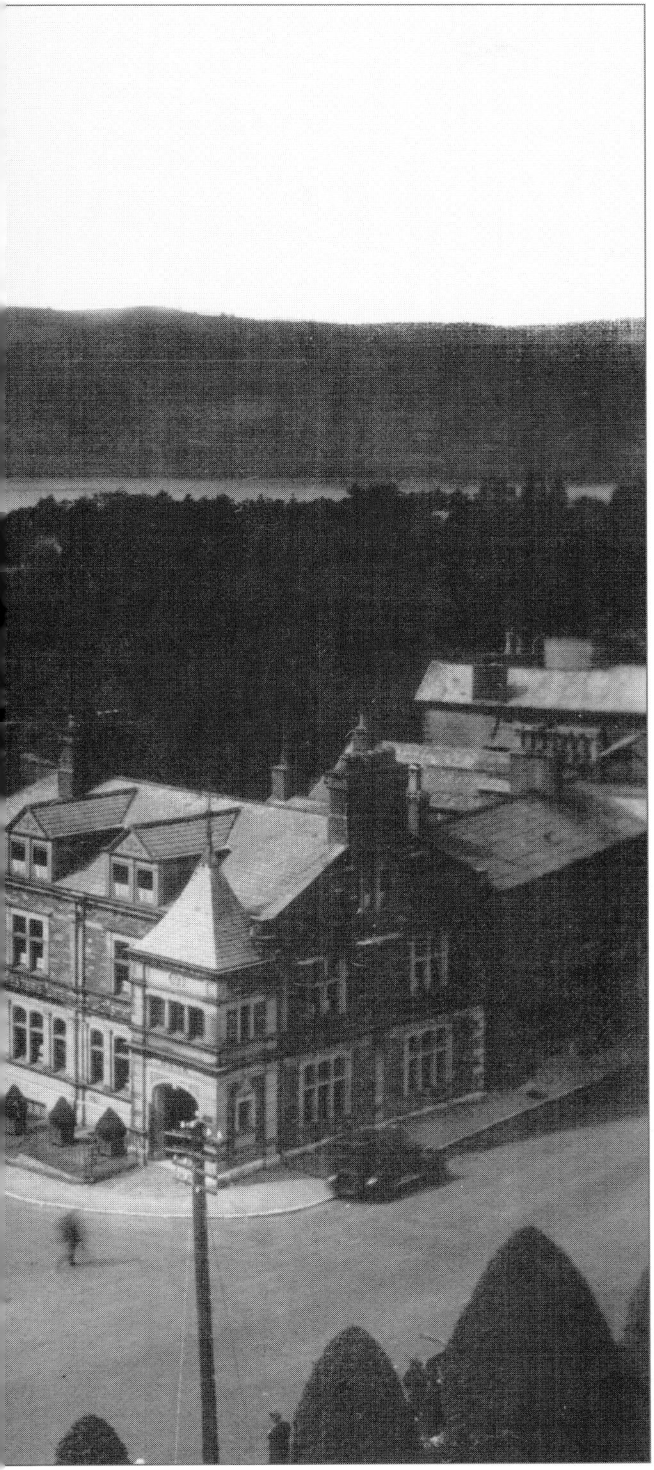

THE VILLAGE of Windermere is almost entirely a Victorian creation. Locally-based building firms rapidly developed the land to the south and west of the railway station from 1847 onwards. Before then, there were only farming hamlets such as Birthwaite and Heathwaite. The not unattractive mixture of houses, shops and inns, solidly stone-built, has since remained largely unchanged except, of course, for shop fronts and signs. The subsequent inevitable expansion of Windermere as a desirable residential area has resulted in its coalescence with the neighbouring settlement of Bowness.

WINDERMERE
The Village 1929 82825

This bird's eye view of the road junction near the railway station is from one of the upper rooms of the Windermere Hotel. There is a notable absence of traffic on the nowadays always busy A591 main road. The ornate drinking fountain in the middle of the junction carries an Ambleside road sign. The impressive building on the right with 'Bank' over its door is still a branch of the National Westminster. The road approach to the railway station, to the left of the fountain, has subsequently been opened out to cope with modern traffic.

▼ **WINDERMERE,** *The Main Street 1929* 82816

This view shows the approach to the village from the south, with the open space of Ellerthwaite Square having no shortage of motor traffic even at this early time, including an omnibus (right). The gardens, barely visible to the right, are those of the big house, Ellerthwaite, which now houses the public library and the Citizen's Advice Bureau.

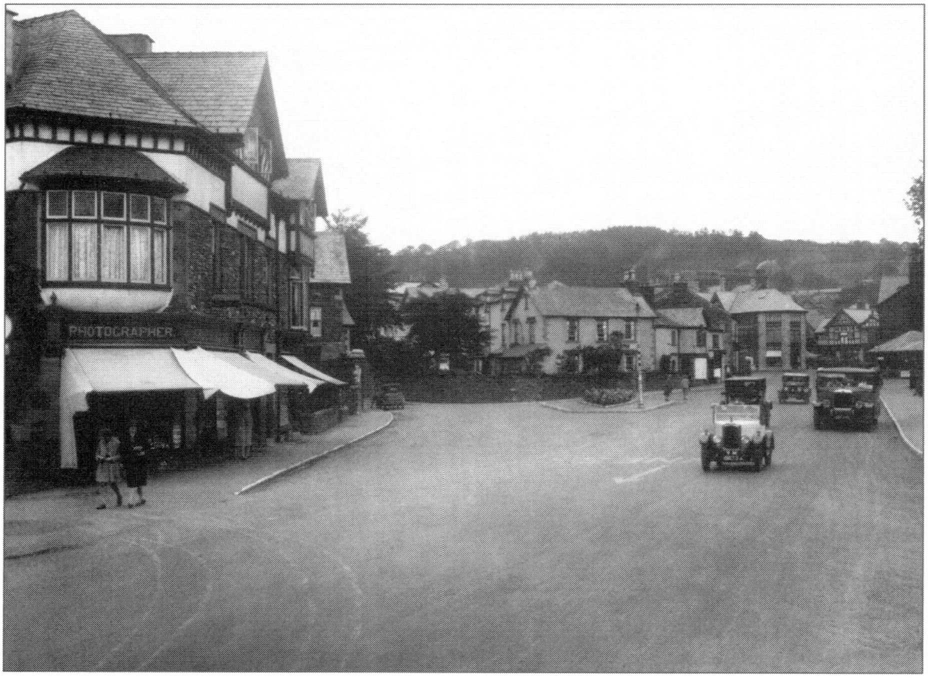

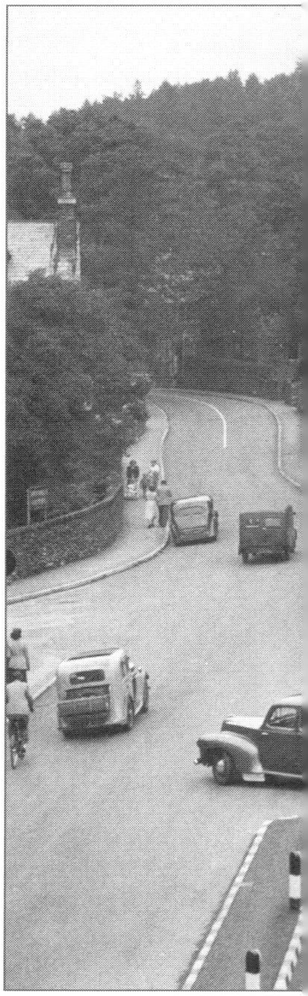

► **WINDERMERE**
Victoria Street 1929
82818

Here we see the junction at the foot of Victoria Street. The Queen's Hotel has since acquired outside seating in front of the building, the antique furniture shop (centre) is an optometrist, the Victoria Café at the end of the road is Jambo, Lishman's (left) is an accountant's premises, and the 'to the station' sign (left) has gone. Otherwise this scene is still much as it was in the late twenties.

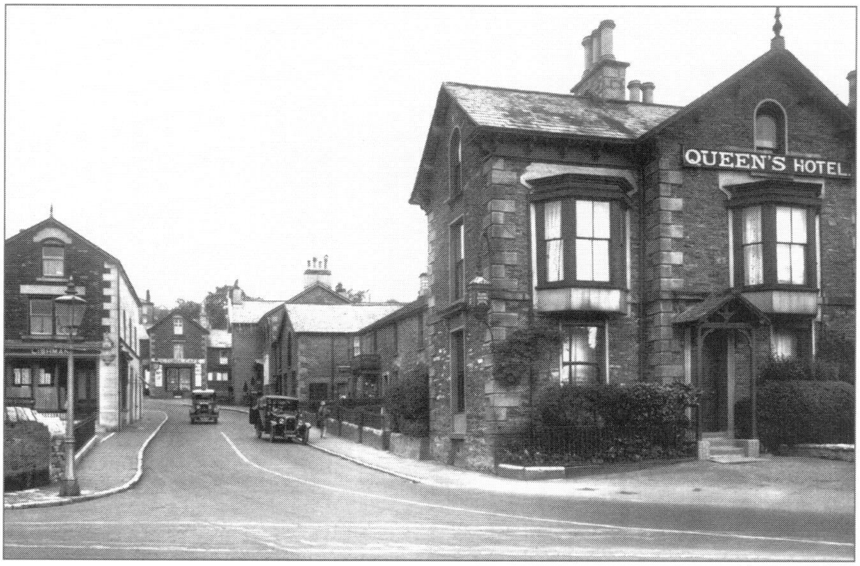

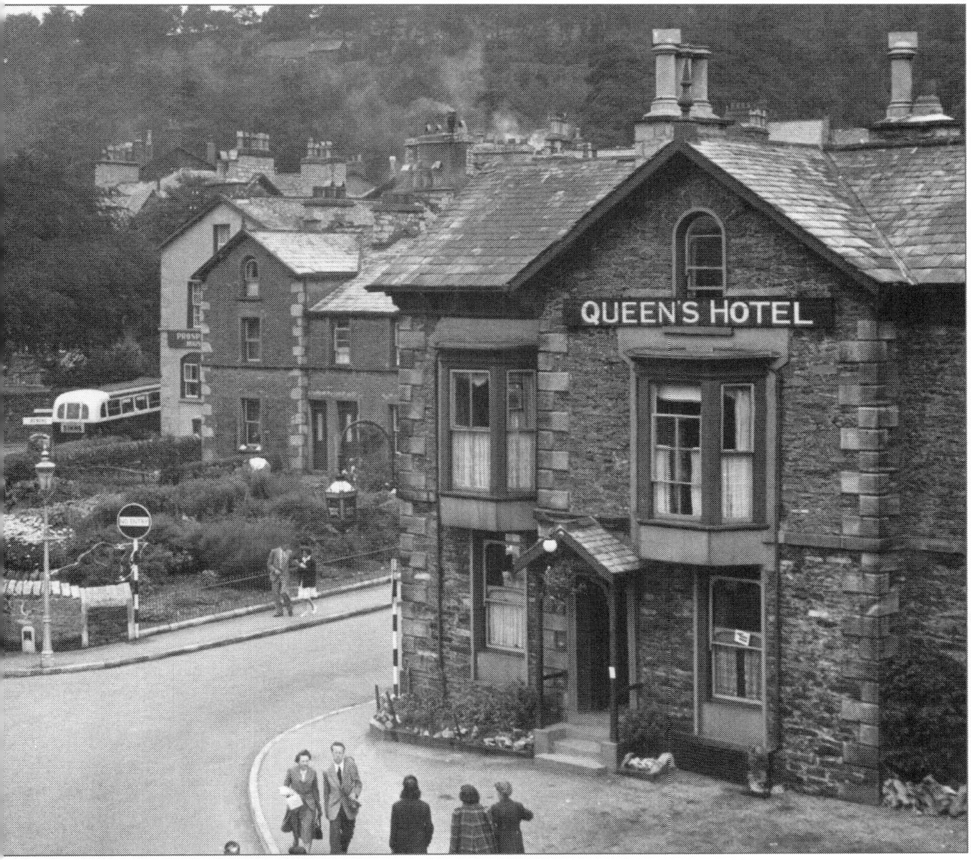

◀ **WINDERMERE**
Orrest Head c1955
W109121

From this elevated viewpoint opposite the Queen's Hotel we see some of the buildings of the village set below the wooded height of Orrest Head, more than eight acres of land gifted to the people of Windermere in memory of A H Heywood of Elleray. The summit is 784ft above sea level. The hotel to the extreme left is now Grays Inn. The sign advertising Binns on the back of the bus (centre) probably refers to the departmental store in Carlisle. Today's traffic scheme would not permit the right turn being made in this picture.

▶ **WINDERMERE**
Rigg's Hotel 1929
82821

The 19th-century entrepreneur Richard Rigg had this spacious hotel constructed by the local Pattinson building company. It stands on the north side of what is now the main A591, opposite the railway station. The hotel was opened on 12 May 1847, the year of the arrival of the railway and the start of mass tourism in Windermere.

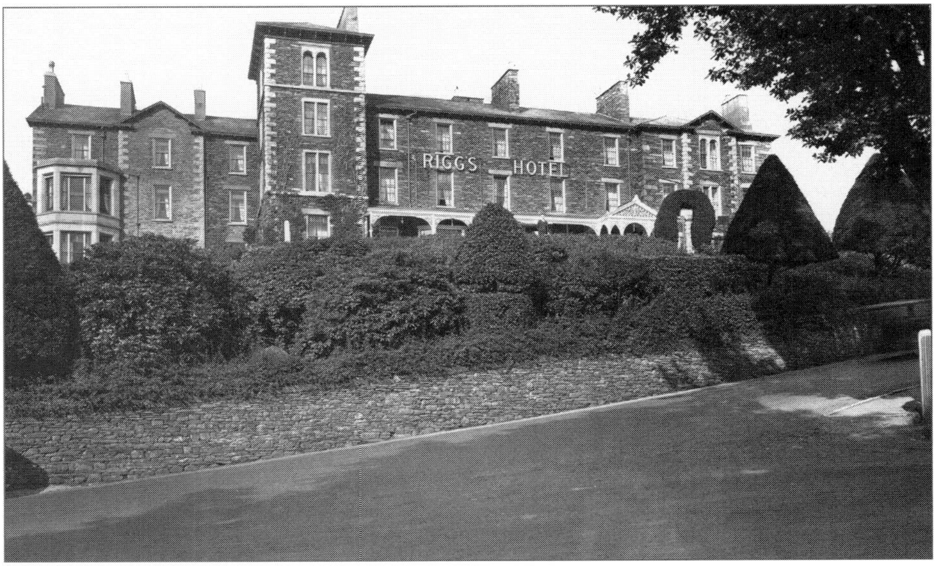

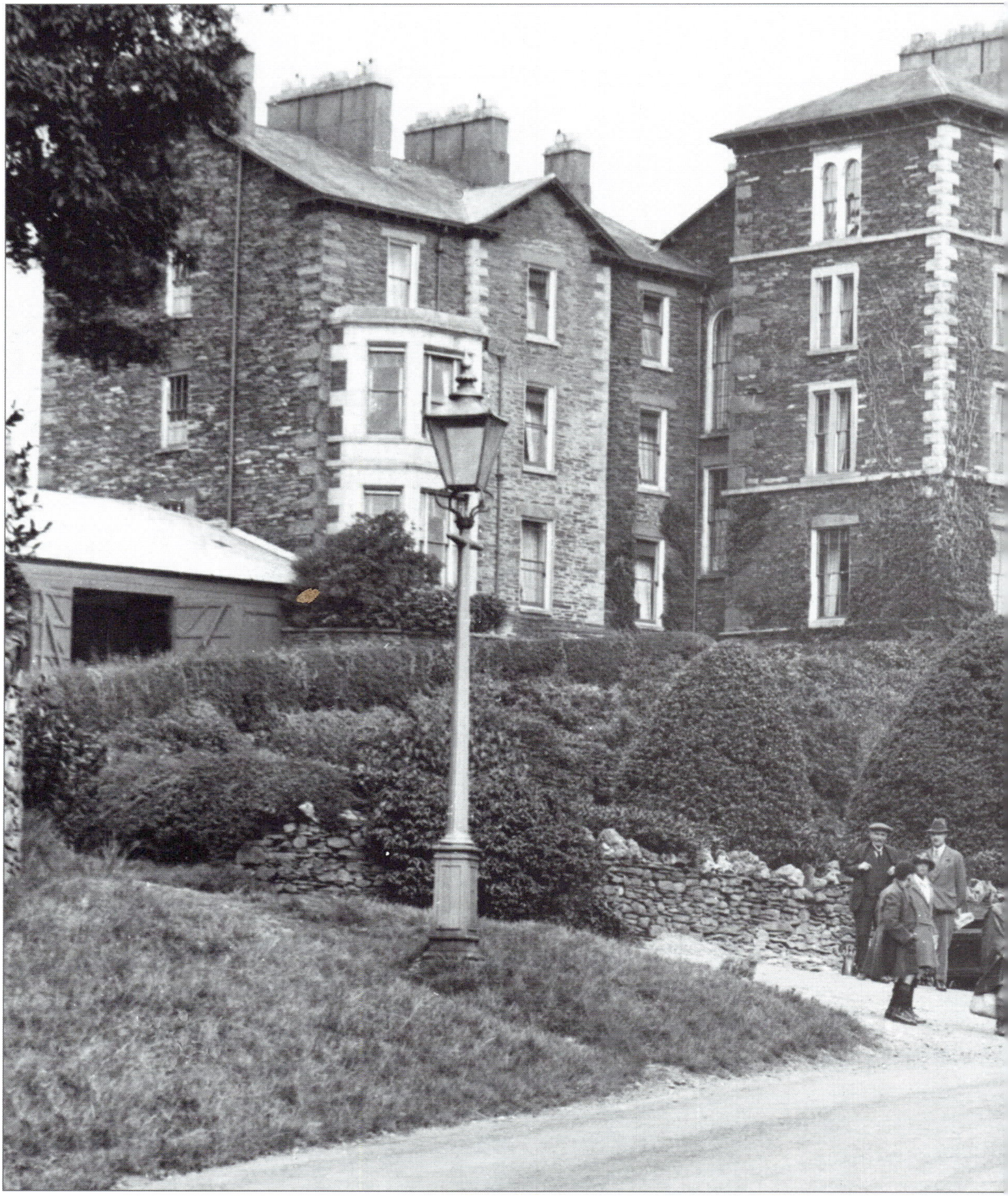

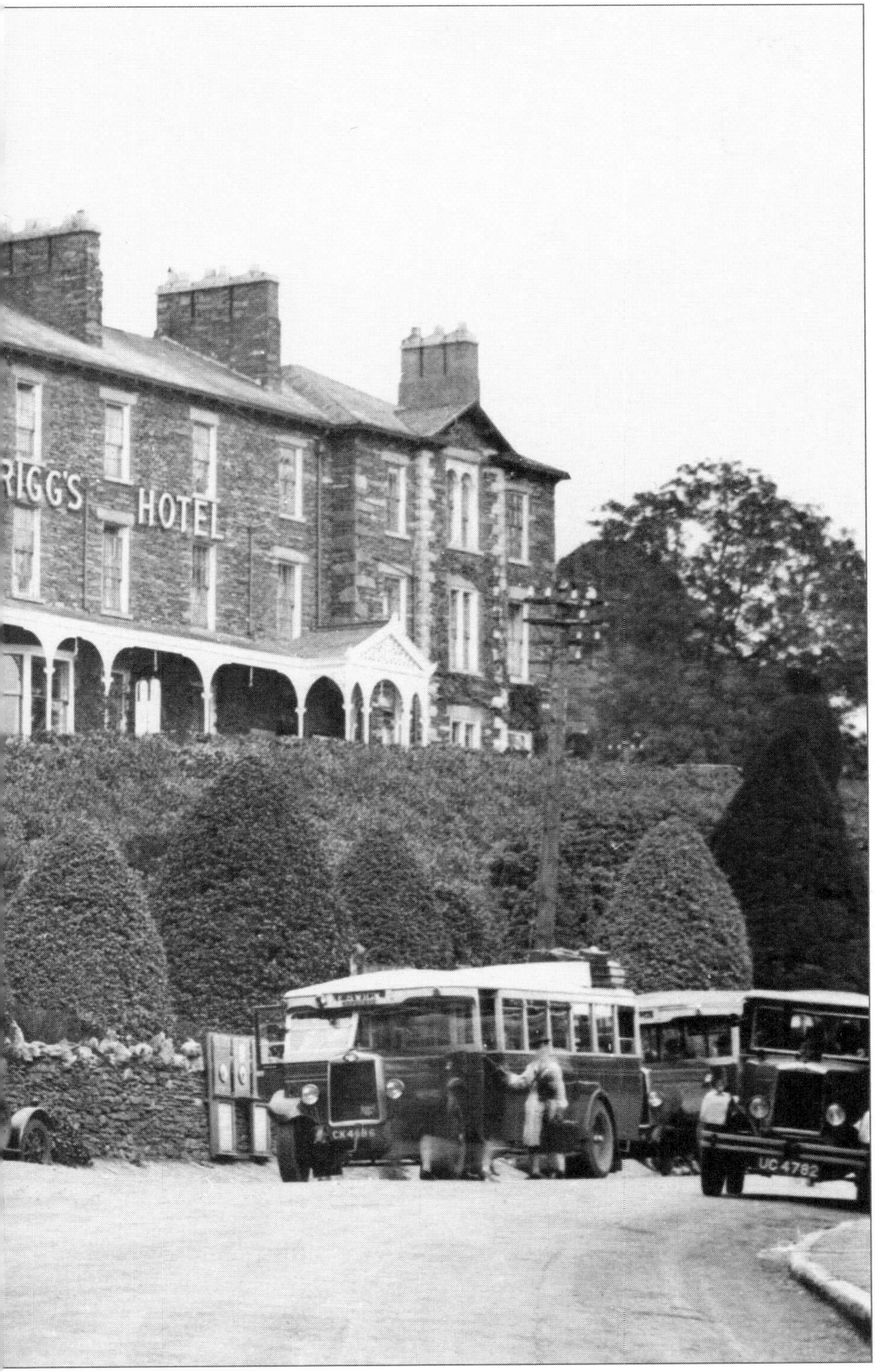

WINDERMERE
Rigg's Hotel 1929 82820

Here we have another view of Rigg's Hotel. In addition to owning the hotel, Rigg operated coaching services across the Lake District to Ambleside, Grasmere and Keswick, and across the Windermere ferry to Hawkshead and Coniston. There were links with the Salutation Inn at Ambleside and the Red Lion Inn at Hawkshead. The motor buses we see here have taken over from Rigg's coaching services - the front one is bound for Keswick. The bus stop is still in the same place, but today's vehicles would certainly not stop on the wrong side of the road!

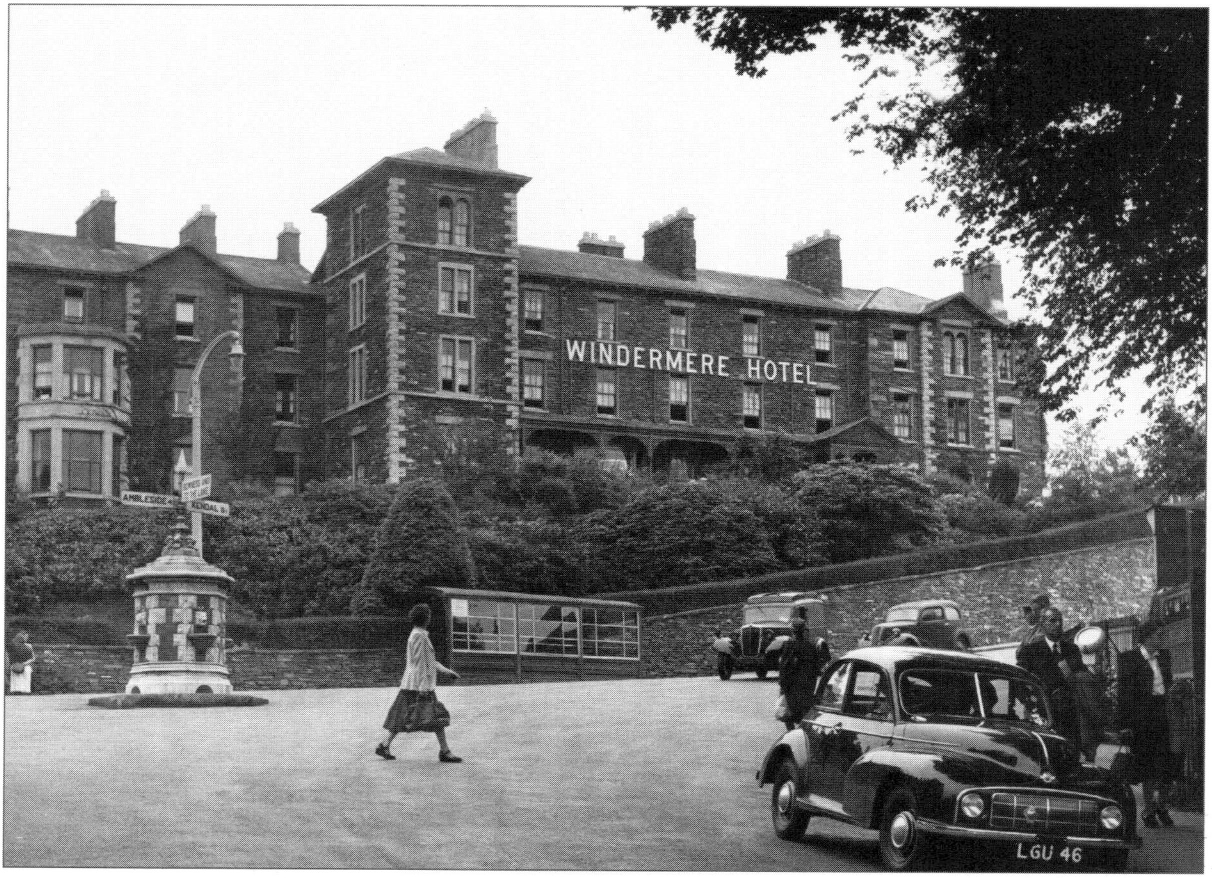

WINDERMERE

The Windermere Hotel c1955 W109124

No longer owned by the Rigg family, the hotel has been re-named in this post-World War II photograph. Otherwise, very little has outwardly changed in the interim years. The ornate drinking fountain with its road signs to Ambleside, Kendal, Bowness and the lake has been removed since 1955 - presumably it was a hazard on this now busy junction. It can now be found in the open area in front of the Brewery Arts Centre in Kendal. The shining example of an early version of the Morris Minor car is a reminder of the advanced design of this vehicle and of its consequent popularity.

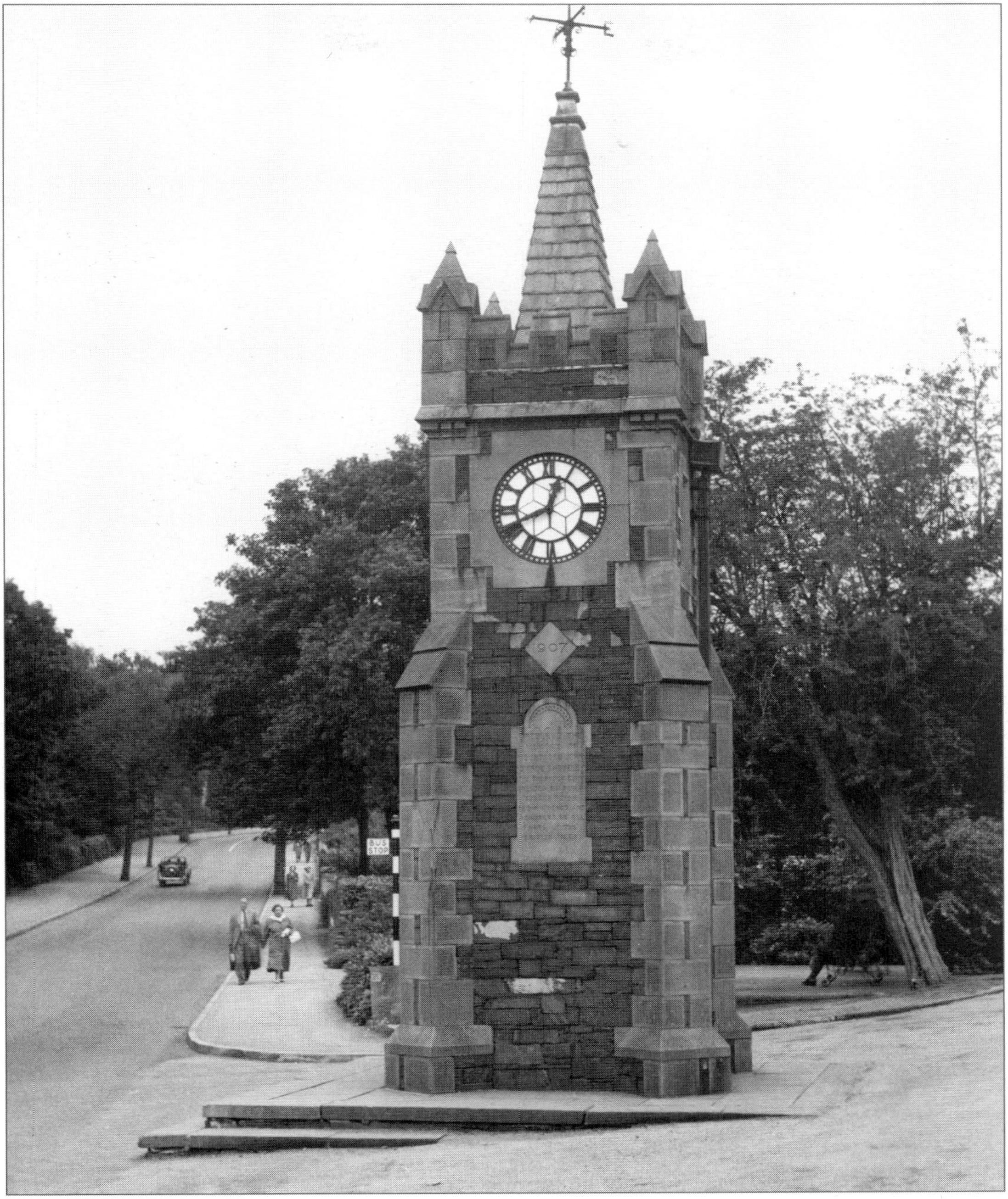

WINDERMERE, *The Baddeley Clock c1955* W109132

This clock is a notable landmark by the side of the road connecting Windermere with Bowness. It was erected in 1907 as a memorial to M J B Baddeley, whose guide books were greatly esteemed at that time and for much of the earlier part of the 20th century. The inscription reads: ' To preserve the memory of Mountford John Byroe Baddeley (the thorough guide), erected by public subscription from friends and admirers in all parts of the British Isles'.

WINDERMERE
The Lake from Orrest Head 1929 82830

This is a sacred spot for all lovers of Lakeland mountains. Here, the legendary A Wainwright, the author of the best-loved and unique series of hand-written mountain guide books, was inspired by his first glimpse of what would become his lifetime interest and obsession - exploring and recording every walking route on every hill and mountain. There has long been an orientation table on this mini summit, which is easily reached by a signposted track starting opposite the National Westminster Bank in Windermere.

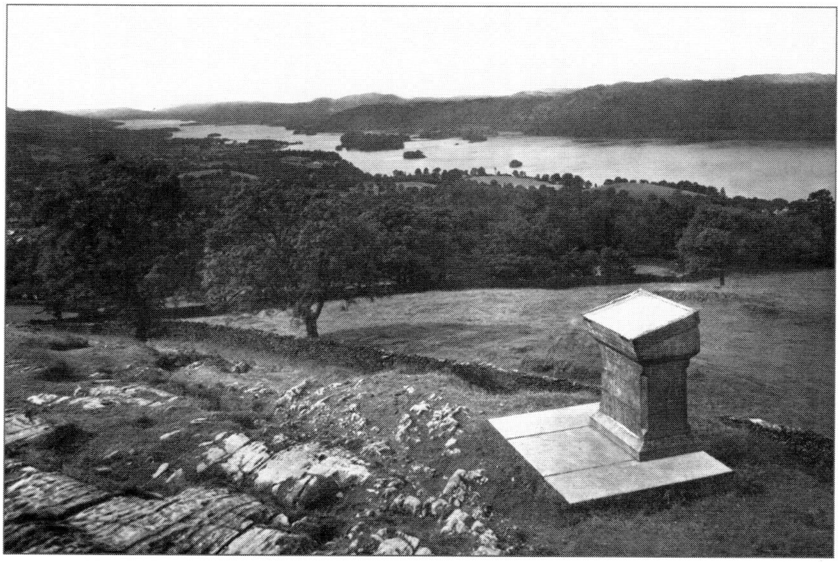

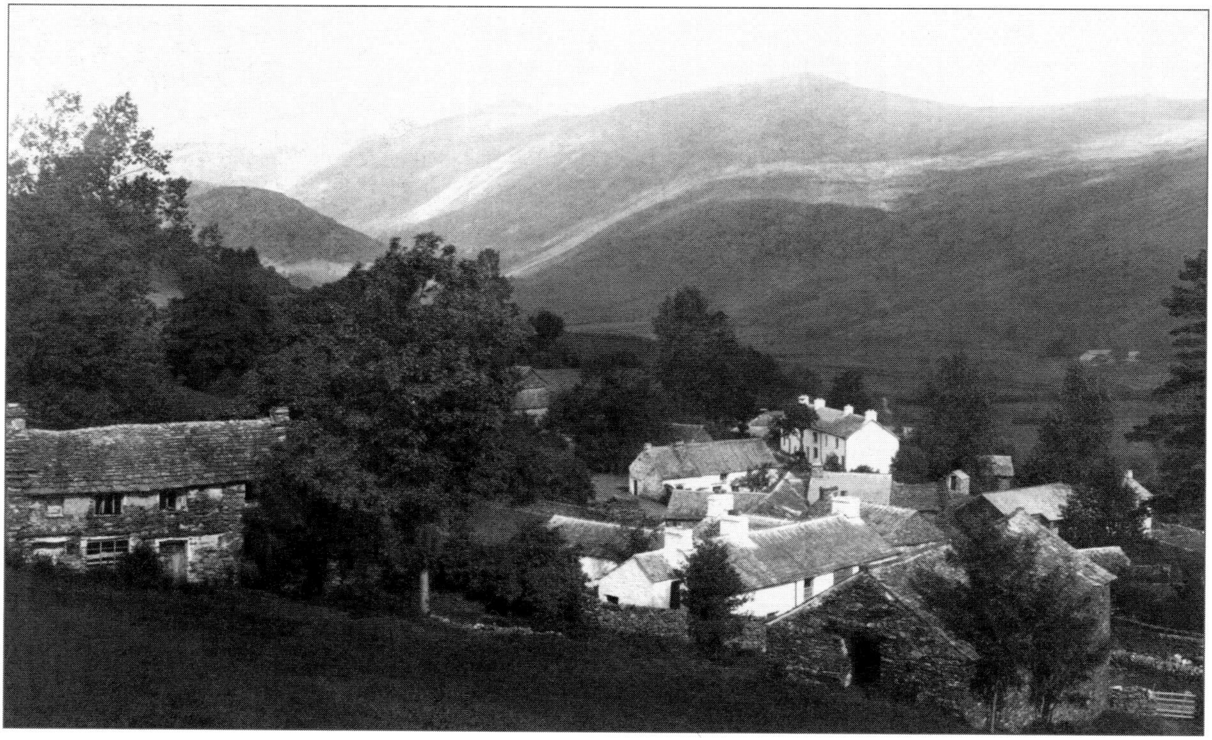

TROUTBECK, *Town Head c1880* 12522

A view over the rooftops of Town Head, the upper portion of the elongated Troutbeck village, sitting below the long high ridge which includes the summits of (from the left) Froswick, Ill Bell and Yoke. The dilapidated building on the left has since been renovated to provide extra accommodation for the adjacent Queen's Head Hotel, itself obscured by the trees.

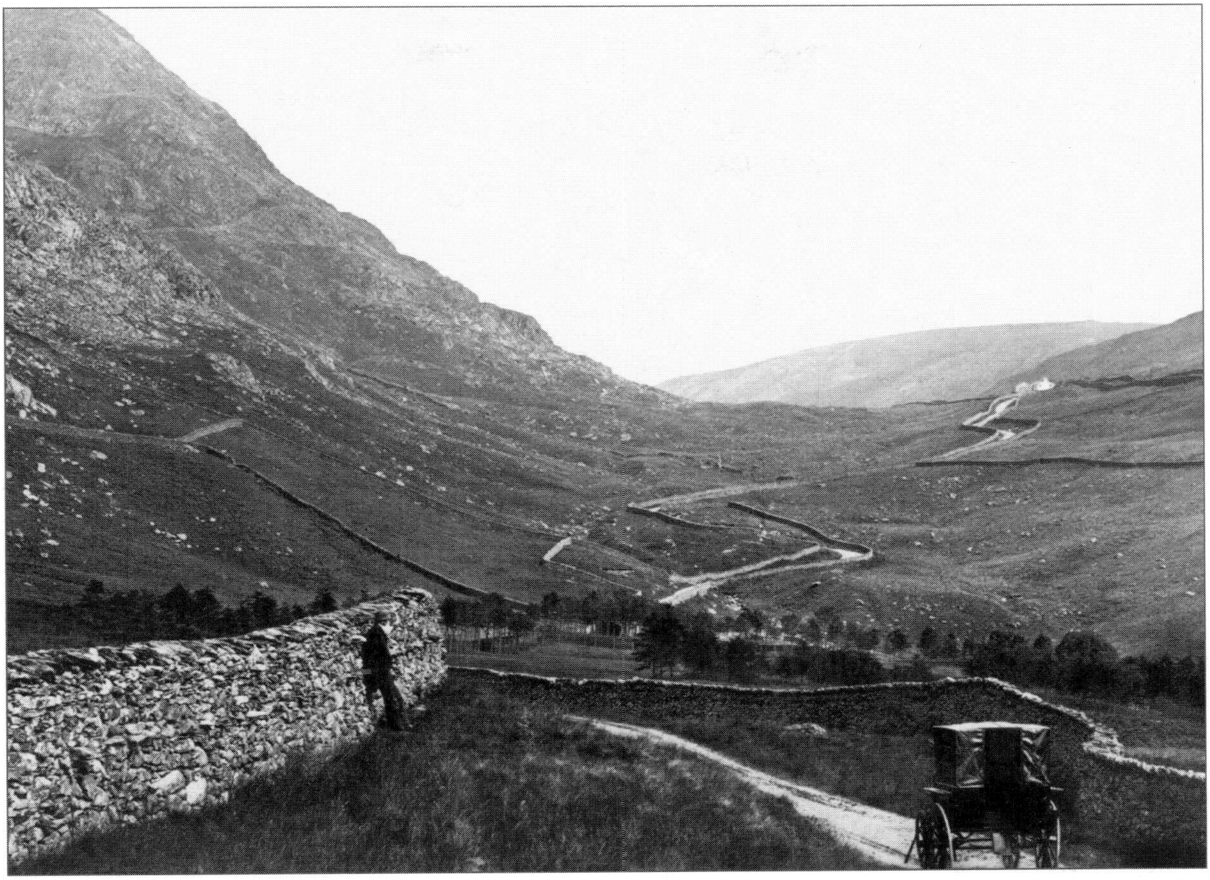

TROUTBECK
The Kirkstone Pass 1886 5010

This little road, climbing steeply from Ambleside through stark countryside to join the main Windermere to Ullswater road at the top of the Kirkstone Pass, has long been known as 'The Struggle'. In the late 19th century it was obviously just a narrow rough track, dominated by the bulk of Red Screes to the left, with Caudale Moor rising above the lonely Kirkstone Inn, just visible ahead. This picture also poses interesting questions - why is the solitary traveller leaning abjectly on the wall, and where is the horse? Perhaps tired of the remorseless ascent, could it have broken free and bolted?

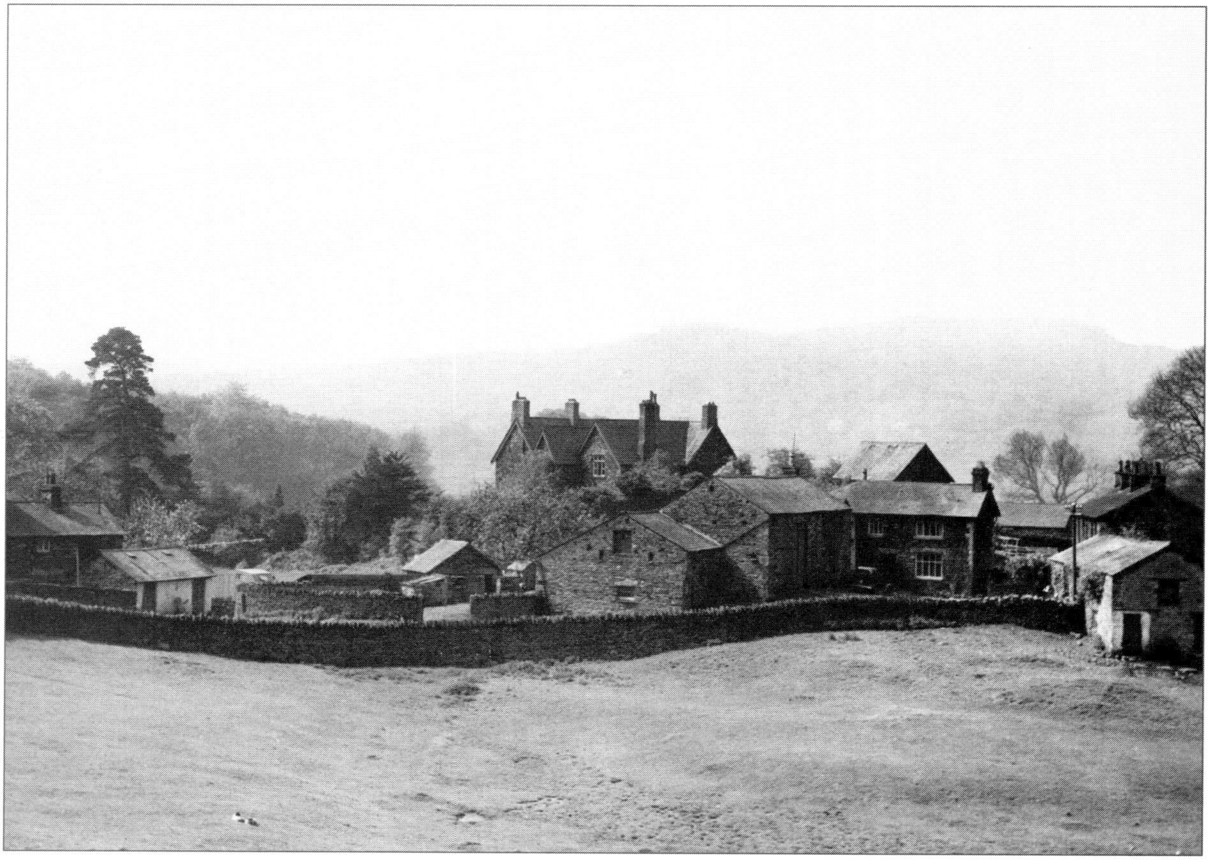

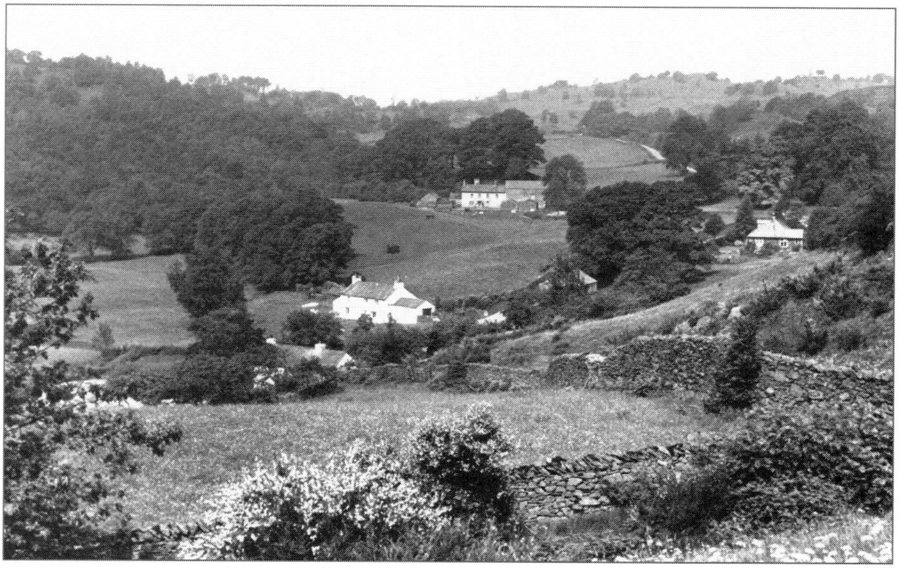

◀**WINSTER**
The Valley c1960
W500001

The unchanging beauty of the Winster Valley, with its meadows, rolling hillsides, dry stone walls and scattered dwellings, is entirely typical of the soft countryside of the southern fringe of the Lake District. The underlying Silurian geology produces a landscape contrasting sharply with the dramatic, craggy nature of the central mountains.

◀ **STAVELEY**
The Village c1955 S831038

Some of the older buildings of the village present a pretty and tranquil picture below the wooded hillsides, although in 1955 the road through the middle of Staveley still carried all the traffic to and from Windermere. Similarly, there is no indication of industrial activity; until the 19th century, this was a dominant feature of Staveley, with bobbin and other mills lining the banks of the River Kent.

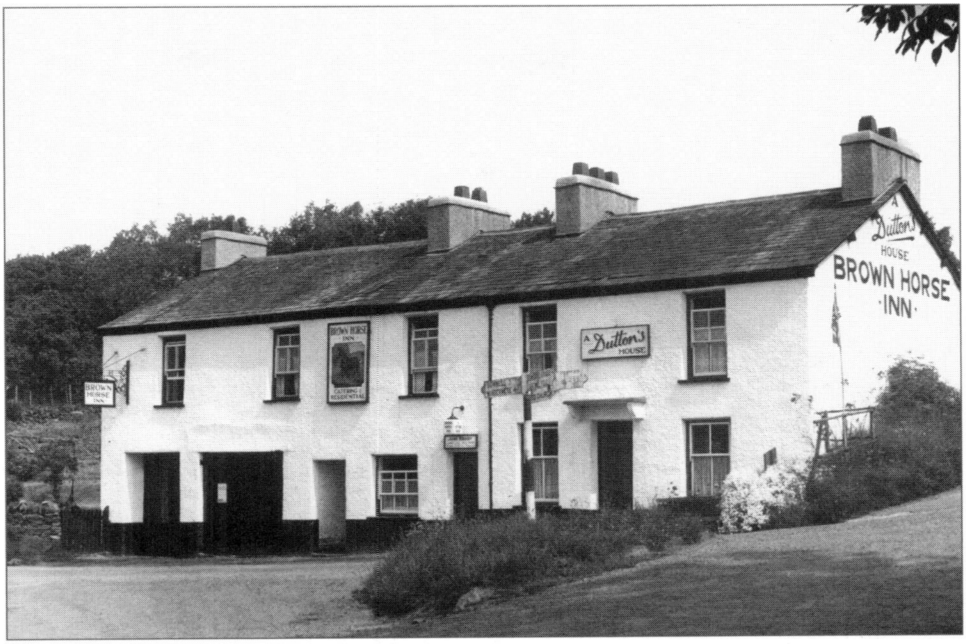

▲ **WINSTER,** *The Brown Horse Inn c1960* W500006

One of the focal points of the scattered village of Winster, the Brown Horse is a well-known local hostelry. The signs leave no doubt that in 1960 the inn was owned by Dutton's Brewery (of Blackburn), and that John Kirkby was the licensee. There have since been a few comparatively minor changes to the structure, most notably the conversion of the garage doors into a double bow window. The signpost still points the way to Windermere and Bowness, Kendal and Lancaster, and Bowland Bridge and Winster Church.

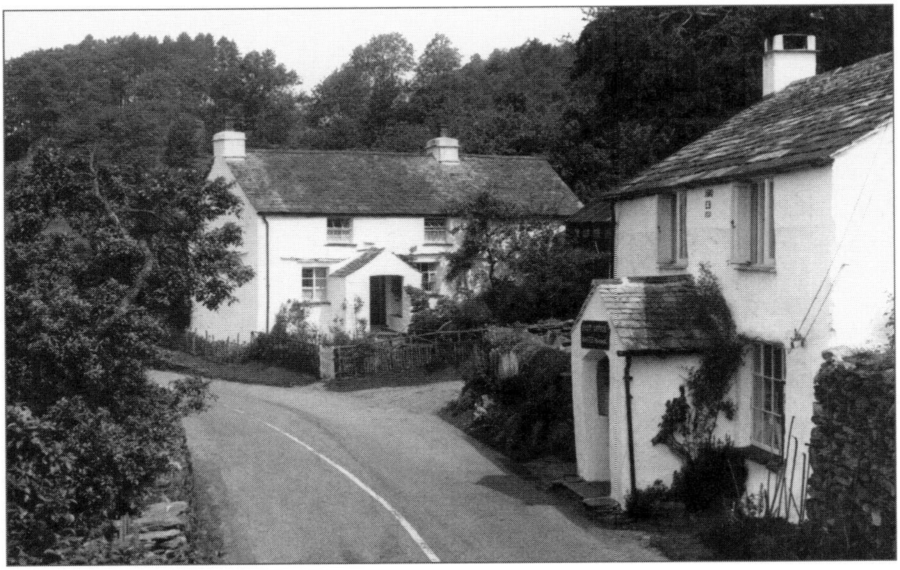

◀ **WINSTER**
The Post Office c1960
W500009

This charming picture shows the Winster post office, formerly another focal point of the scattered village. Alas, in 1984 the office was closed, but apart from the loss of the stone porch on the adjacent building, the scene remains the same. The post office cottage is inscribed '1600 EB 1950'.

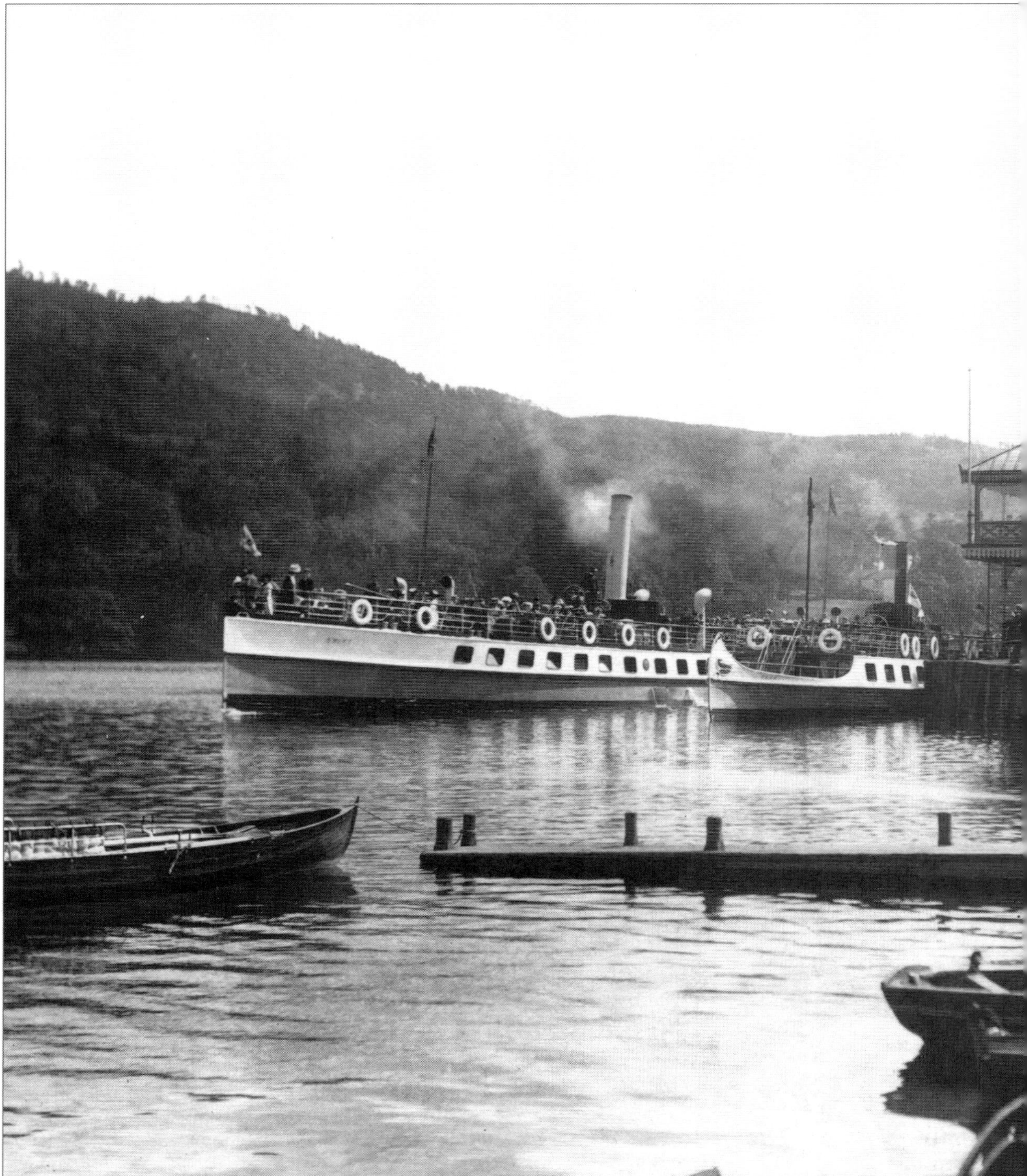

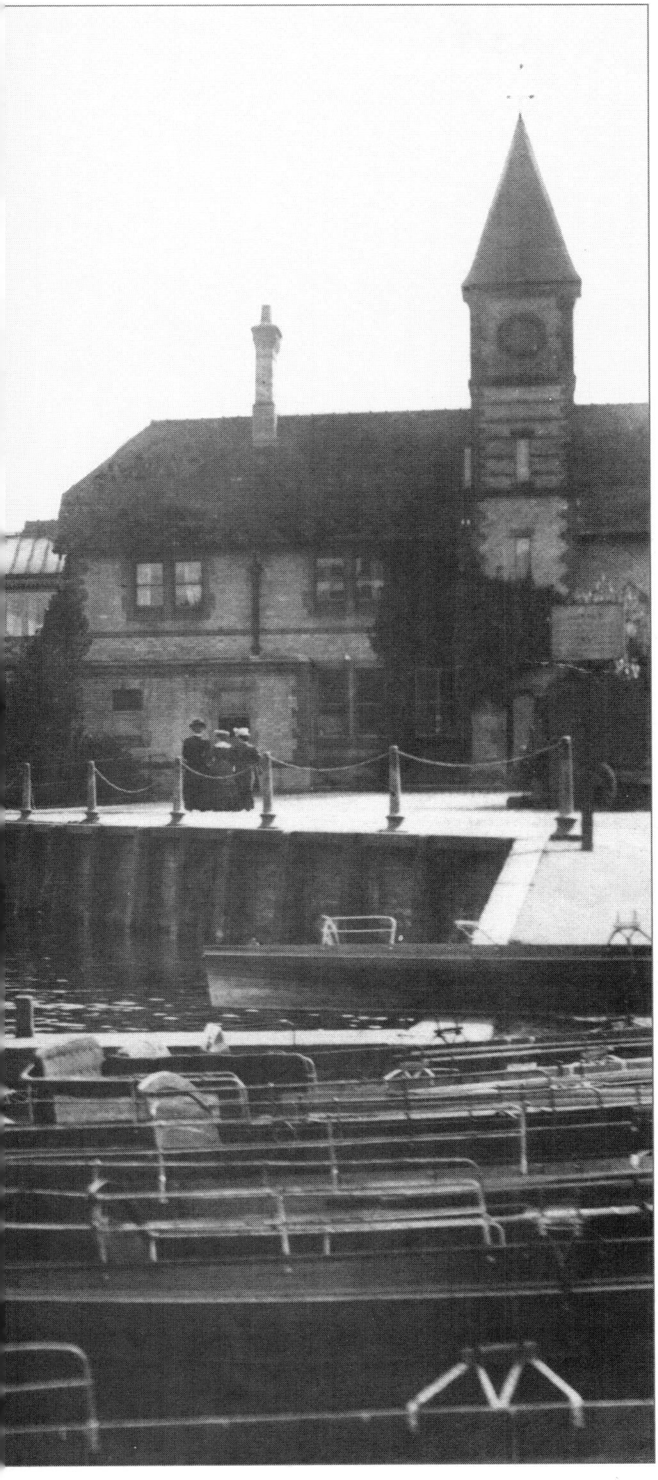

LAKESIDE AND NEWBY BRIDGE

LAKESIDE is the settlement furthest away from the Lakeland mountains, but it is historically important as the entry point for large numbers of day visitors from 1868, when the Furness Railway constructed the terminal linking railway and steamer services. It has continued to be the southern terminus of timetabled services on the lake, resuming its role as a link between train and steamer following the opening of the Lakeside and Haverthwaite Railway.

Nearby, the historic Newby Bridge spans the outfall from Windermere, a communication link between settlements on the west and the east sides of the water, its importance marked by the presence of the large Swan Hotel at one end of the bridge.

LAKESIDE
The Terminal 1907 59150

This picture captures well the activity at the Lakeside steamer/railway exchange terminal constructed by the Furness Railway near the foot of the lake. The 'Swift' has just departed, whilst the slighter smaller and older 'Tern' waits at the quayside. The 'Tern' no longer has the bird emblem which is just visible on her prow in this photograph, but she has remained in service to the present day, now converted to diesel propulsion. The terminal still exists, but the buildings are more utilitarian; the main building with the tower has been replaced.

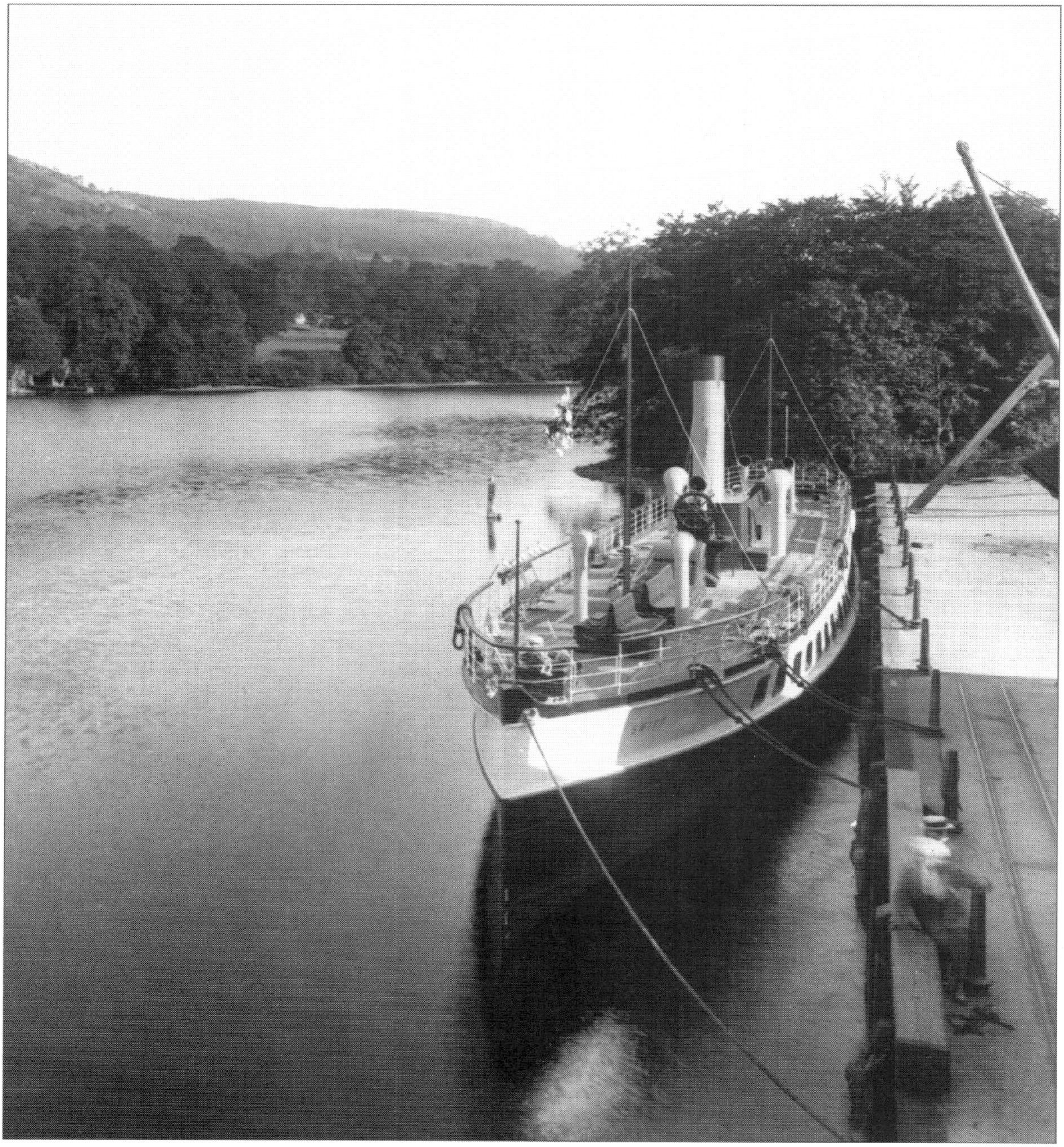

LAKESIDE, *The 'Swift' 1921* 70689

Moored at the Lakeside steamer terminal is the 'Swift', 150ft long, 21ft wide and claimed to be capable of carrying 780 passengers. Launched in 1900, she was at that time the biggest boat ever to sail on the lake. Visible across the lake is the large boathouse and the grounds at Fell Foot, the estate formerly owned by Col Ridehalgh, a great boating enthusiast. It is now owned and managed as a visitor attraction by the National Trust.

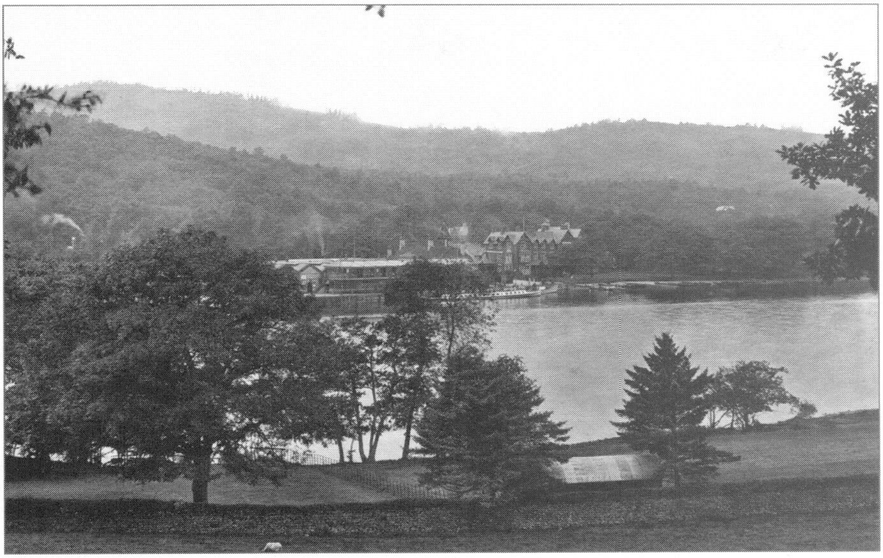

LAKESIDE
From Fell Foot 1914
67420

This view from Fell Foot is across the lake to the steamer/railway exchange terminal, with the bulk of the Lakeside New Hotel next to it. There are two steam boats at the quayside. Although the Lakeside branch railway line was closed by British Rail in the 1960s, it was subsequently partially re-opened as a visitor attraction by the Lakeside and Haverthwaite Railway Co. The terminal still functions as an interchange between boat and train.

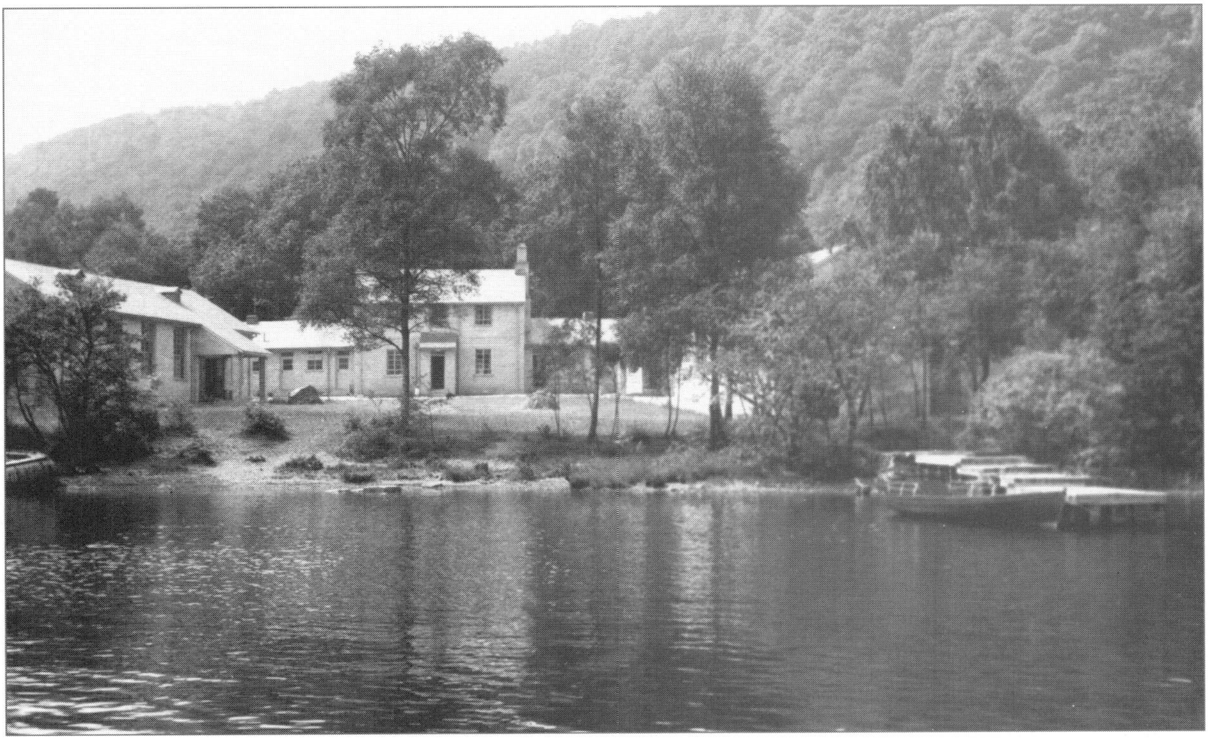

LAKESIDE, *The YMCA National Camp from the Lake c1960* L455001

The YMCA outdoor activities centre on the western shore of Windermere a little distance north of Lakeside occupies 240 acres, with a lake frontage of half a mile. It was established in 1953, and its activities now extend beyond the 'National' element of the title. Likewise, the many permanent buildings on the site belie its description as a camp.

▶ **LAKESIDE**
Woodland Tent Site, YMCA National Camp c1960 L455009

Much of the large area included in the centre is woodland. Here the 'camp' title is well justified by the neatly erected tents, with two people folding ground sheets (left).

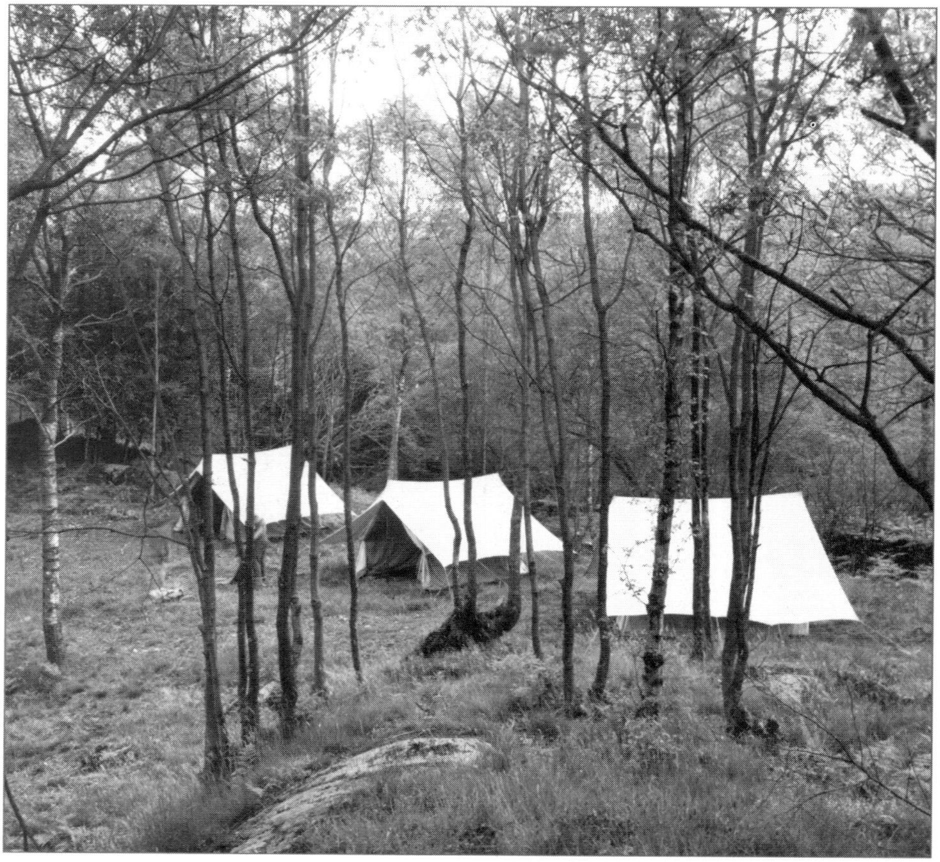

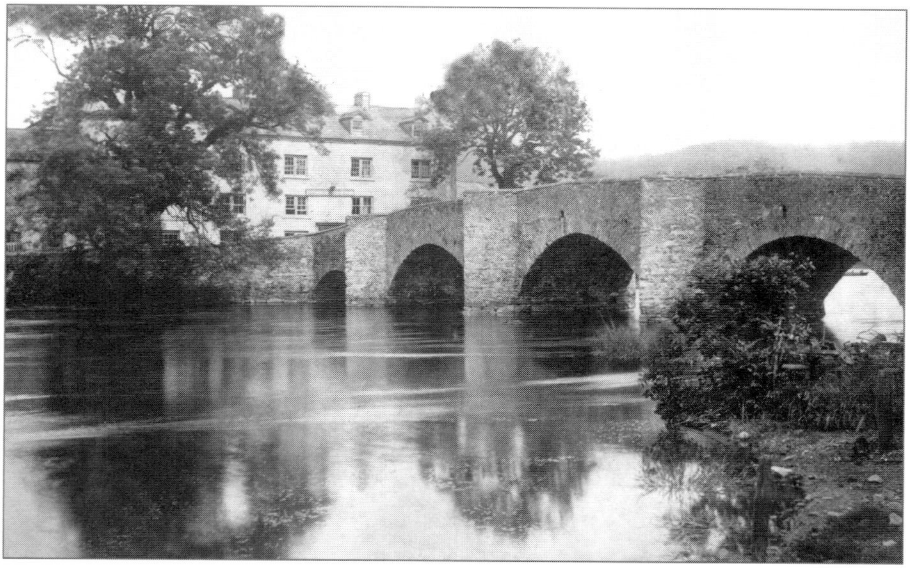

◀ **NEWBY BRIDGE**
The Swan Hotel 1888
20476

Newby Bridge is an old five-arched structure spanning the outflow from Windermere just above the weir which regulates the water level in the lake. Downstream, to the left, the River Leven reaches Morecambe Bay in a few miles. At the end of the bridge the old Swan Hotel is a noted landmark.

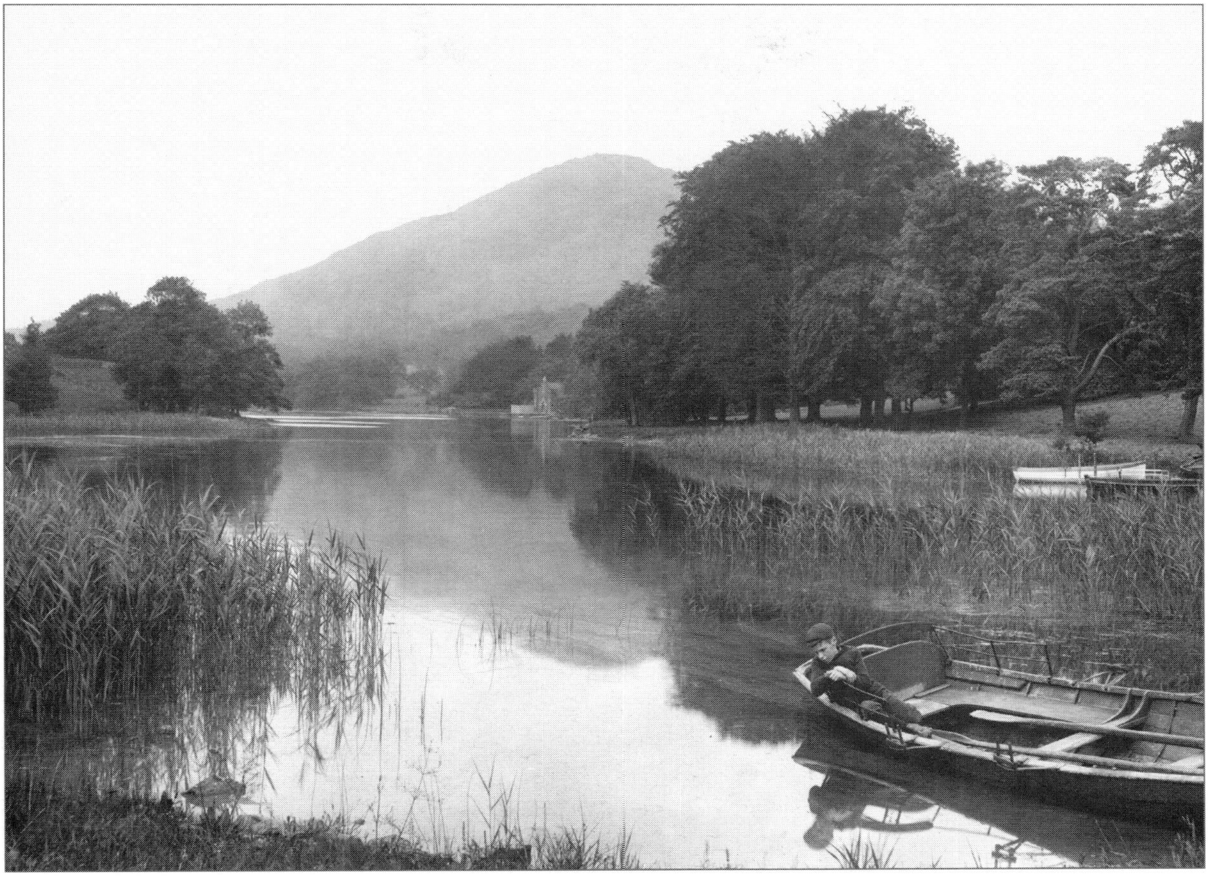

NEWBY BRIDGE
Nickle Landing Stage 1914 67419

A short distance downstream from Fell Foot, a young boy watches for fish in the shallow, reed-grown water by the shore, apparently in charge of a large rowing boat. Gummer's How rises to a summit of 1054ft behind the Fell Foot boathouse. All the area of land to the right is part of the Fell Foot estate, now owned by the National Trust.

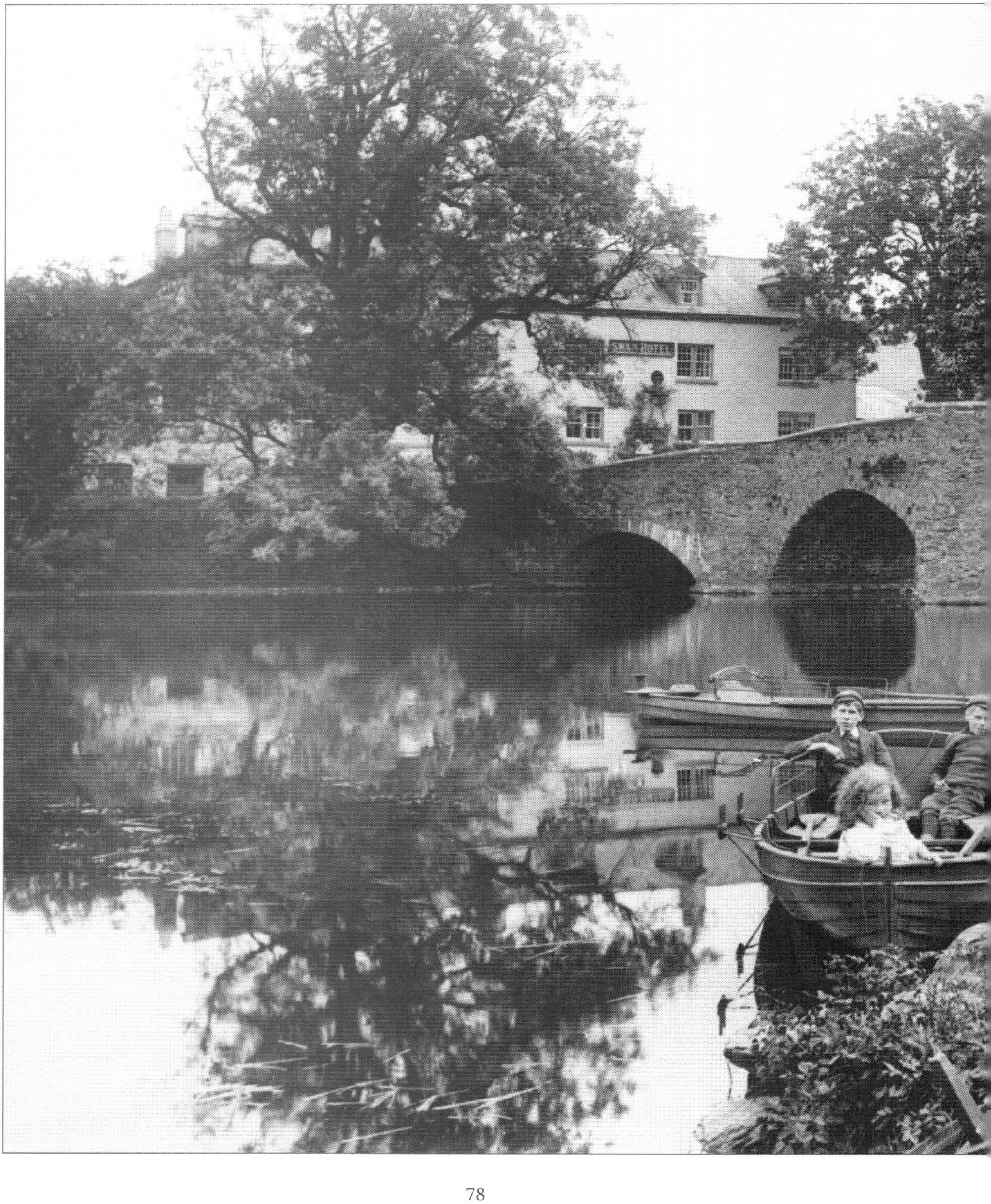
SWAN HOTEL

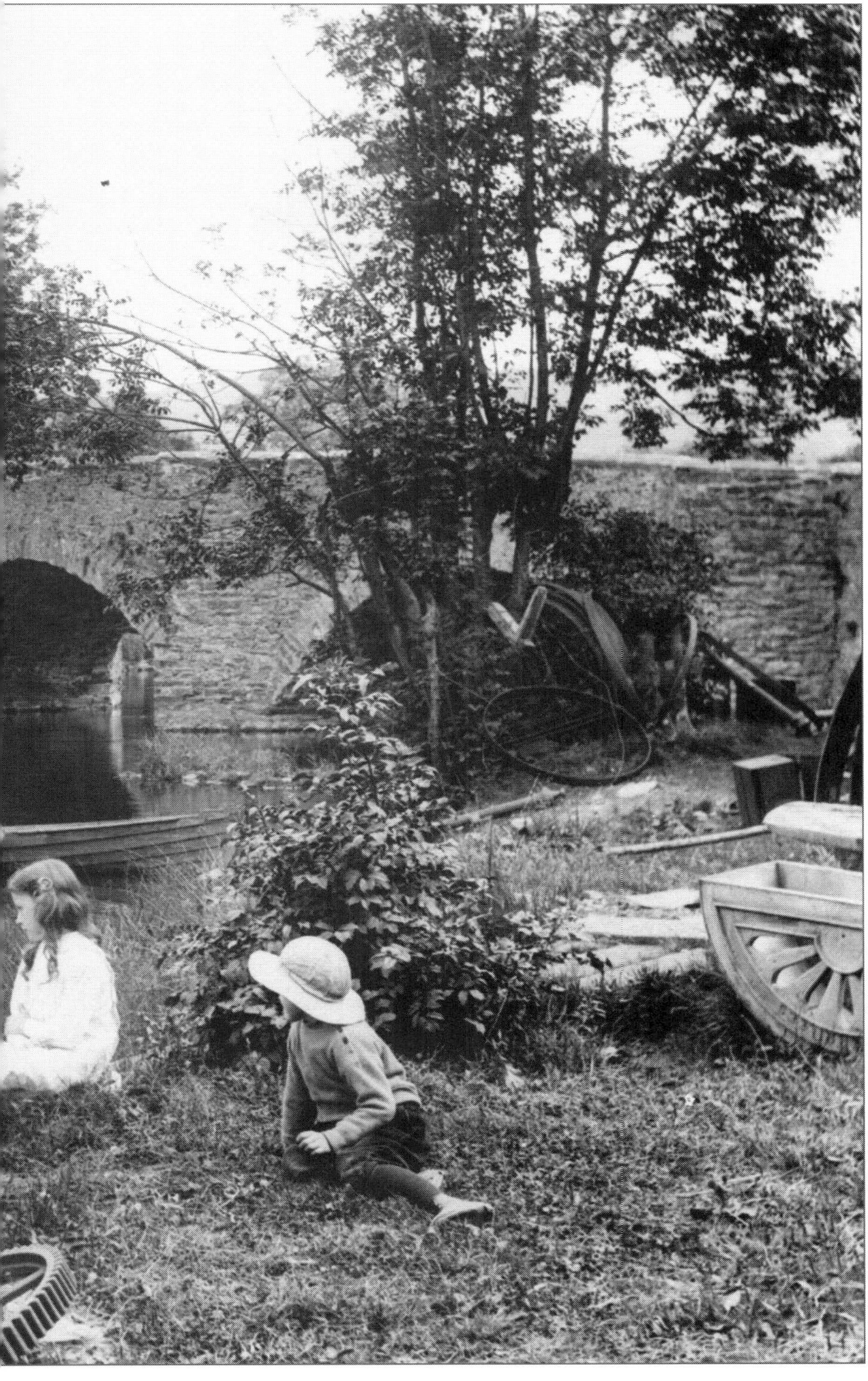

NEWBY BRIDGE
The Swan Hotel 1914
67414

Twenty-six years after 20476 (page 76) was taken, we see the bridge and the hotel from the same viewpoint, but with the added interest of a group of children, apparently in charge of a rowing boat. The tree to the right has certainly grown during the ensuing years, and the assorted rubbish is evidence of a workshop just out of the picture.

NEWBY BRIDGE
The Swan Hotel c1940 N15003

Taken from the roadway over the bridge, this view shows the Swan Hotel at the outbreak of World War II, still very much as it was in the late 19th century. This part of the building has hardly changed since 1940 - there is still a swan over the door - but to the right the outbuildings we see here have been replaced by a large extension wing.

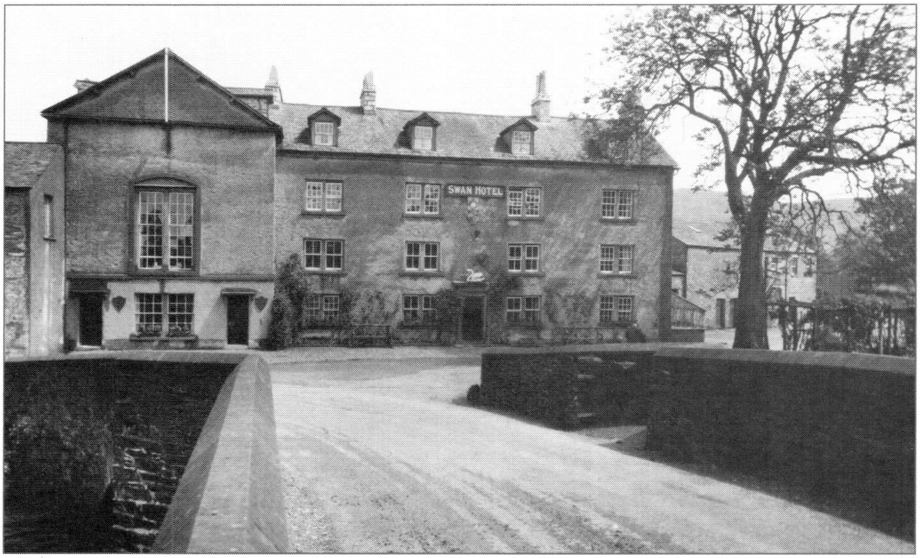

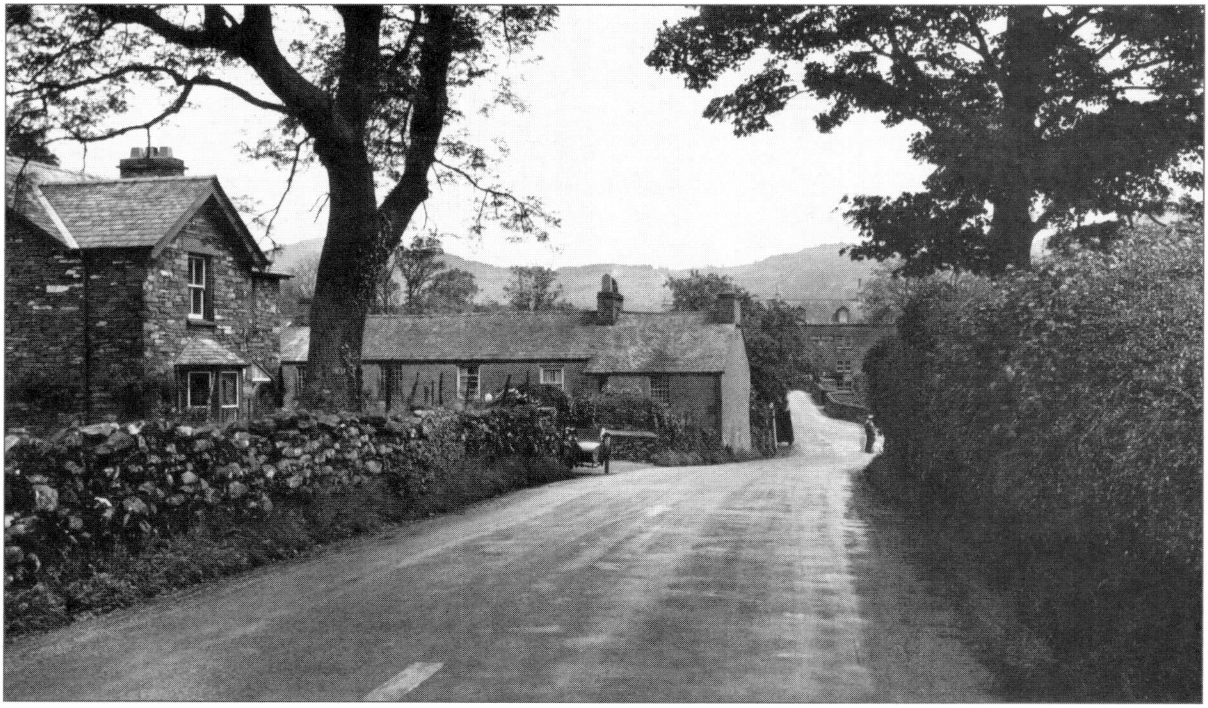

NEWBY BRIDGE, *Bridge Approach c1940* N15007

This is the approach road from the Barrow in Furness direction to Newby Bridge, now the A590, with the Swan Hotel on the far side of the bridge. The main road, widened in more recent years, swings to the right at the junction where the solitary pedestrian is standing in what would now be a suicidal position. The roadside house (Newby Bridge House), the big tree and the cottages are virtually unchanged since 1940, but the motor bike and sidecar (centre) are very much of the 1930s.

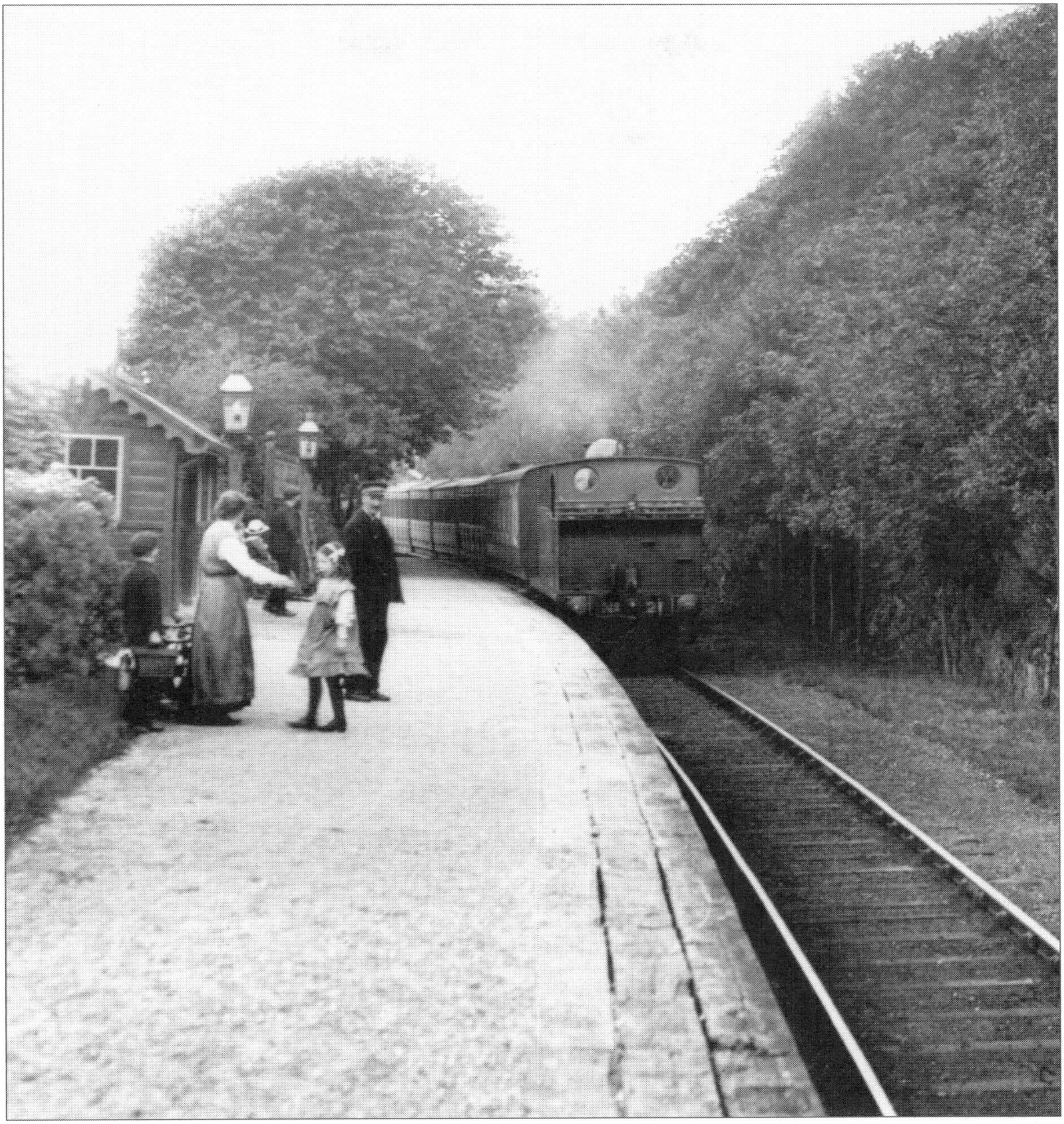

NEWBY BRIDGE, *The Railway Station 1914* 67417

Here we have a quintessential country branch line railway station scene, with the Furness Railway Greenodd to Lakeside train approaching the platform. The stationmaster watches carefully as the little girl is brought back from the edge of the platform by her mother, whilst the boy clutches his wicker basket. Following the closure of the line by British Rail in 1968, the station has been brought back into use as part of the Lakeside and Haverthwaite Railway; the building has been replaced, and only the columns remain of the distinctive platform lamps.

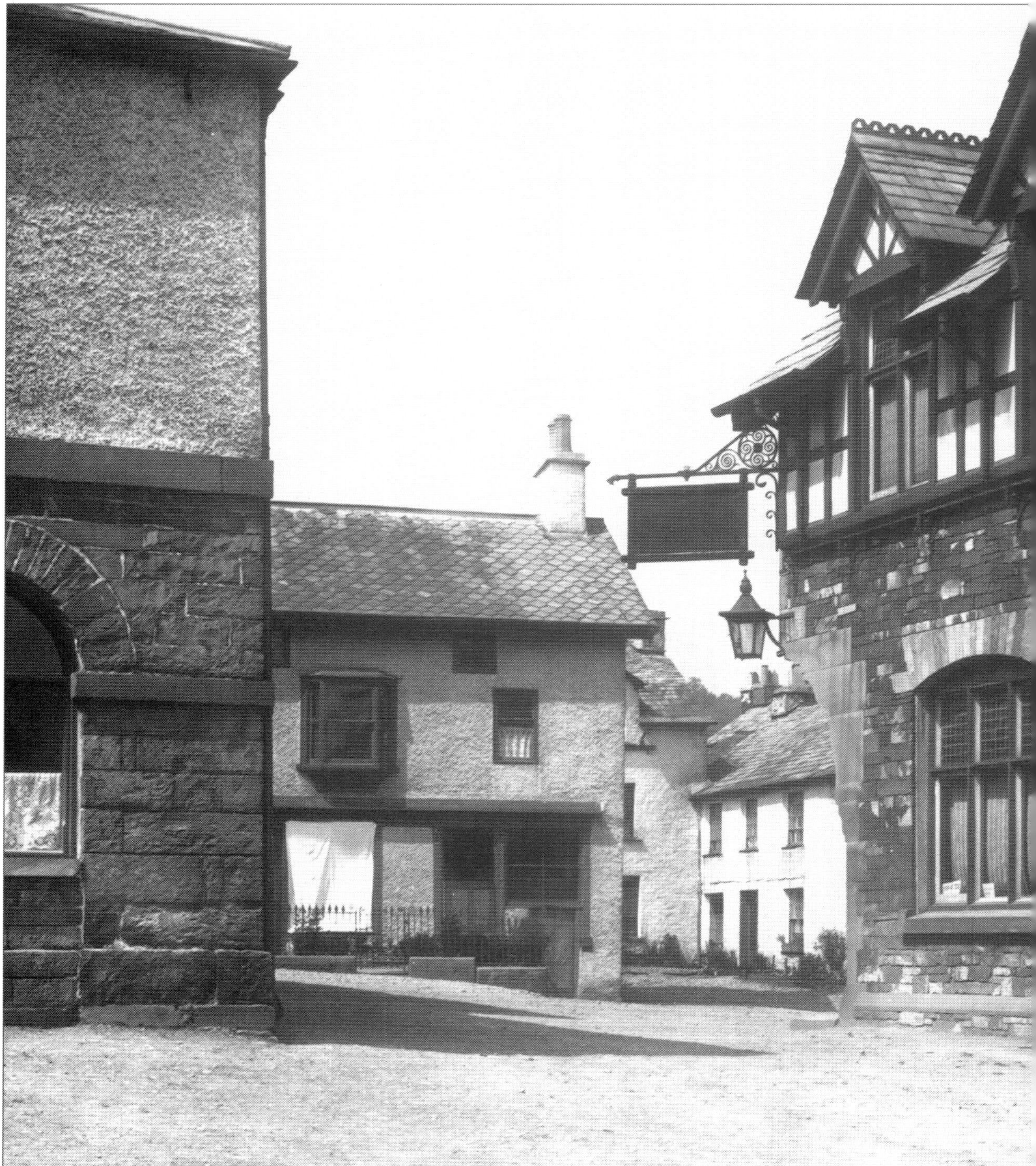

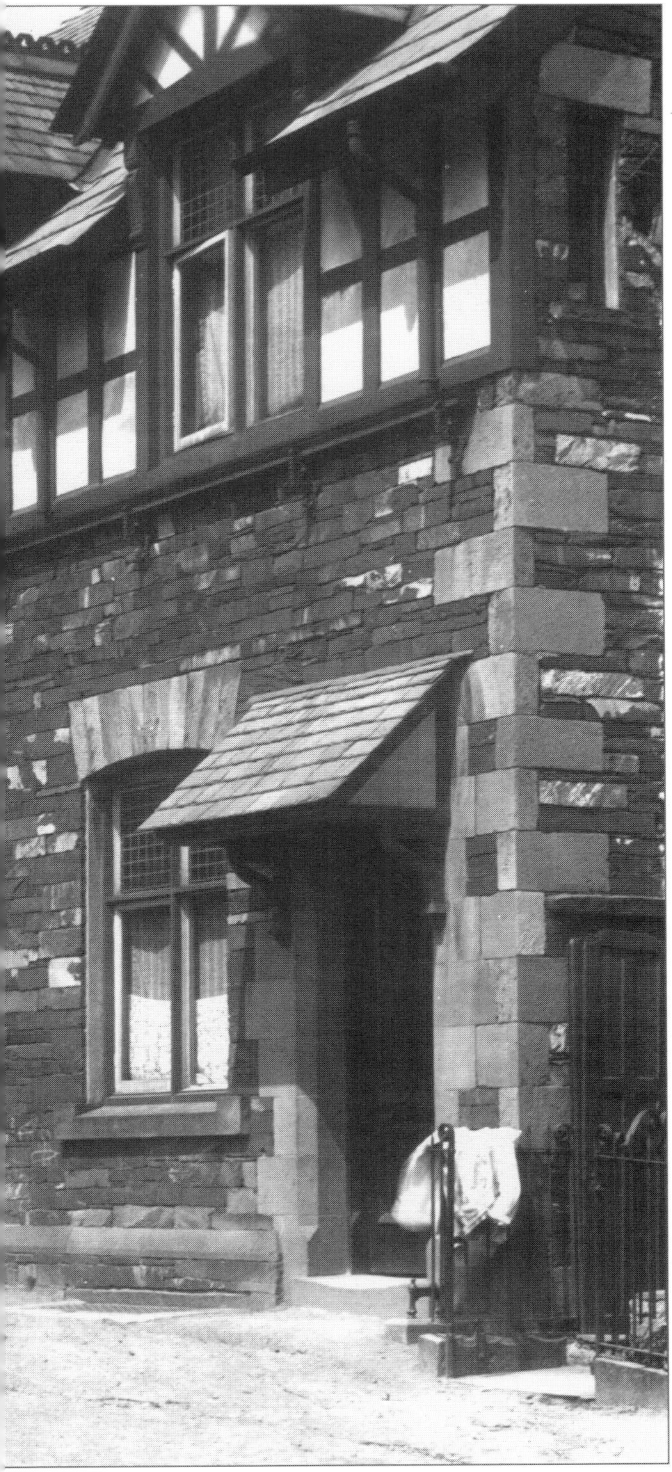

HAWKSHEAD

UNTIL comparatively recent times, Hawkshead was a largely self-sufficient small town. Originally an outpost of Furness Abbey, it was granted its own market charter after the 16th-century Dissolution of the Monasteries by King Henry VIII, trading over a wide area by means of pack-horses. With its tight-knit little squares and streets, it is quite unlike any other Lake District settlement. The strong associations with William Wordsworth and with Beatrix Potter add greatly to its popularity with visitors.

HAWKSHEAD
The Village Centre 1892 30539

The attractively crowded buildings in the centre of Hawkshead village are well displayed by this early photograph, with the former Market Hall on the left. The Lakeland stone structures were built to last, and apart from changes to shop fronts, little has changed over the years. The 'cup of tea' offered by a small sign in the second window from the right has developed into several tea/coffee shops.

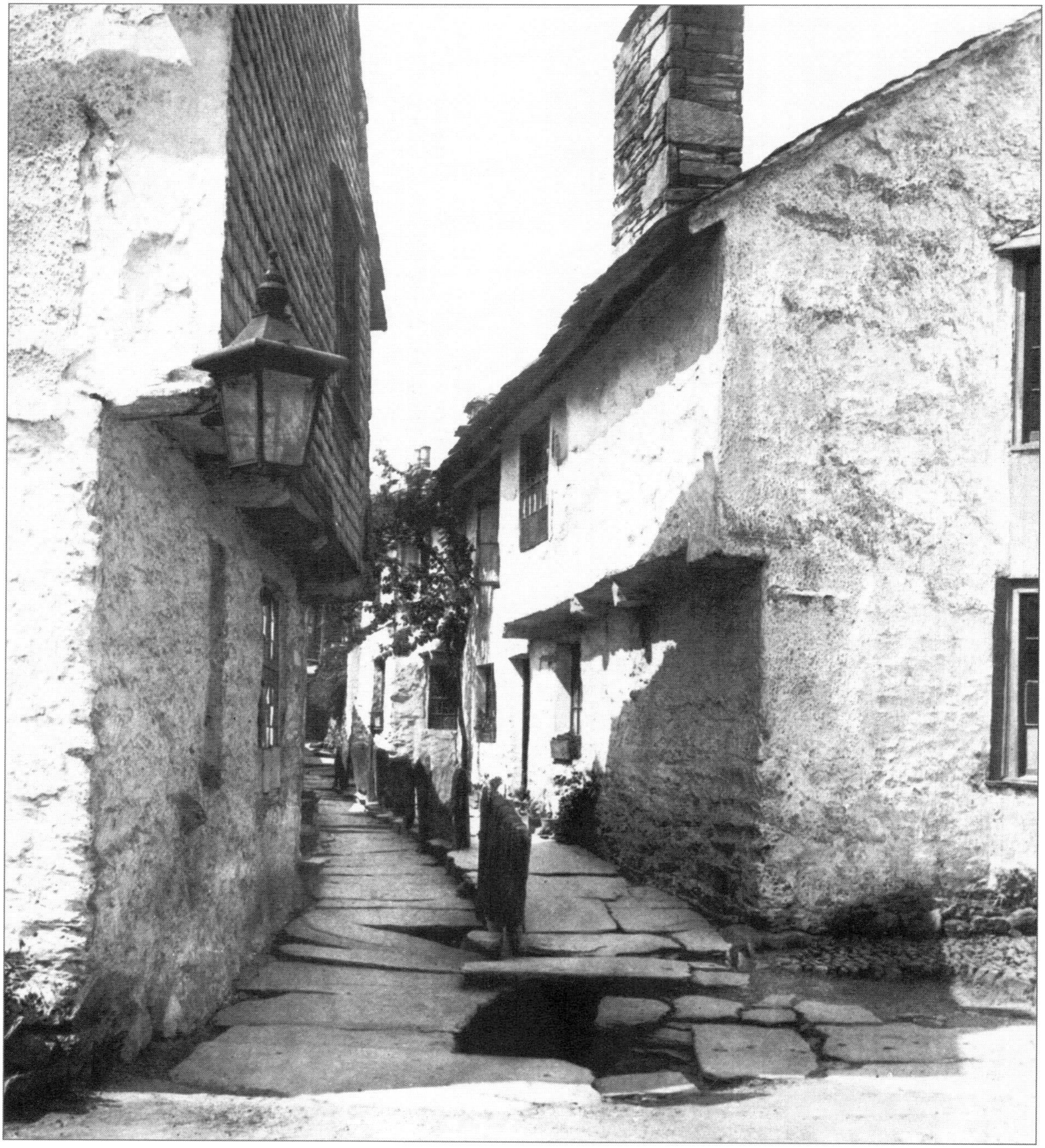

HAWKSHEAD, *Flag Street 1892* 30537

Hawkshead's most characterful street makes a charming picture. Houses with overhanging upper storeys are rare in the Lake District. The street name derives from the large stone paving flags, which cover a small watercourse running just below street level. The flags, the central barriers and the ornate lamp have all disappeared since 1892.

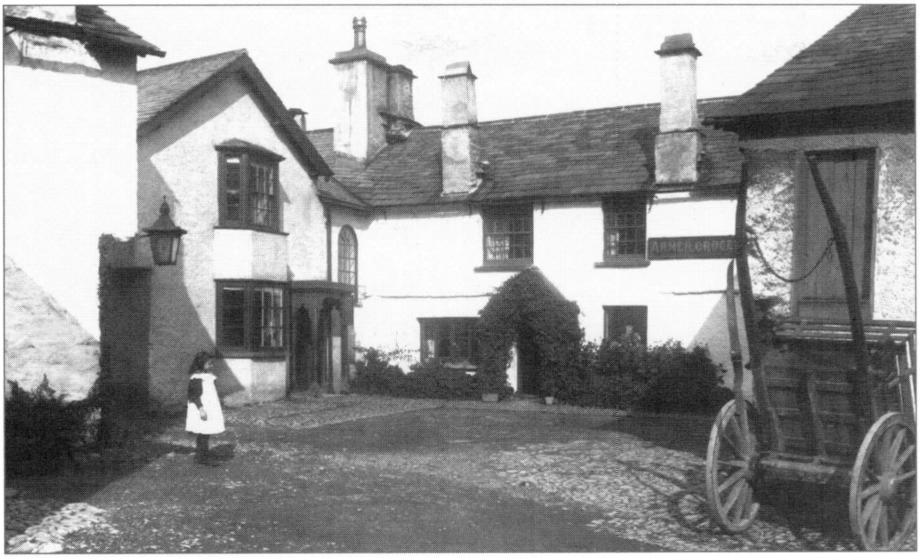

HAWKSHEAD
The Square 1896
38828

This is one of the three small interlocking squares flanked by very old buildings which form the centre of the village, still partially cobbled as we see here. Armer's grocer's shop (centre), with wares apparently displayed in the window on the right, has become the Minstrel's Gallery Café whilst the gable-fronted building at right-angles is now the Methodist Chapel.

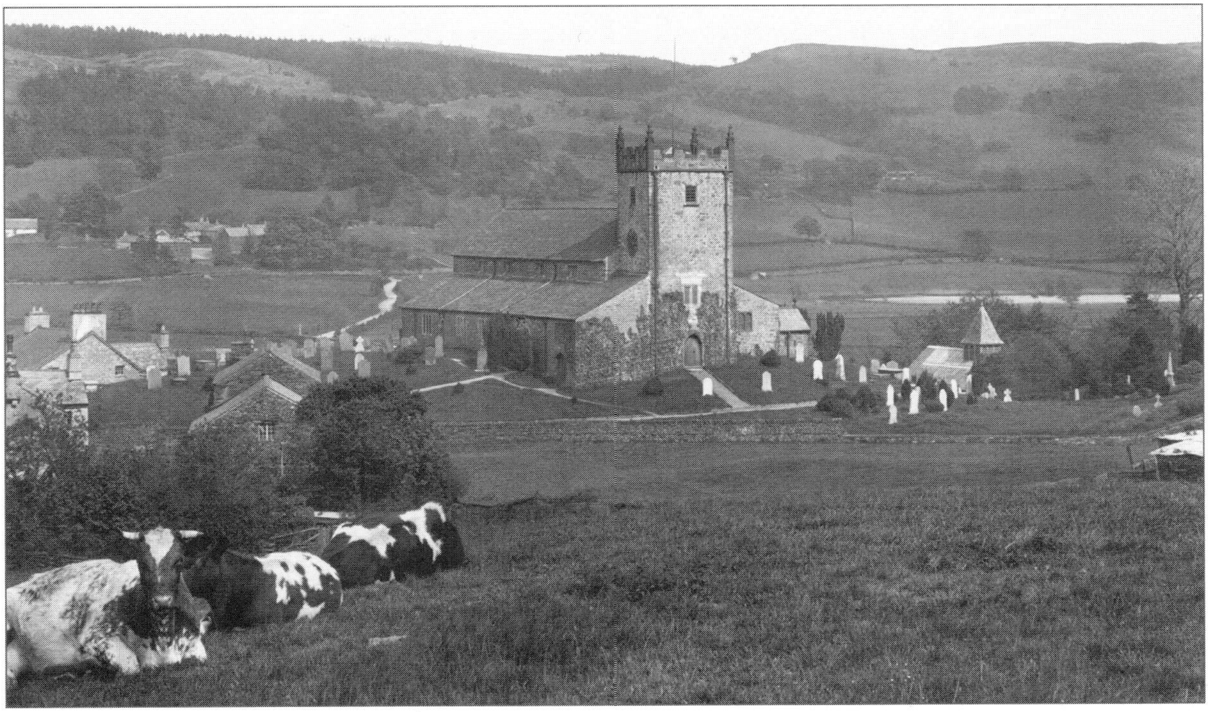

HAWKSHEAD, *The Church 1912* 64297

The famous church at Hawkshead sits on a little knoll above the village. William Wordsworth's 'snow white church upon her hill' lost its white rendering in 1876. In view is Colthouse hamlet, tucked into the foot of the western side of Claiffe Heights; to the right we can see part of the roof of the Grammar School attended by Wordsworth, and also the end of Esthwaite Water.

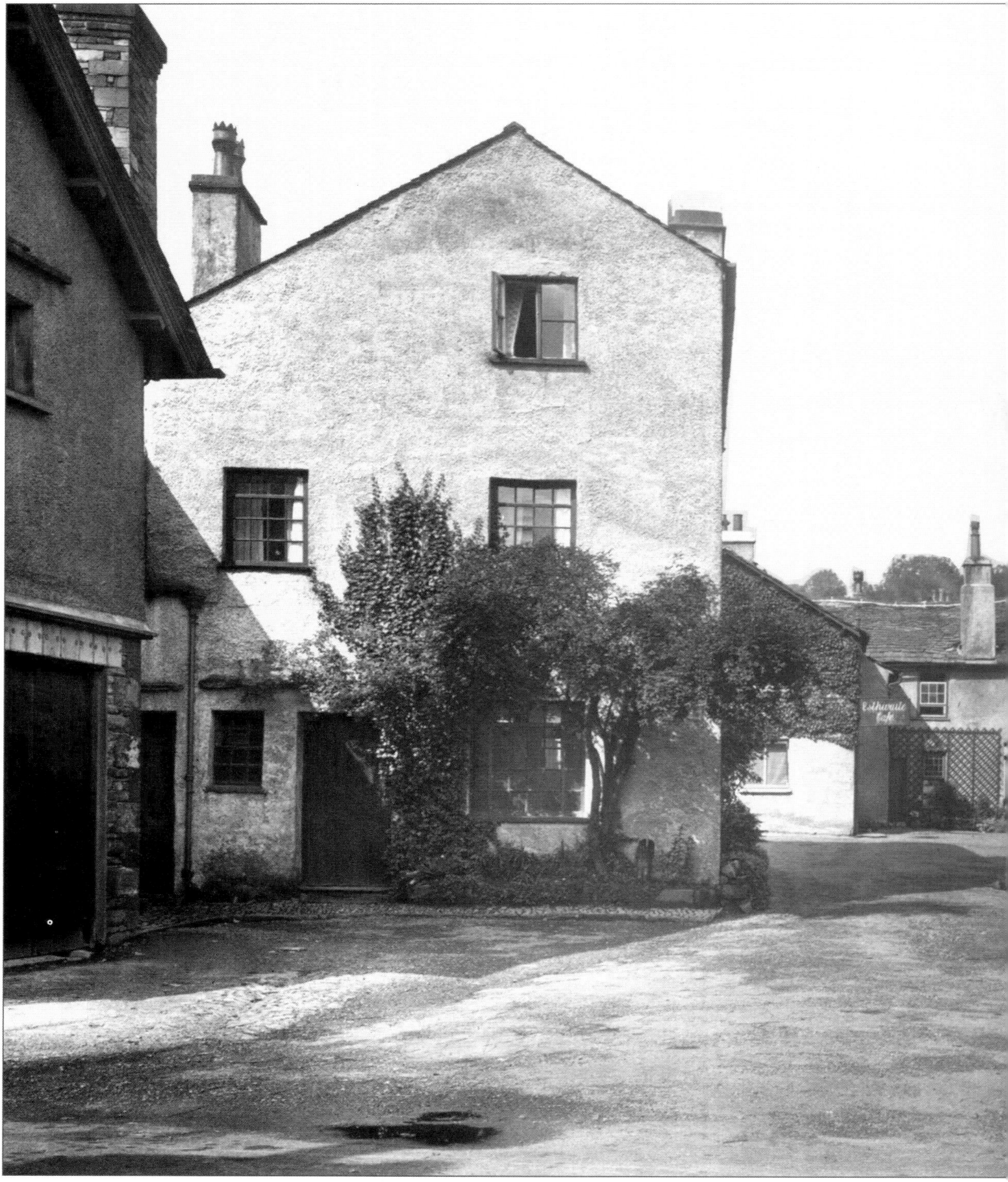

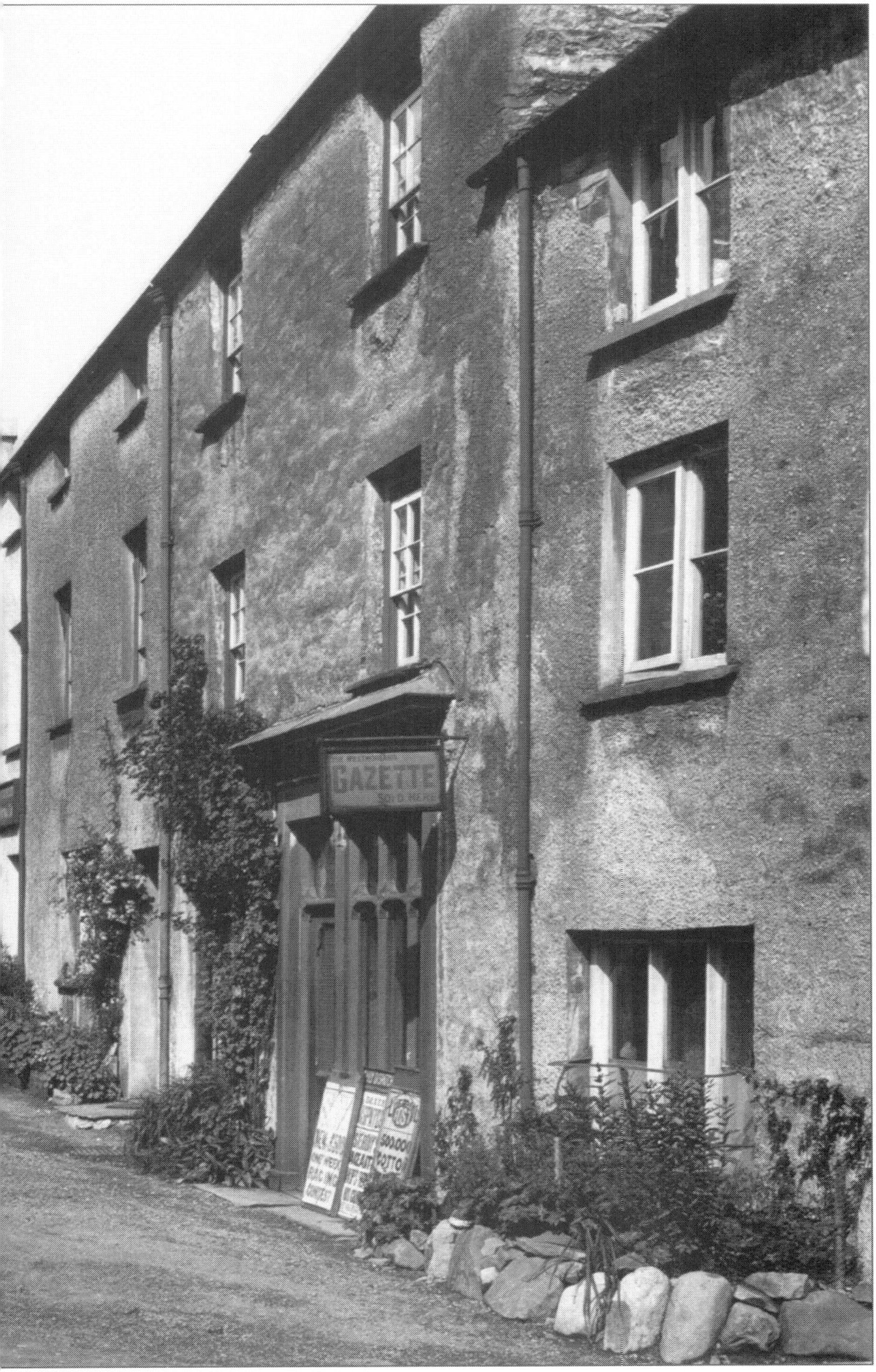

HAWKSHEAD
Laburnum Street 1929
82369

The various advertisements outside the newsagent's on the right add to the period flavour of this village centre scene. The Daily Dispatch is long gone, but the Westmorland Gazette endures, as it has for more than 150 years. A coffee shop now occupies the 'pure ices' premises beyond, whilst the gable-fronted building has since become a book shop.

HAWKSHEAD
The Pillared Cottage
1930 82370

The rather unusual construction of the front part of this old cottage, which stands beside the slope leading up to the church, is not entirely apparent from this picture, which groups it with an adjacent dwelling and another stone building beyond which has since been converted into a house. Is the elderly lady picking flowers from the front garden?

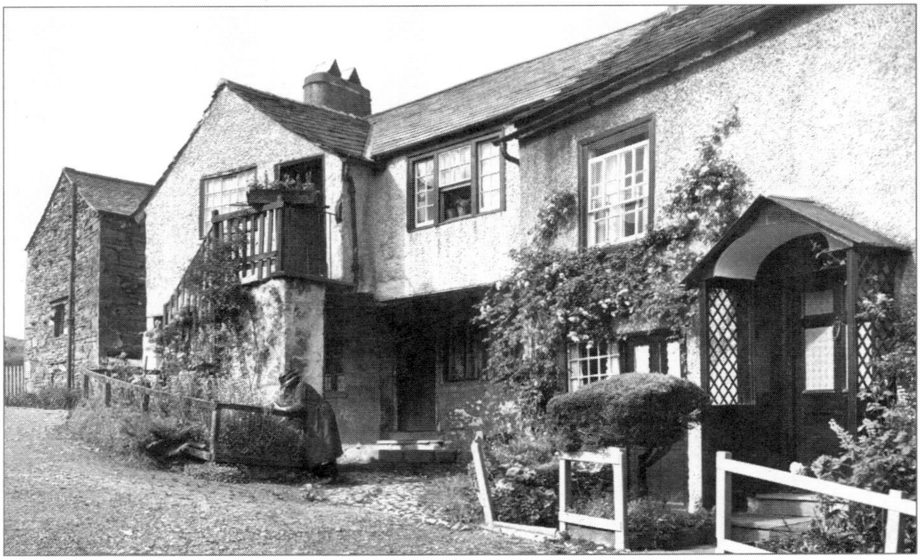

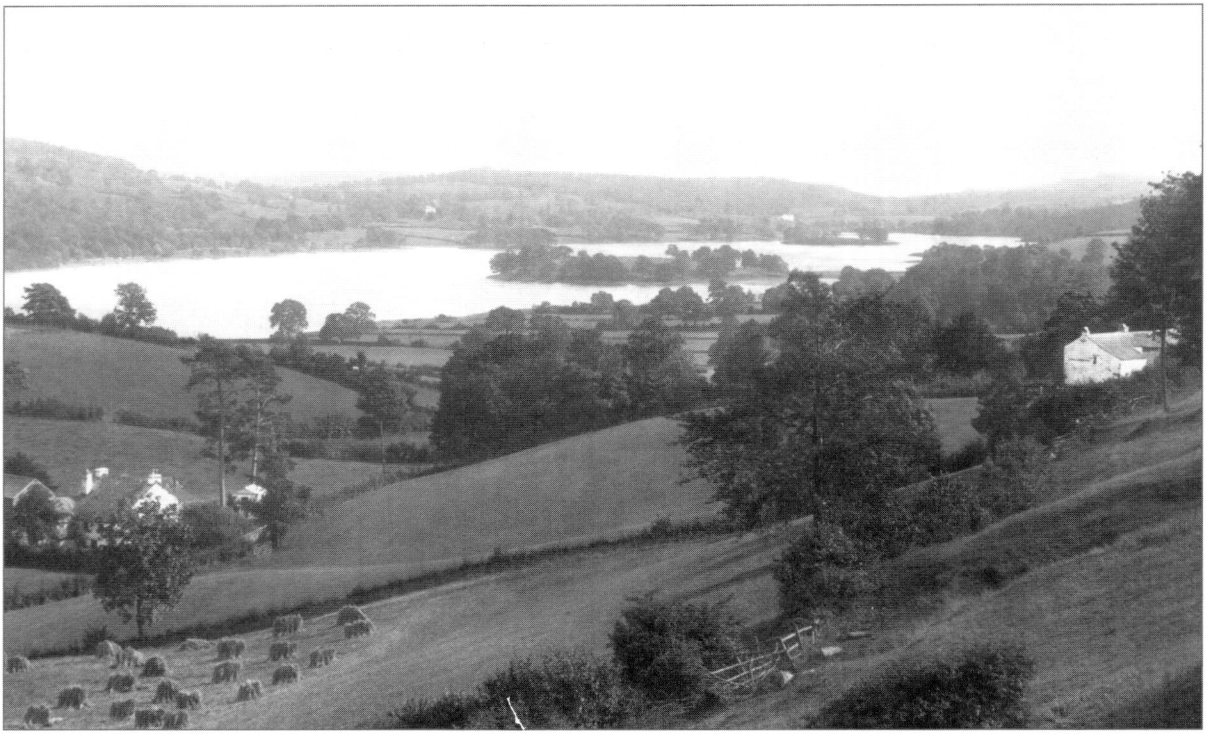

ESTHWAITE WATER *1896* 38814

Esthwaite Water, near Hawkshead, is surrounded by comparatively gentle countryside, typical of the soft Silurian landscape of the southern Lakeland fringe. Sloping meadows, scattered woodlands and nestling farmsteads all contribute to the pastoral scene. Despite appearances, there are no islands in Esthwaite Water.

INDEX

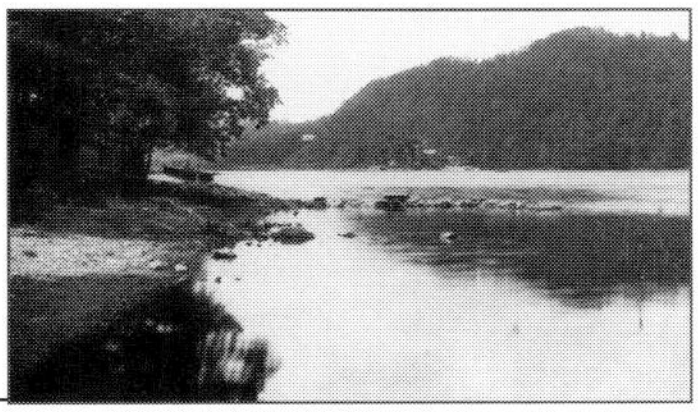

Frith Book Co Titles

www.francisfrith.co.uk

The Frith Book Company publishes over 100 new titles each year. A selection of those currently available are listed below. For latest catalogue please contact Frith Book Co.
Town Books 96 pages, approximately 100 photos. ***County and Themed Books*** 128 pages, approximately 150 photos (unless specified). All titles hardback with laminated case and jacket, except those indicated pb (paperback)

Amersham, Chesham & Rickmansworth (pb)	1-85937-340-2	£9.99
Andover (pb)	1-85937-292-9	£9.99
Aylesbury (pb)	1-85937-227-9	£9.99
Barnstaple (pb)	1-85937-300-3	£9.99
Basildon Living Memories (pb)	1-85937-515-4	£9.99
Bath (pb)	1-85937-419-0	£9.99
Bedford (pb)	1-85937-205-8	£9.99
Bedfordshire Living Memories	1-85937-513-8	£14.99
Belfast (pb)	1-85937-303-8	£9.99
Berkshire (pb)	1-85937-191-4	£9.99
Berkshire Churches	1-85937-170-1	£17.99
Berkshire Living Memories	1-85937-332-1	£14.99
Black Country	1-85937-497-2	£12.99
Blackpool (pb)	1-85937-393-3	£9.99
Bognor Regis (pb)	1-85937-431-x	£9.99
Bournemouth (pb)	1-85937-545-6	£9.99
Bradford (pb)	1-85937-204-x	£9.99
Bridgend (pb)	1-85937-386-0	£7.99
Bridgwater (pb)	1-85937-305-4	£9.99
Bridport (pb)	1-85937-327-5	£9.99
Brighton (pb)	1-85937-192-2	£8.99
Bristol (pb)	1-85937-264-3	£9.99
British Life A Century Ago (pb)	1-85937-213-9	£9.99
Buckinghamshire (pb)	1-85937-200-7	£9.99
Camberley (pb)	1-85937-222-8	£9.99
Cambridge (pb)	1-85937-422-0	£9.99
Cambridgeshire (pb)	1-85937-420-4	£9.99
Cambridgeshire Villages	1-85937-523-5	£14.99
Canals And Waterways (pb)	1-85937-291-0	£9.99
Canterbury Cathedral (pb)	1-85937-179-5	£9.99
Cardiff (pb)	1-85937-093-4	£9.99
Carmarthenshire (pb)	1-85937-604-5	£9.99
Chelmsford (pb)	1-85937-310-0	£9.99
Cheltenham (pb)	1-85937-095-0	£9.99
Cheshire (pb)	1-85937-271-6	£9.99
Chester (pb)	1-85937-382 8	£9.99
Chesterfield (pb)	1-85937-378-x	£9.99
Chichester (pb)	1-85937-228-7	£9.99
Churches of East Cornwall (pb)	1-85937-249-x	£9.99
Churches of Hampshire (pb)	1-85937-207-4	£9.99
Cinque Ports & Two Ancient Towns	1-85937-492-1	£14.99
Colchester (pb)	1-85937-188-4	£8.99
Cornwall (pb)	1-85937-229-5	£9.99
Cornwall Living Memories	1-85937-248-1	£14.99
Cotswolds (pb)	1-85937-230-9	£9.99
Cotswolds Living Memories	1-85937-255-4	£14.99
County Durham (pb)	1-85937-398-4	£9.99
Croydon Living Memories (pb)	1-85937-162-0	£9.99
Cumbria (pb)	1-85937-621-5	£9.99
Derby (pb)	1-85937-367-4	£9.99
Derbyshire (pb)	1-85937-196-5	£9.99
Derbyshire Living Memories	1-85937-330-5	£14.99
Devon (pb)	1-85937-297-x	£9.99
Devon Churches (pb)	1-85937-250-3	£9.99
Dorchester (pb)	1-85937-307-0	£9.99
Dorset (pb)	1-85937-269-4	£9.99
Dorset Coast (pb)	1-85937-299-6	£9.99
Dorset Living Memories (pb)	1-85937-584-7	£9.99
Down the Severn (pb)	1-85937-560-x	£9.99
Down The Thames (pb)	1-85937-278-3	£9.99
Down the Trent	1-85937-311-9	£14.99
East Anglia (pb)	1-85937-265-1	£9.99
East Grinstead (pb)	1-85937-138-8	£9.99
East London	1-85937-080-2	£14.99
East Sussex (pb)	1-85937-606-1	£9.99
Eastbourne (pb)	1-85937-399-2	£9.99
Edinburgh (pb)	1-85937-193-0	£8.99
England In The 1880s	1-85937-331-3	£17.99
Essex - Second Selection	1-85937-456-5	£14.99
Essex (pb)	1-85937-270-8	£9.99
Essex Coast	1-85937-342-9	£14.99
Essex Living Memories	1-85937-490-5	£14.99
Exeter	1-85937-539-1	£9.99
Exmoor (pb)	1-85937-608-8	£9.99
Falmouth (pb)	1-85937-594-4	£9.99
Folkestone (pb)	1-85937-124-8	£9.99
Frome (pb)	1-85937-317-8	£9.99
Glamorgan	1-85937-488-3	£14.99
Glasgow (pb)	1-85937-190-6	£9.99
Glastonbury (pb)	1-85937-338-0	£7.99
Gloucester (pb)	1-85937-232-5	£9.99
Gloucestershire (pb)	1-85937-561-8	£9.99
Great Yarmouth (pb)	1-85937-426-3	£9.99
Greater Manchester (pb)	1-85937-266-x	£9.99
Guildford (pb)	1-85937-410-7	£9.99
Hampshire (pb)	1-85937-279-1	£9.99
Harrogate (pb)	1-85937-423-9	£9.99
Hastings and Bexhill (pb)	1-85937-131-0	£9.99
Heart of Lancashire (pb)	1-85937-197-3	£9.99
Helston (pb)	1-85937-214-7	£9.99
Hereford (pb)	1-85937-175-2	£9.99
Herefordshire (pb)	1-85937-567-7	£9.99
Herefordshire Living Memories	1-85937-514-6	£14.99
Hertfordshire (pb)	1-85937-247-3	£9.99
Horsham (pb)	1-85937-432-8	£9.99
Humberside (pb)	1-85937-605-3	£9.99
Hythe, Romney Marsh, Ashford (pb)	1-85937-256-2	£9.99
Ipswich (pb)	1-85937-424-7	£9.99
Isle of Man (pb)	1-85937-268-6	£9.99
Isle of Wight (pb)	1-85937-429-8	£9.99
Isle of Wight Living Memories	1-85937-304-6	£14.99
Kent (pb)	1-85937-189-2	£9.99
Kent Living Memories(pb)	1-85937-401-8	£9.99
Kings Lynn (pb)	1-85937-334-8	£9.99

Available from your local bookshop or from the publisher

Frith Book Co Titles (continued)

Lake District (pb)	1-85937-275-9	£9.99
Lancashire Living Memories	1-85937-335-6	£14.99
Lancaster, Morecambe, Heysham (pb)	1-85937-233-3	£9.99
Leeds (pb)	1-85937-202-3	£9.99
Leicester (pb)	1-85937-381-x	£9.99
Leicestershire & Rutland Living Memories	1-85937-500-6	£12.99
Leicestershire (pb)	1-85937-185-x	£9.99
Lighthouses	1-85937-257-0	£9.99
Lincoln (pb)	1-85937-380-1	£9.99
Lincolnshire (pb)	1-85937-433-6	£9.99
Liverpool and Merseyside (pb)	1-85937-234-1	£9.99
London (pb)	1-85937-183-3	£9.99
London Living Memories	1-85937-454-9	£14.99
Ludlow (pb)	1-85937-176-0	£9.99
Luton (pb)	1-85937-235-x	£9.99
Maidenhead (pb)	1-85937-339-9	£9.99
Maidstone (pb)	1-85937-391-7	£9.99
Manchester (pb)	1-85937-198-1	£9.99
Marlborough (pb)	1-85937-336-4	£9.99
Middlesex	1-85937-158-2	£14.99
Monmouthshire	1-85937-532-4	£14.99
New Forest (pb)	1-85937-390-9	£9.99
Newark (pb)	1-85937-366-6	£9.99
Newport, Wales (pb)	1-85937-258-9	£9.99
Newquay (pb)	1-85937-421-2	£9.99
Norfolk (pb)	1-85937-195-7	£9.99
Norfolk Broads	1-85937-486-7	£14.99
Norfolk Living Memories (pb)	1-85937-402-6	£9.99
North Buckinghamshire	1-85937-626-6	£14.99
North Devon Living Memories	1-85937-261-9	£14.99
North Hertfordshire	1-85937-547-2	£14.99
North London (pb)	1-85937-403-4	£9.99
North Somerset	1-85937-302-x	£14.99
North Wales (pb)	1-85937-298-8	£9.99
North Yorkshire (pb)	1-85937-236-8	£9.99
Northamptonshire Living Memories	1-85937-529-4	£14.99
Northamptonshire	1-85937-150-7	£14.99
Northumberland Tyne & Wear (pb)	1-85937-281-3	£9.99
Northumberland	1-85937-522-7	£14.99
Norwich (pb)	1-85937-194-9	£8.99
Nottingham (pb)	1-85937-324-0	£9.99
Nottinghamshire (pb)	1-85937-187-6	£9.99
Oxford (pb)	1-85937-411-5	£9.99
Oxfordshire (pb)	1-85937-430-1	£9.99
Oxfordshire Living Memories	1-85937-525-1	£14.99
Paignton (pb)	1-85937-374-7	£7.99
Peak District (pb)	1-85937-280-5	£9.99
Pembrokeshire	1-85937-262-7	£14.99
Penzance (pb)	1-85937-595-2	£9.99
Peterborough (pb)	1-85937-219-8	£9.99
Picturesque Harbours	1-85937-208-2	£14.99
Piers	1-85937-237-6	£17.99
Plymouth (pb)	1-85937-389-5	£9.99
Poole & Sandbanks (pb)	1-85937-251-1	£9.99
Preston (pb)	1-85937-212-0	£9.99
Reading (pb)	1-85937-238-4	£9.99
Redhill to Reigate (pb)	1-85937-596-0	£9.99
Ringwood (pb)	1-85937-384-4	£7.99
Romford (pb)	1-85937-319-4	£9.99
Royal Tunbridge Wells (pb)	1-85937-504-9	£9.99
Salisbury (pb)	1-85937-239-2	£9.99
Scarborough (pb)	1-85937-379-8	£9.99
Sevenoaks and Tonbridge (pb)	1-85937-392-5	£9.99
Sheffield & South Yorks (pb)	1-85937-267-8	£9.99
Sherborne (pb)	1-85937-301-1	£9.99
Shrewsbury (pb)	1-85937-325-9	£9.99
Shropshire (pb)	1-85937-326-7	£9.99
Shropshire Living Memories	1-85937-643-6	£14.99
Somerset	1-85937-153-1	£14.99
South Devon Coast	1-85937-107-8	£14.99
South Devon Living Memories (pb)	1-85937-609-6	£9.99
South East London (pb)	1-85937-263-5	£9.99
South Somerset	1-85937-318-6	£14.99
South Wales	1-85937-519-7	£14.99
Southampton (pb)	1-85937-427-1	£9.99
Southend (pb)	1-85937-313-5	£9.99
Southport (pb)	1-85937-425-5	£9.99
St Albans (pb)	1-85937-341-0	£9.99
St Ives (pb)	1-85937-415-8	£9.99
Stafford Living Memories (pb)	1-85937-503-0	£9.99
Staffordshire (pb)	1-85937-308-9	£9.99
Stourbridge (pb)	1-85937-530-8	£9.99
Stratford upon Avon (pb)	1-85937-388-7	£9.99
Suffolk (pb)	1-85937-221-x	£9.99
Suffolk Coast (pb)	1-85937-610-x	£9.99
Surrey (pb)	1-85937-240-6	£9.99
Surrey Living Memories	1-85937-328-3	£14.99
Sussex (pb)	1-85937-184-1	£9.99
Sutton (pb)	1-85937-337-2	£9.99
Swansea (pb)	1-85937-167-1	£9.99
Taunton (pb)	1-85937-314-3	£9.99
Tees Valley & Cleveland (pb)	1-85937-623-1	£9.99
Teignmouth (pb)	1-85937-370-4	£7.99
Thanet (pb)	1-85937-116-7	£9.99
Tiverton (pb)	1-85937-178-7	£9.99
Torbay (pb)	1-85937-597-9	£9.99
Truro (pb)	1-85937-598-7	£9.99
Victorian & Edwardian Dorset	1-85937-254-6	£14.99
Victorian & Edwardian Kent (pb)	1-85937-624-X	£9.99
Victorian & Edwardian Maritime Album (pb)	1-85937-622-3	£9.99
Victorian and Edwardian Sussex (pb)	1-85937-625-8	£9.99
Villages of Devon (pb)	1-85937-293-7	£9.99
Villages of Kent (pb)	1-85937-294-5	£9.99
Villages of Sussex (pb)	1-85937-295-3	£9.99
Warrington (pb)	1-85937-507-3	£9.99
Warwick (pb)	1-85937-518-9	£9.99
Warwickshire (pb)	1-85937-203-1	£9.99
Welsh Castles (pb)	1-85937-322-4	£9.99
West Midlands (pb)	1-85937-289-9	£9.99
West Sussex (pb)	1-85937-607-x	£9.99
West Yorkshire (pb)	1-85937-201-5	£9.99
Weston Super Mare (pb)	1-85937-306-2	£9.99
Weymouth (pb)	1-85937-209-0	£9.99
Wiltshire (pb)	1-85937-277-5	£9.99
Wiltshire Churches (pb)	1-85937-171-x	£9.99
Wiltshire Living Memories (pb)	1-85937-396-8	£9.99
Winchester (pb)	1-85937-428-x	£9.99
Windsor (pb)	1-85937-333-x	£9.99
Wokingham & Bracknell (pb)	1-85937-329-1	£9.99
Woodbridge (pb)	1-85937-498-0	£9.99
Worcester (pb)	1-85937-165-5	£9.99
Worcestershire Living Memories	1-85937-489-1	£14.99
Worcestershire	1-85937-152-3	£14.99
York (pb)	1-85937-199-x	£9.99
Yorkshire (pb)	1-85937-186-8	£9.99
Yorkshire Coastal Memories	1-85937-506-5	£14.99
Yorkshire Dales	1-85937-502-2	£14.99
Yorkshire Living Memories (pb)	1-85937-397-6	£9.99

Frith Products & Services

Francis Frith would doubtless be pleased to know that the pioneering publishing venture he started in 1860 still continues today. Over a hundred and forty years later, The Francis Frith Collection continues in the same innovative tradition and is now one of the foremost publishers of vintage photographs in the world. Some of the current activities include:

Interior Decoration

Today Frith's photographs can be seen framed and as giant wall murals in thousands of pubs, restaurants, hotels, banks, retail stores and other public buildings throughout the country. In every case they enhance the unique local atmosphere of the places they depict and provide reminders of gentler days in an increasingly busy and frenetic world.

Product Promotions

Frith products are used by many major companies to promote the sales of their own products or to reinforce their own history and heritage. Frith promotions have been used by Hovis bread, Courage beers, Scots Porage Oats, Colman's mustard, Cadbury's foods, Mellow Birds coffee, Dunhill pipe tobacco, Guinness, and Bulmer's Cider.

Genealogy and Family History

As the interest in family history and roots grows world-wide, more and more people are turning to Frith's photographs of Great Britain for images of the towns, villages and streets where their ancestors lived; and, of course, photographs of the churches and chapels where their ancestors were christened, married and buried are an essential part of every genealogy tree and family album.

Frith Products

All Frith photographs are available Framed or just as Mounted Prints and Posters (size 23 x 16 inches). These may be ordered from the address below. From time to time other products - Address Books, Calendars, Table Mats, etc - are available.

The Internet

Already fifty thousand Frith photographs can be viewed and purchased on the internet through the Frith websites and a myriad of partner sites.

For more detailed information on Frith companies and products, look at these sites:

www.francisfrith.co.uk
www.francisfrith.com
(for North American visitors)

See the complete list of Frith Books at:

www.francisfrith.co.uk

This web site is regularly updated with the latest list of publications from the Frith Book Company. If you wish to buy books relating to another part of the country that your local bookshop does not stock, you may purchase on-line.

For further information, trade, or author enquiries please contact us at the address below:

The Francis Frith Collection, Frith's Barn, Teffont, Salisbury, Wiltshire, England SP3 5QP.
Tel: +44 (0)1722 716 376 Fax: +44 (0)1722 716 881 Email: sales@francisfrith.co.uk

See Frith books on the internet at www.francisfrith.co.uk

HOW TO ORDER YOUR FREE MOUNTED PRINT

and other Frith prints at half price

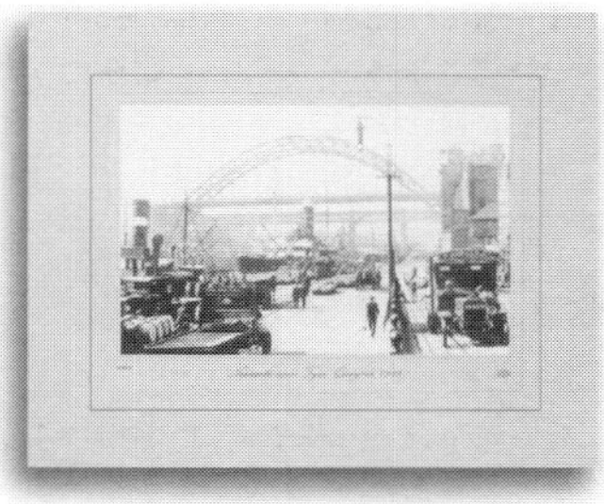

Mounted Print
Overall size 14 x 11 inches

Fill in and cut out this voucher and return it with your remittance for £2.25 (to cover postage and handling to UK addresses).
For overseas addresses please include £4.00 post and handling.
Choose any photograph included in this book.
Your SEPIA print will be A4 in size. It will be mounted in a cream mount with a burgundy rule line (overall size 14 x 11 inches).

Order additional Mounted Prints at HALF PRICE (only £7.49 each*)

If you would like to order more Frith prints from this book, possibly as gifts for friends and family, you can buy them at half price (with no additional postage and handling costs).

Have your Mounted Prints framed

For an extra £14.95 per print* you can have your mounted print(s) framed in an elegant polished wood and gilt moulding, overall size 16 x 13 inches (no additional postage and handling required).

*** IMPORTANT!**

These special prices are only available if you order at the same time as you order your free mounted print. You must use the ORIGINAL VOUCHER on this page (no copies permitted). We can only despatch to one address.

Voucher

for ***FREE***
and Reduced Price
Frith Prints

Please do not photocopy this voucher. Only the original is valid, so please fill it in, cut it out and return it to us with your order.

Picture ref no	Page number	Qty	Mounted @ £7.49	Framed + £14.95	Total Cost
		1	Free of charge*	£	£
			£7.49	£	£
			£7.49	£	£
			£7.49	£	£
			£7.49	£	£
			£7.49	£	£
Please allow 28 days for delivery			* Post & handling (UK)		£2.25
			Total Order Cost		£

Title of this book ....

I enclose a cheque/postal order for £ ....
made payable to 'The Francis Frith Collection'

OR please debit my Mastercard / Visa / Switch / Amex card
(credit cards please on all overseas orders), details below

Card Number

Issue No (Switch only) Valid from (Amex/Switch)

Expires Signature

Name Mr/Mrs/Ms ....
Address ....
....
....
.... Postcode ....
Daytime Tel No ....
Email ....

Valid to 31/12/05

Send completed Voucher form to:
The Francis Frith Collection, Frith's Barn, Teffont, Salisbury, Wiltshire SP3 5QP

Free Print - see overleaf

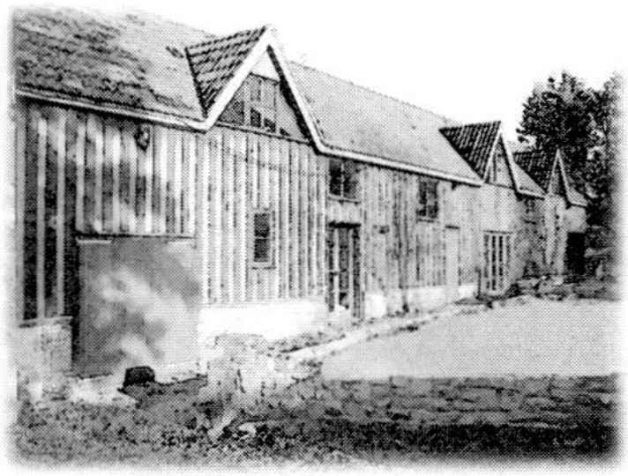

Would you like to find out more about Francis Frith?

We have recently recruited some entertaining speakers who are happy to visit local groups, clubs and societies to give an illustrated talk documenting Frith's travels and photographs. If you are a member of such a group and are interested in hosting a presentation, we would love to hear from you.

Our speakers bring with them a small selection of our local town and county books, together with sample prints. They are happy to take orders. A small proportion of the order value is donated to the group who have hosted the presentation. The talks are therefore an excellent way of fundraising for small groups and societies.

Can you help us with information about any of the Frith photographs in this book?

We are gradually compiling an historical record for each of the photographs in the Frith archive. It is always fascinating to find out the names of the people shown in the pictures, as well as insights into the shops, buildings and other features depicted.

If you recognize anyone in the photographs in this book, or if you have information not already included in the author's caption, do let us know. We would love to hear from you, and will try to publish it in future books or articles.

Our production team

Frith books are produced by a small dedicated team at offices in the converted Grade II listed 18th-century barn at Teffont near Salisbury, illustrated above. Most have worked with the Frith Collection for many years. All have in common one quality: they have a passion for the Frith Collection. The team is constantly expanding, but currently includes:

Jason Buck, John Buck, Douglas Mitchell-Burns, Ruth Butler, Heather Crisp, Isobel Hall, Maureen Harrison, Julian Hight, Peter Horne, James Kinnear, Karen Kinnear, Tina Leary, David Marsh, Sue Molloy, Kate Rotondetto, Dean Scource, Eliza Sackett, Terence Sackett, Sandra Sampson, Adrian Sanders, Sandra Sanger, Julia Skinner, Lewis Taylor, Shelley Tolcher, and Lorraine Tuck.